TECHNIQUE IN
THE TALES OF
Henry James

TECHNIQUE IN THE TALES OF

Henry James

KRISHNA BALDEV VAID

HARVARD UNIVERSITY PRESS

CAMBRIDGE, MASSACHUSETTS

1964

Distributed in Great Britain by Oxford University Press, London

Publication of this volume has been aided
by a grant from the Ford Foundation

Quotations from the New York Edition of James's works (Charles Scribner's Sons, 1907-1909; copyright 1964 by Henry James) are reprinted by arrangement with Paul R. Reynolds Inc., 599 Fifth Avenue, New York 17, New York. Quotations from the London edition of James's works (Macmillan, 1921-1923) are reprinted by permission of John Farquharson Ltd., 15 Red Lion Square, London WC1, England.

Library of Congress Catalog Card Number: 64-22723

Printed in the United States of America

THIS BOOK IS FOR

Harry Levin

Acknowledgments

IN THE making of this book I have been generously helped, through both personal encouragement and professional advice, by Leon Edel, Harry Levin, Kenneth S. Lynn, Richard Poirier, and I. A. Richards—to all of whom I am very grateful. My special indebtedness to Harry Levin is but imperfectly conveyed by the dedication of the book to him. The warmth of my other friends at Harvard University contributed a great deal to the sense of essential harmony I experienced in spite of being away from home.

My wife, like most good wives under similarly trying circumstances, showed exemplary patience both when she was with me in Cambridge and when for two brief spells she allowed me to absent myself from the felicity of her company.

I am thankful to Jean Whittemore, who typed the final draft at a pace that allowed me to make several last-minute changes, and to Joyce Lebowitz of Harvard University Press for her expert editorial guidance.

Finally, I am deeply grateful to Chadbourne Gilpatric of the Rockefeller Foundation, Richard Park of the Asia Foundation, and the directors of the Social Science Fund for providing me with fellowships and travel grants that enabled me to stay at Harvard and finish the work.

K.B.V.

Chandigarh, Panjab
December 1963

Contents

ix

TECHNIQUE IN
THE TALES OF
Henry James

Introduction

THE PURPOSE of this study is to examine, through a close analysis of several carefully chosen specimens, the relatively neglected half of Henry James's fiction. In all, James produced one hundred and twelve tales; although a few of these have been fortuitous victims of overinterpretation bordering occasionally on misinterpretation, in journals both learned and not so learned, the vast majority has been either ignored or dismissed as a mere tributary to the "mainstream" of his novels. Thus, despite the striking proliferation of books on James, there is only one little book on his shorter fiction; even that one has a misleading title and is based on a confused notion of the Jamesian distinction between a novel and a nouvelle, between a nouvelle and a short story.[1] The implicit assumption seems to be that James was a novelist who also wrote tales, by way of necessary apprenticeship in the early years and because of professional contingencies and occupational weariness in the later.

This assumption seems to me ill founded and unjust. James was a writer whose creative energies and formal concerns were devoted in almost equal measure to his novels and his tales. The tales, then, deserve serious and sustained critical attention in their own right. Even if James had produced nothing but the tales he did, I believe that he could have laid an indisputable claim to a seat among the Olympians. Hence I do not agree with the invidious comparison implied in the statement that "the novels of James are more interesting than his tales."[2] Writing of Maupassant, James once said, "He has published less than half a dozen novels and more than a hundred tales, and it is upon his tales that his reputation will mainly rest."[3] Of James himself it seems perfectly sound to predict that his reputation will ultimately rest upon his novels *and* his tales.

One important elementary fact is that James's concern with the writing of tales, unlike his short painful bout with the theater, was continuous and life-long. In an early letter to Charles Eliot Norton on January 16, 1871, he wrote, "To write a series of good little tales I deem ample work for a life-time."[4] During another phase of his career, he made repeated resolutions to concentrate only on tales. Writing to Robert Louis Stevenson on July 31, 1888, he said, "After that [finishing *The Tragic Muse*], with God's help, I propose, for a longish period, to do nothing but short lengths. I want to leave a multitude of pictures of my time, projecting my small circular frame upon as many different spots as possible and going in for number as well as quality, so that the number may constitute a total having a certain value as observation and testimony."[5] A similar plan is recorded in the *Notebooks* on May 19, 1889, where he mentions "the wish and dream that have lately grown stronger than ever in me—the desire that the literary heritage, such as it is, poor thing, that I may leave, shall consist of a large number of perfect *short* things, *nouvelles* and tales illustrative of ever so many things in life."[6] A year later, May 16, 1890, he writes to William James that *"The Tragic Muse* is to be my last long novel. For the rest of my life I hope to do lots of short things with irresponsible spaces between."[7] Again in the *Note-*

books, July 13, 1891, he gives himself an "artistic" reason for the desire to concentrate on short things, the other reason being that he wanted to keep himself free for his theatrical experiment: "What I call *the* artistic [reason] *par excellence* is simply the consideration that by doing short things I can do so many, touch so many subjects, break out in so many places, handle so many of the threads of life."[8] In still another letter to Stevenson, on October 30, 1891: "I mean never to write another novel; I mean I have solemnly dedicated myself to a masterly brevity. I have come back to it, as to an early love."[9] The culmination, as it were, of this preoccupation with shorter forms is reached in a letter to Howells on January 22, 1895: "I shall never again write a *long* novel; but I hope to write six immortal short ones—and some tales of the same quality."[10]

James's subsequent performance was to prove him false, for three of his longest, and greatest, novels were done after the 1890s. As a matter of fact, we can trace his return to the longer form through two illuminating entries in the *Notebooks.* In the first, August 30, 1893, possessed by "the desire to escape from the cramp of the too intensely short," he is bracing himself up by "excellent examples of the short novel" done by Maupassant and Octave Feuillet.[11] In the second entry, January 27, 1899, he rejoices in the decision to take up the long novel once again: "How, through all hesitations and conflicts and worries, *the* thing, the desire to get back only to the *big* (scenic, constructive, 'architectural' effects) seizes me and carries me off my feet: making me feel that it's a far deeper economy of time to sink, at *any* moment, into the evocation and ciphering out of *that,* than into any other *small* beguilement at all. Ah, once more, to let myself go!"[12] But this return to the novel, fortunately, did not mean a neglect of short fiction. It is important to note that between 1888 (the year in which he resolved to concentrate on the tales) and 1910 (the year of his last fictional product), he published as many as sixty-five tales, including all of his greatest. Even in the "severely sifted"[13] New York Edition, six whole volumes are given to the tales, with three others divided among tales and three short novels.[14]

I have sufficiently stressed the point that with James the writing of the tales was not just an intermittent refuge from the more exacting labor of novel writing. In the *Notebooks* we see his constant awareness of the need to adjust to, and sometimes to defy, the existing preconceptions about the form of the "short story." These meditations are dispersed throughout the *Notebooks*. They are often so closely related to specific *données,* several of which are either abandoned or developed into short and long novels, that the task of adducing them here is likely to be tedious. However, this formal concern is more systematically reflected in the prefaces, where James attempts several formulations of the two categories of his tales—the nouvelle and the anecdote. I shall make numerous references to these formulations later.

Here I must refer to the problem of deciding upon an apposite nomenclature that can be used consistently to designate James's shorter fictions and to distinguish them clearly from his novels. There is no simple way out of the current confusion on this matter. One critic's short story is another's short novel. "The Beast in the Jungle" is a short story in the collections of Clifton Fadiman and Quentin Anderson and a short novel in Philip Rahv's.[15] Occasionally the same writer has used two different terms for the same piece, almost in the same breath.[16] This casualness in the use of terminology would not be so serious an offense perhaps, if it caused no confusion in the critical appreciation of James's tales. But evidently it does cause a considerable dislocation of norms and standards. Take, for instance, Elizabeth Bowen's remark that "the short stories of James and Hardy show . . . *qua* the short story, no urgent aesthetic necessity; their matter does not dictate their form. Their shortness is not positive; it is non-extension. They are great architects' fancies, little buildings on an august plan. They have no emotion that is abrupt or special; they do not give mood or incident a significance outside the novelist's power to explore."[17] Miss Bowen's observations proceed from those restrictive assumptions about the "ideal" short story that James spent a lifetime in refuting; besides, they are relevant, if at all, only to a very limited number of his tales, those which he himself chose to call anecdotes. The best of these again, regardless of the trouble they caused their author, do have emotions that are "abrupt or special." The fact of the matter, however, is that most of James's characteristic fictions are beyond the narrow embrace of the rubric "short story."

So, in order to avoid confusion and inconsistency, I have adopted the terminology preferred by James himself. In his letters, the *Notebooks*, prefaces, and other critical writings, James almost always used the term "tale" in connection with fictions of shorter length. He did not confuse his short novels with his long tales. The outer limit of the Jamesian tale is clearly demarcated by *The Reverberator*, which according to James "falls into the category of Shorter Novels—under an indulgence not extended to several of its compeers."[18] I consider it significant —in view of his habitual care in the choice of names for characters, places, individual pieces, and books—that James should have called his New York Edition, *The Novels and Tales of Henry James*. "Short novel" is a misleading equivalent for a James nouvelle, and "short story" is accompanied by confusing associations even when used for a James anecdote. I have therefore retained both these terms (nouvelle and anecdote) and, following James's practice and preference, used "tale" as a general substitute for both throughout this study.

In the preface to *Roderick Hudson* James defines a novel as "a long fiction with a 'complicated' subject."[19] It is a simple enough definition but it works, the essential element being a combination of length and complications. A short novel, according to James, is a piece of fiction ranging from about 80,000 to 100,000 words;[20] and since he singled out *The Reverberator* as one of the shorter novels, the problem of the maximum dimensional reach of a Jamesian nouvelle is definitively settled. The main distinction between a novel and a short novel is indicated by their comparative lengths, complications being common to both. The nouvelle is defined by James in greater detail in several of his prefaces. It is a "picture" consisting of "richly summarised and foreshortened effects"; it is a "fine type of composition" permitting "shades and differences, varieties and styles, the value above all of the idea happily developed"; its "main merit and sign is the effort to do the complicated thing with a strong brevity and lucidity—to arrive, on behalf of the multiplicity, at a certain science of control"; it is a form whose "achieved iridescence from within works, I feel sure, more kinds of magic."[21] In short, the nouvelle is the treatment of a complicated subject in a form that compared to the novel is exiguous.

James reveled in the nouvelle—"the beautiful and blest *nouvelle*"[22]—and regretted the Anglo-Saxon indifference to its possibilities. He frequently groaned under the restrictions imposed on him by the magazine notions of a short story: "In that dull view a 'short story' was a 'short story,' and that was the end of it."[23] At the same time, however, he was fascinated by the challenge to produce such stories. (This is not to deny the part played by financial motives, for it was easier to place stories of very short length.) He had a fairly normal theoretical conception of what a short story ought to be and equated it with a "concise anecdote."[24] The anecdote, moreover, "consists, ever, of something that has oddly happened to some one, and the first of its duties is to point directly to the person whom it so distinguishes."[25] James knew that he "must take, and take only, the single incident," that he must "try to make use, for the brief treatment, of nothing, absolutely *nothing*, that isn't ONE, as it were—that doesn't begin and end in its little self."[26] He did produce a few excellent anecdotes—"Brooksmith," "The Visits," "Flickerbridge," "Greville Fane," "The Two Faces." But more often than not even his anecdotes are compressed nouvelles. The subjects that generally occurred to him required, or at least were amenable to, development, and yet the form that he chose for them was sometimes anecdotic, which gave him "too little room to turn around."[27]

James was conscious of the strain to which he put himself in order to arrange so many marriages between a developmental subject and the anecdotic form. Most of these unions were successful to the point of giving him an immense, sometimes even disproportionate, satisfaction. In the New York Edition he included those anecdotes in which he had been able to treat his subject successfully, despite the inherent congestedness of the form as he used it. In most cases, however, he had to exert "a ferocious" though, "far from fruitless ingenuity" to keep them from becoming nouvelles.[28] Speaking of "The Middle Years," he says: "The form of 'The Middle Years' is not that of the *nouvelle,* but that of the concise anecdote; whereas the subject treated would perhaps seem one comparatively demanding 'developments'—if indeed, amid these mysteries, distinctions were so absolute." A few sentences further: "Treating a theme that 'gave' much in a form that, at the best, would give little, might indeed represent a peck of troubles; yet, who, none the less, beforehand, was to pronounce with authority such and such an idea anecdotic and such and such another developmental?"[29] It would seem that here James snatches the very ground from under the question of anecdotal versus developmental by postulating a fundamental uncertainty. As a matter of fact, his own practice does suggest that there is no method whereby you can lay down hard and fast rules on this matter. We know from the *Notebooks* how James promptly mentions the approximate stretch of the tale or the novel that is to proceed from a given situation, and in how few cases his estimate is even reasonably correct. As the editors of the *Notebooks* have pointed out: "We can observe him, again and again, conceiving his theme as 'a thing of a tiny kind,' only to have it expand, once he began to treat it, far beyond his reckoning. Short stories became *nouvelles,* and *nouvelles* became novels."[30] The moral of all this seems to be that the critic of fiction, even more than the writer of fiction, should not start with preconceived notions about the dimensional potentialities of this, that, or the other theme. His best course is to examine the given piece of fiction and to evaluate its success or failure on its own terms. The moral is especially relevant to James's anecdotes, the best of which were arrived at after "innumerable repeated chemical reductions and condensations that tend to make the very short story . . . one of the costliest, even if, like the hard, shining sonnet, one of the most indestructible, forms of composition in general use."[31] This is a triumphant sigh of relief at having mastered a form that seldom came easily to him.

The general procedure of this study requires some explanation. It is deliberately selective rather than exhaustive, the latter course often being a misnomer for a rapid survey of a vast range of material. The surveyor, more acceptable as he is generally, cannot quite resist the temptation (or avoid the necessity) of making short work of the numerous, not-so-easily perceptible subtleties in the voluminous work of an artist as self-conscious as James was. Besides, the shape of a book naturally emerges from its intention. Since my intention was to examine in detail the working of James's method, I found it imperative to concentrate on a few representative specimens. Except for the two chapters on the early tales, the rest of the book is devoted to an analysis of some of the major tales published after 1888. This choice may seem arbitrary but, for the purpose of understanding James at his characteristic best, these tales seem to me to be richer and more rewarding. An effort has been made to suggest, without forcing the point, that the earliest tales of James do contain in seed form his later technical, thematic, and artistic preoccupations. But a full developmental approach would have taken me too far from my real subject. Within the chosen period, selection was governed by considerations of variety in narrative technique, thematic emphasis, and achieved effect. In spite of this rather "narrow" approach, however, it was borne in mind that the generalizations derived from an analysis of the tales actually chosen would not be radically altered or invalidated by a study of those left out.

The division of the study into two parts was also motivated by the desire to spotlight the distinctions—in structure, style, tone, even content, and of course total effect—that stem from James's two main narrative methods. Within each part the varieties of narrative experiments are thus more clearly demonstrable. The same desire has induced me to attempt a close textual analysis of all the tales discussed. Fiction, it is true, does not generally lend itself to such close scrutiny, its values being diffuse, its structures often loose, its effects dependent more on stock devices and responses. James, however, is supreme among the few who can only gain by a focused look of the kind that is now usually directed to poetry. But most Jamesian studies have been concerned with "larger" matters—the thematic patterns and the ideological content, the philosophical influences and the biographical insights.[32] The predominant tendency seems to be that about his art James himself said all that we need to know, and that whatever little remained was exhausted long ago by Beach in *The Method of Henry James* and by Lubbock in *The Craft of Fiction*. Although I have unqualified admiration for these two studies, the tendency mentioned above seems to be an excuse for ignoring the most important single aspect of James—his method or craft. This aspect has been taken too much for granted; the themes of James have been discussed too often and too much in isolation from the technique that discovered them; and what James called "the *accessory* facts" have been given too much free play. This study purports to be—if I may use a phrase of Stevenson's made famous by association with James—a "humble remonstrance."

PART ONE

THE AUTHOR'S
DEPUTY

CHAPTER I

Three Early Tales

AS INDICATED in the Introduction, this part of the book is devoted to a discussion of James's method in his first-person tales. In this chapter I have selected for examination three out of the few "early brevities"[1] admitted by James into the New York Edition. They strike me as the best examples of his first-person narrative technique in the early phase. The first of these—"The Madonna of the Future" (1873)—belongs to a small group, thirteen in number and spanning all but the last decade of his career as a teller of tales, in which he adopted the device of prefacing the actual narrative by a brief prologue.[2] This method of framing the narrative seems to have gone out of currency now, but James made good use of it in some of his most effective first-person tales, such as "The Turn of the Screw" (1898). The prologue in these tales is spoken by an anonymous person who appears for a short time and, having set the scene or mentioned the occasion of the tale, leaves the floor to the real narrator.

It would be difficult to maintain that these prologues are quite indispensable. The only definite exception seems to be "The Turn of the Screw" where, as we shall see, the prologue cannot be ignored without misinterpreting the tale. On the other hand, only in "Gabrielle de Bergerac" (1869) and "The Sweetheart of M. Briseux" (1873) does this dilatory method of opening the tale strike the reader as an altogether avoidable narrative blandishment. In other tales it is employed with an unobtrusive nonchalance and often looks like an amiable ritualistic bow to an older convention. If it incidentally gives a more authentic ring to the subsequent narrative, the effect is achieved without an excessive effort to create an illusion of actuality, for James seldom renders in its entirety or with undue realistic elaboration the scene of the first hearing of the tale. At its best, the prologue succeeds in arousing the reader's curiosity to an adequate pitch and in drawing him into the promised narrative.

The Madonna of the Future

The first narrator of "The Madonna of the Future" informs us of the occasion that produced the tale, makes an identifying remark about H—, the real narrator—"a clever man who had seen much of men and manners and had a great stock of reminiscences" (XIII, 437)—and withdraws after noting with gentle irony the effect of the tale on his charming hostess: "When the catastrophe was reached she glanced across and showed me a tear in each of her beautiful eyes" (XIII, 438).[3] Through this glimpse he anticipates the pathetic conclusion of the tale, even as he gives us a subtle warning lest our own response take a similarly demonstrative course. After this the real narrator takes over.

The tale told by H— is not an autobiographical story. He does not say more about himself than is absolutely necessary for his function as the narrator of a particular experience in which the chief character is someone else, Theobald. In other words, H—, like most Jamesian firstperson narrators, is more of a method and less of a character. He is the medium through which our interest in Theobald and his dilemma is to be aroused, the device through which this dilemma is to be dramatically rendered. For all his ostensible involvement in the action, H— remains only a partially individualized witness

who contributes to the case mainly a certain amount of criticism and interpretation of it. Again and again, on review, the shorter things in especial that I have gathered into this Series have ranged themselves not as my own impersonal account of the affair in hand, but as my account of somebody's impression of it—the terms of this person's access to it and estimate of it contributing thus by some fine little law to intensification of interest. The somebody is often, among my shorter tales I recognize, but an unnamed, unintroduced and (save by right of intrinsic wit) unwarranted participant, the impersonal author's concrete deputy or delegate, a convenient substitute or apologist for the creative power otherwise so veiled and disembodied.[4]

In this excerpt from the preface to *The Golden Bowl* James is referring particularly to his first-person tales included in the New York Edition. In the omniscient-narrator tales the witness is often a combination of the impersonal author and the central character himself; the detached observer is either nonexistent or appears as a peripheral figure, a *ficelle,* or else as an occasional hypothetical spectator.

Thus the attributes of H— are primarily those of a generic character. His wit, skepticism, curiosity, and sympathy are common to all Jamesian narrators in varying degree. To be a good raconteur, he has to be witty enough to compel our attention. His situation in this respect is analogous to that of a public lecturer who is always well advised in making his seriousness, if he has any, palatable through a proper seasoning of wit. H— is not a monster of curiosity like the narrators of *The Sacred Fount* (1901) and "The Aspern Papers" (1888); but without a certain measure of unusual curiosity he will not be the busybody he has to be in order to explore the given case. Skepticism is a necessary ballast both for the narrator's curiosity and his sympathetic attitude. Without a touch of disbelief, curiosity may deteriorate into vulgar nosiness and sympathy into maudlin sentimentality. Very often this skepticism is only a pose by which the narrator anticipates, as well as accentuates, the skepticism of the reader—this invests the narrative with tension and suspense. The more marvelous the nature of the incidents and characters involved, the more gradual is the process by which the narrator sheds his skepticism and arrives at a final understanding of what he has been observing and commenting upon. This understanding is often the crux of the story, the point that James wants to put across to the reader. The Jamesian narrator thus has a persuasive effect on the reader, whose response is carefully controlled through an unobtrusive artifice. Finally, H— is a thoroughly reliable witness. As a matter of fact, James rarely used a first-person narrator as an ironic center of revelation or self-revelation: "A Light Man" (1869), "The Aspern Papers" (1888), and "The Figure in the Carpet" (1896) seem to be the only exceptions to this rule. ("The Turn of the Screw" is highly controversial in this respect and will be discussed later.)

These generic attributes of the narrator shape the structure and tone of the tale. The structure corresponds to the process of the narrator's own growing comprehension of the experience embodied in the tale. Of course, the order and the pace of this process vary according to the position at which the author chooses to place his deputy, as well as to the predesigned nature and order of complications. In other words, H— is not a mere reporter of all he saw and felt; he has to exercise the selectivity and skill expected of a "professional" craft-conscious narrator. So far as it is consistent with this general limitation, he proceeds with an apparent autonomy, in the manner of a person relating events to which he was an actual witness. His narrative thus assumes the appearance of an unedited step-by-step account of a succession of meetings with the hero; it is interspersed by his own independent investigations, comments, and conclusions. The artistry of selection and organization is in this way cunningly concealed, and an air of spontaneity given to the march of the tale. The tone in almost all the first-person narratives of James is always light without being frivolous, however serious the subject itself may be. A solemn first-person narrative, James knew, is generally a bore.

With these general observations in mind, let us look more closely at "The Madonna." The sketch of Florence in the long opening paragraph by H— is not so much an attempt at local color as an effort to provide the necessary atmosphere for his first meeting with the odd stranger "hovering in that consecrated background" (XIII, 439). Subsequent meetings between the narrator and Theobald can gain in inevitability and interest only if the first is spectacular enough to provoke the narrator's, and the reader's, curiosity. So we have a marked emphasis on the strangeness of the "romantic, fantastic, slightly unreal" Theobald (XIII, 439). The narrator's reported impressions must be confirmed by our own direct view. Hence the important portions of the exchange between the narrator and Theobald are rendered dramatically, in the form of a dialogue. H— is at first puzzled by Theobald's moon-struck rhapsody about the Florentine past; presently he makes his first intuitive conjecture about his interlocutor: "The mystery was suddenly solved; my friend was the most characteristic of compatriots. He would *have* to be one of 'us,' of the famished race—for we were at least a pair—to take the situation so to heart" (XIII, 441).

Here it may be mentioned that all first-person narrators

in James are gifted with a striking capacity for intuition. The ultimate refinement of this gift is seen in the governess of "The Turn of the Screw." It is a device by which James achieves economy in presentation, for the alternative course would be to portray the entire slow process by which the narrator gathers his information. The numerous intuitions of the narrator also lead to carefully manipulated alternations of mystification and recognition. The device does not look arbitrary, since an intuitive perception is one of the normal functions of an inquiring mind. However, to avoid ambiguity James almost always has the intuitive flights of his narrators corroborated by subsequent events. H—'s guess about Theobald's national origin soon turns out to be true: "He confessed with a melancholy but an all-respectful headshake to an origin identical with my own" (XIII, 442). This is followed by Theobald's famous speech:

We're the disinherited of Art! We're condemned to be superficial! We're excluded from the magic circle! The soil of American perception is a poor little barren artificial deposit! Yes, we're wedded to imperfection! An American, to excel, has just ten times as much to learn as a European! We lack the deeper sense! We have neither taste nor tact nor force! How *should* we have them! Our crude and garish climate, our silent past, our deafening present, the constant pressure about us of unlovely conditions, are as void of all that nourishes and prompts and inspires the artist as my sad heart is void of bitterness is saying so! We poor aspirants must live in perpetual exile. (XIII, 442)

This, no doubt, is the impassioned voice of a genuine American expatriate, whose "sad heart is void of bitterness" and whose criticism of his own country is at the same time very profound. However, this is only one view of the "complex fate" of being an American. The other side is equally well represented in the answer provided by H—:

You seem fairly at home in exile . . . and Florence seems to me a very easy Siberia. But do you know my own thought? Nothing is so idle as to talk about our want of a nursing air, of a kindly soil, of opportunity, of inspiration, of the things that help. The only thing that helps is to do something fine. There's no law in our glorious Constitution against that. Invent, create, achieve. No matter if you've to study fifty times as much as one of these. What else are you an artist for? Be you our Moses . . . and lead us out of the house of bondage! (XIII, 442)

Theobald is thrown on the defensive: "Don't take me, in heaven's name, for one of your barren complainers, of the falsely fastidious, who have neither talent nor faith! I'm at work!" (XIII, 443). But he soon revives through a brief hymn of praise to Florence, which is followed by a matter-of-fact question from H—: "And have you been very productive all this time?" (XIII, 444). This evokes from Theobald his second significant speech, embodying an extension of the major theme—the expatriate is also an implacable idealist in regard to Art:

Not in the vulgar sense! I've chosen never to manifest myself by imperfection. The good in every performance I've re-absorbed into the generative force of new creations; the bad—there's always plenty of that—I've religiously destroyed. I may say with some satisfaction that I've not added a grain to the rubbish of the world. As a proof of my conscientiousness . . . I've never sold a picture! "At least no merchant traffics in my heart!" Do you remember that divine line in Browning? (XIII, 444)

H— does not make a direct comment on the perfectionist stand taken by Theobald, but to the reader he confesses to a sense of relief on reaching his hotel, "for

I had begun to feel unequal to the society of a genius of this heroic strain" (XIII, 444). In this dialogue, the structural backbone of the tale, along with the gradual revelation of the central character we have a corresponding revelation of the theme. H— secures our identification with his own point of view without presenting Theobald's case in so exaggerated a manner as to make it ridiculous. Such a course would have prematurely alienated our sympathy and deprived us of the capacity to enjoy the accumulating tension of further argument.

The dialogue between H— and Theobald is continued during their second accidental meeting which, in an intended contrast with the first moonlight meeting, takes place in "common daylight" (XIII, 444). The romantic visionary of the previous occasion now strikes H— "as haggard as an actor by daylight" (XIII, 445). But the narrator soon realizes that, appearances apart, Theobald is the same impassioned soul with fire undimmed: "A very little talk, however, cleared his brow and brought back his flow" (XIII, 446). The essential purpose of this meeting is to throw further light on the aesthetic idealism of Theobald. Theobald theorizes eloquently about Art and Taste, while H— reflects sanely that he "inclined more than I approved to the sentimental proposition" (XIII, 446), till they come to Raphael's "Madonna of the Chair" and Theobald pours forth characteristically, ending in a theatrical invocation: "Lovely Madonna, model at once and muse, I call you to witness that I too am an idealist!" (XIII, 449). We notice a further exaggeration of manner in Theobald's effusions. Meanwhile, H— continues to probe into his opinions through a series of deflating questions. The point at issue now is not the rival claims of America and Europe, but the complex relation between reality and art. Here H— is not in much fundamental disagreement with Theobald, and we find him only "sow-ing the false to reap the true" (XIII, 450). However, it is necessary that this dialogue should also move the narrative on toward greater complication. This is done when H— remarks slyly: "Unless I'm mistaken *you* have a master-piece on the stocks. If you put all that in you'll do more than Raphael himself did. Let me know when your picture's finished, and wherever in the wide world I may be I'll post back to Florence and pay my respects to—the *Madonna of the Future!*" (XIII, 452). Once again, it happens that his guess is correct. Theobald has a Madonna in progress, but he detests "this modern custom of pre-mature publicity" (XIII, 452). The section comes to a close with the artist's pathetic appeal for sympathy: "My dear young man . . . I'm worthy of respect. Whatever my limitations may be I'm honest. There's nothing grotesque in a pure ambition or in a life devoted to it" (XIII, 453). The appeal rings out at the end of the tale again, as if to season the reader's final judgment of the deluded artist.

The second section is very brief, a compositional varia-tion, a pause in which the narrator, before going on to the next phase of the story, explicitly connects the extreme idealism of Theobald with the fact of his being an Ameri-can expatriate:

It was hard to have to accept him as of our own hard-headed stock; but after all there could be no better sign of his American star than the completeness of his reaction in favour of vague profits. The very heat of his worship was a mark of conversion; those born within sight of the temple take their opportunities more for granted. He had moreover all our native mistrust for intellectual discretion and our native relish for sonorous superlatives. (XIII, 456)

H—, we notice, has not been taken in by the enthusiasm of his compatriot; besides, Theobald's personal life and his masterpiece are still shrouded in mystery.

In the opening pages of the next and last section, H—
confronts us with another and, it ironically turns out, a
brutally correct version of Theobald's case. This comes
from Mrs. Coventry, who "enjoyed the dignity of a social
high-priestess of the arts" (XIII, 458) and for whom the
reader, on the basis of what he is told by the narrator, has
not much respect: "I shouldn't myself be surprised if,
when one runs him to earth, one finds scarce more than in
that terrible little tale of Balzac's—a mere mass of inco-
herent scratches and daubs, a jumble of dead paint!"
(XIII, 461). Here, incidentally, James points out the
partial thematic affinity of "The Madonna" with Balzac's
"Le Chef-d'oeuvre inconnu."[5] Mrs. Coventry's malicious
but plausible conjecture sharpens the narrator's curiosity
and gives an added urgency to his quest for Theobald's
Madonna. He is soon disenchanted by the stout Serafina,
whose beauty he had been given to believe was "a revelation, a lesson, a morality, a poem!" (XIII, 464). He is also
intrigued by her "attempt to establish an understanding
with me at the expense of our companion" (XIII, 466).
As they leave Serafina's apartment, Theobald reminisces
fondly about the history of his relations with her and tells
H— that now at last he will invite her to sit for him. The
factual part of his reminiscences is perhaps slightly overdone, for it serves no artistic purpose to tell us how he met
Serafina. H—, who has been holding back his disappointment, now breaks into "a headlong exclamation . . . 'My
poor friend, . . . you've *dawdled!* She's an old, old woman
—for a maiden mother'" (XIII, 472). He tries to remedy
his indiscretion but the lifelong illusion of Theobald has
been shattered: "The poor fellow's sense of wasted time, of
vanished opportunity, surged in upon his soul in waves of
darkness. He suddenly dropped his head and burst into
tears" (XIII, 473-474). H— thus becomes instrumental to

the drama by initiating the recognition. This is one of the ways in which James is able to justify the presence of his persona in the tale.

To carry the narrative successfully beyond this point is a hard test of the writer's narrative ingenuity, for any reiteration of Theobald's disillusionment is likely to be anticlimactic. James tries to overcome this difficulty in several ways. He holds out a faint possibility that Theobald may still finish his masterpiece: "'I'll finish it,' he vowed, 'in a month! No, no, in a fortnight! After all I have it *here!*' And he smote his forehead" (XIII, 474). But this by itself is too faint to sustain our interest, particularly in view of the prologue which told us that the hero is not to paint his masterpiece. However, this unconvincing resolve explains, for H——, the disappearance of Theobald from his usual haunts. We know about the ultimate failure of the artist, but we are still interested in how that becomes known to H——. So, for a while, our interest shifts to the narrator's unabated curiosity and to his remorse, a new factor that is reflected in a modulation of tone. Our interest, moreover, in how Theobald himself will face his disillusionment still remains. James also introduces a new focus of interest through his narrator's second visit to Serafina's, where he meets the other artist, the "jaunty Juvenal of the chimney-piece" (XIII, 482). This artist is an obvious foil to Theobald: his proliferations are completely devoid of any serious artistic intention; his promiscuous relations with the madonna Serafina contrast glaringly with Theobald's attachment; his cynical comments upon his "creations" are at the opposite pole of Theobald's idealism; and his success is unmistakable. The narrator might have listened to Theobald's pious effusions with amused skepticism, but he is disgusted by this other artist's loquacious exposition of a vulgar creed, even as he fails to be amused by his vulgar statuettes: "Caricature, burlesque, *la charge,* has hitherto been confined to paper, to pen and pencil. Now it has been my inspiration to introduce it into statuary. . . . What do you say to my types, signore? The idea's bold; does it strike you as happy? Cats and monkeys—monkeys and cats—all human life is there!" (XIII, 481-482). After a brief pause: "My figures are studied from life! I've a little menagerie of monkeys whose frolics I follow by the hour. As for the cats, one has only to look out of one's back window! Since I've begun to examine these expressive little brutes I've made many profound observations. Speaking, signore, to a man of imagination, I may say that my little designs are not without a philosophy of their own. Truly, I don't know whether the cats and monkeys imitate us, or whether it is we who imitate them" (XIII, 483).

The second glimpse of Serafina herself in such promiscuous proximity with the "jaunty Juvenal" disenchants H— more completely than before: "She was coarse and her poor adorer a poet" (XIII, 478). As he leaves her place he "turned an eye on Madonna Serafina, wondering whether she had a sense for contrasts. She had picked up one of the little couples [the vulgar statuettes] and was tenderly dusting it with a feather broom" (XIII, 483-484). H—'s skepticism with regard to Theobald is thus transfigured into compassion. He perceives with unreserved sympathy the extent to which Theobald has been duped by his fond illusions and by his unworthy enchantress. In this way, apart from its intrinsic charm, the episode is vitally important to the full sympathetic exploration of Theobald's case and the theme it exemplifies. After this point the narrator's tone changes completely. Instead of an amused disapproval of Theobald's excessive idealism, he now shows an understanding that is unhampered by the sense of his own intellectual superiority. A corresponding change also takes place in the attitude of the reader, which is a measure of the control the narrator has over the reader's response.

The narrator's visit to Theobald's poor lodgings and the unveiling of the unattempted Madonna, "a canvas that was a mere dead blank cracked and discoloured by time" (XIII, 485), are a natural sequel to the above episode. The prophecy of Mrs. Coventry has come true. Theobald remains faithful to his character until the end and delivers his last terrible speech, which sums up his whole life and is a lesson of the might-have-been Master. The fact that it comes from Theobald and not from the narrator rescues it from the obtrusive extraneousness of an undigested moral:

"You were right," he said with a pitiful smile, "I'm a dawdler! I'm a failure! I shall do nothing more in this world. You opened my eyes, and though the truth is bitter I bear you no grudge. Amen! . . . Since I've been sitting here taking stock of my intellects I've come to believe that I've the material for a hundred masterpieces. But my hand's paralysed now and they'll never be painted. I never began! I waited and waited to be worthier to begin—I wasted my life in preparation. While I fancied my creation was growing it was only dying. I've taken the whole business too hard. . . . I suppose we're a genus by ourselves in the providential scheme—we talents that can't act, that can't do nor dare! We take it out in talk, in study, in plans and promises, in visions! . . . I'm the half of a genius! Where in the world is my other half? Lodged perhaps in the vulgar soul, the cunning ready fingers of some dull copyist or some trivial artisan who turns out by the dozen his easy prodigies of touch! But it's not for me to sneer at him; he at least does something. He's not a dawdler. Well for me if I had been vulgar and clever and reckless, if I could have shut my eyes and taken my leap." (XIII, 485-487)

The speech conforms to the general tenor of the tale so far; it comes as the culminating note and gathers up in its fold and pitch the total meaning of this rhapsodic tale. It is significant that Theobald does not refer to his nationality. Thus the final impression we have of Theobald is not that of an American, but that of a disillusioned artist; his national extraction, and the part played by this in his failure, recedes into the background.

After such a high-pitched speech, the account of the last silent stroll through the Pitti Gallery is refreshing. But the details of Theobald's death and funeral, of the narrator's rudeness to Mrs. Coventry, of his last meeting with Serafina, even his last glimpse of the other artist and his "inimitable 'combinations'"—all these are unnecessary accumulations and round off the narrative a bit too neatly. In this matter of the ending, Balzac's "Le Chef-d'oeuvre inconnu" has an advantage over "The Madonna": "Porbus, in anxiety, went again on the morrow to see Frenhofer, and learned that he had died in the night after burning his canvases."[6] Despite some differences of emphasis, the central idea in both tales is very much the same: the tragic consequence for an artist of the severance between aesthetic theory and artistic practice. But James singles it out in the end as *the* point of his tale. In Balzac's tale the idea is explicitly expressed not by the hero but by Porbus toward the end of a long speech addressed to Poussin: "A sublime painter! but, unluckily for him, he was born to riches, and so he has leisure to follow his fancies. Do not you follow his example! Work! Painters have no business to think, except brush in hand."[7] Theobald was not born to riches; his "misfortune" is more fundamental, and that is why perhaps his fate is more terrible than that of Balzac's Frenhofer. Hawthorne's "The Artist of the Beautiful" must also have been in James's mind as he wrote "The Madonna," but there is not much more than a peripheral thematic resemblance between the two tales.

Furthermore, although both are told in a parable-like manner, James's tale by comparison seems a fully realistic work.

Of course, the urgency behind the theme of "The Madonna" would seem to have a personal basis. Through the created example of Theobald, James may have been forewarning himself against a personally apprehended destiny, in view of his own perfectionist obsession even in the early years. As Cornelia Pulsifer Kelley points out, H— and Theobald "represent the two sides which James felt in himself, and the story is devoted to showing the futility of Theobald's side which talked and lamented but did not act."[8] Needless to say, James in his own practice as a writer successfully avoided the tragic error of Theobald —he produced at an astonishing rate and yet adhered to his perfectionist bias. He kept clear of the divorce between theory and practice without ever having to sink to the prolific vulgarity of the "jaunty Juvenal of the chimney-piece." It may not be too fanciful to suggest that "The Madonna of the Future" had its share in clarifying the issues.

A Passionate Pilgrim

"A Passionate Pilgrim" (1871) has several claims to our attention. It has the distinction of being James's earliest piece in the New York Edition. It belongs to the phase of his immaturity and yet, like its close successors, "The Madonna of the Future" and "Madame de Mauves" (1874), it stands out among his early productions because it fore-shadows the later thematic as well as technical concerns of James. We have only to compare it with some other early first-person tales—for instance, "My Friend Bingham" (1867), "Guest's Confession" (1872), and "Adina" (1874)— to realize this. Thematically, it is significant because the "international department"[9] that it virtually inaugurates is to occupy so vast an area of James's fictional territory. It is extremely rich as a clue to the personal history of James, since it is the earliest fictional projection of his ambivalence toward America and Europe. Finally, it must have had a certain charm as a composition, for it kept attracting James's revisionary attention until it was finally included, with one last revision, in the canon.[10]

Of all these distinctions, the one that concerns us most here is the last. James sets himself a very difficult task in this early tale: to portray sympathetically the last days of a man irremediably on the way to dissolution and death. James was to face a similar problem much later in *The Wings of the Dove,* but by then his awareness of this and other artistic difficulties, not to mention the resources developed to overcome them, had become much greater. He was able to solve the problem of *The Wings* in the way described in his preface: "With the clearness I have just noted, accordingly, the last thing in the world it proposed to itself was to be the record predominantly of a collapse. . . . My young woman would *herself* be the opposition— to the catastrophe announced by the associated Fates."[11] The same problem is confronted, and not completely mastered, by James in the later part of *Roderick Hudson,* where the spectacle of collapse, because it is inadequately motivated and has a defective time-scheme, causes disproportion in the structure of the novel.[12] Much closer to "A Passionate Pilgrim," however, is "The Madonna of the Future." There are several similarities between the two tales: the attitude of the protagonists to their home country and to the country of their dreams is similar; both tales are told by a narrator who is not in complete sympathy or in complete disagreement with the hero's position; both protagonists are given to long speeches full of self-analysis and self-pity. But in "The Madonna" the death of the hero is not the main point. It is the shock of his disillusionment that becomes the focal issue; the collapse follows the turning point of the story. Furthermore, the attitude of the narrator is much more distinctly defined so that the dialogue between him and Theobald upholds the structural framework.

In "A Passionate Pilgrim," however, there is neither a precise turning point nor an explicit confrontation between two sharply defined attitudes. Clement Searle starts his pilgrimage without the slightest hold on life: "A cold fatal gentlemanly weakness was expressed indeed in his attenuated person. His eye was restless and deprecating; his whole physiognomy, his manner of shifting his weight from foot to foot, the spiritless droop of his head, told of exhausted intentions, of a will relaxed. His dress was neat and 'toned down'—he might have been in mourning" (XIII, 338). This impression is confirmed by the conversation between Clement Searle and his lawyer friend. There are gusts of despair throughout this conversation. The hero is incurably sick—the disease remains unspecified— and constantly haunted by intimations of mortality. An additional depressing factor is that he is penniless; apparently he does not have even passage money for the return journey. That, in the context of James's other Americans abroad, is an unusual kind of disability. Few of his later pilgrims suffer from this degree of impecuniosity, however dim or unspecified or providential the sources of their funds may be.

The passion of this pilgrim thus is overburdened with an ironic pathos right from the start. The problem is to keep the irony sufficiently under control, for a mocking tone in regard to a dying person is a violation which no degree of cynicism will justify. James accomplishes this difficult feat of tightrope walking between cynicism and sentimentality by a clever manipulation of the narrator's role. One way of using the narrator effectively for this purpose would have been the familiar Jamesian device of showing a gradual change in his response, starting from a mildly skeptical curiosity. The culminating point of this change would then be coincidental with the turning point of the story, and the element of suspense would have been made integral to the unfolding of events in the story. But in "A Passionate Pilgrim" the narrator does not undergo any such gradual or even a sudden change. His role is confined primarily to that of a sympathetic companion in the last days of a sick man. For a very short interval, of course, the narrator perhaps hopes that Clement may get his share of the ancestral estate to which he is a claimant, and that his cousin, "the Sleeping Beauty," may marry him and everything turn out all right. But this hope is very slight; it is neither adequately built up to nor much emphasized. Moreover, it runs its brief course a little before the middle, after which the tale again resumes its downhill direction.

The narrator does not get involved in an explicit argument with Clement Searle whereby the reader may observe a contrast between his attitude and the protagonist's. In one way this is a mark of subtlety: the author does not make the contrast as clear as he does, for instance, in "The Madonna," where the dialogue between Theobald and H— presents two opposing points of view in dialectical juxtaposition. The absence of this dialogue, however, does not work totally in favor of "A Passionate Pilgrim," for the subtlety is achieved at the expense of a structural imbalance between the long mournful rhapsodies of Clement Searle and the mute gentle disapproval of the narrator. Some balance, nevertheless, is restored in an indirect way. The narrator, it must be stressed, is also a passionate pilgrim. He is Clement Searle's spiritual kinsman insofar as his mind's eye also has long cherished the sights he is now actually seeing during a short stay in England. The point, however, is that his passion, though equally strong, is redeemed by greater discrimination. He too has come to "extract the romantic essence" of "the motherland" (XIII, 335) but, apart from the fact that he is not sick and bankrupt, his attitude to England as well as to America is more percipient. So there is an implicit contrast between his point of view and that of the protagonist.

For one thing, the narrator is going back to America, a detail that is casually mentioned in the opening sentence of the narrative: he has not despaired of his country altogether. Again, the tone of his reflections throughout the tale indicates a greater maturity: "The latent preparedness of the American mind even for the most characteristic features of English life was a matter I meanwhile failed to get to the bottom of. The roots of it are indeed so deeply buried in the soil of our early culture that, without some great upheaval of feeling, we are at a loss to say exactly when and where and how it begins. It makes an American's enjoyment of England an emotion more searching than anything Continental" (XIII, 335-336). These essay-like statements indirectly establish the contrast between the narrator and the protagonist. Or take another example. While wandering through the apartments of Hampton Court, the narrator sees Clement Searle "standing motionless before a simpering countess of Sir Peter Lely's creation." After they have recognized each other as fellow lodgers in the Red Lion, Clement "appealed, rather timidly, as to my opinion of the lady. 'Well,' said I, not quite timidly enough perhaps, 'I confess she strikes me as no great matter'" (XIII, 349). As they walk away, "he stole a sidelong glance of farewell at his leering shepherd-ess" (XIII, 349). And after they have been engaged in some talk, unreported, the narrator remarks about his companion: "It was an honest mind enough, with no great cultivation but with a certain natural love of excellent things" (XIII, 350). This deliberately ambiguous reference to Clement's honest mind also indicates the superiority of the narrator.

But this point is quite obvious. The narrator, after all, is a reliable persona projected by the author, and his very presence is a comment upon the poor infatuated invalid, a necessary corrective to Clement's sentimental outpourings. The success of the tale lies in its holding to a mid-position between severity and total approval. One of the ways in which this is accomplished is by the implied distinction between the febrile emotions of the hero and the stable response of the narrator as they give themselves up to the English countryside. Again and again the narrator's poetic descriptions give the tale the melody of an eclogue;[13] again and again the hero's responses show us the different order of his passion and romanticism. The narrator provides, through his evocation of idyllic scenes, an objective correlative to the emotions of his companion, whose own rhapsodies are always excessive, in keeping with his diseased mind. Take, for instance, this excerpt from the long passage in which the narrator describes one of their "vague undirected strolls" (XIII, 362) before proceeding to Lackley Park:

Beyond the stile, across the level velvet of a meadow, a foot-path wandered like a streak drawn by a finger over a surface of fine plush. We followed it from field to field and from stile to stile; it was all adorably the way to church. At the church we finally arrived, lost in its rook-haunted churchyard, hidden from the work-day world by the broad stillness of pastures—a grey, grey tower, a huge black yew, a cluster of village-graves with crooked headstones and protrusions that had settled and sunk. The place seemed so to ache with consecration that my sensitive companion gave way to the force of it.

"You must bury me here, you know"—he caught at my arm. "It's the first place of worship I've seen in my life. How it makes a Sunday where it stands!" (XIII, 364-365)

Clement's demand is of course pathetic, but at the same time it is perilously close to producing a comic effect. The chief technical achievement of the tale is this constant juxtaposition of two levels of sensibility exemplified by the narrator and the protagonist.

There are other beautiful touches that contribute to the richness of the tale's texture. There is, for instance, the picturesque beggar who appears to the two companions in the early part of the tale. "In one hand he had a stick; and on his arm he bore a tattered basket, with a handful of withered vegetables at the bottom. His face was pale haggard and degraded beyond description—as base as a counterfeit coin, yet as modelled somehow as a tragic mask. He too, like everything else, had a history. From what height had he fallen, from what depth had he risen? He was the perfect symbol of generated constituted baseness; and I felt before him in presence of a great artist or actor" (XIII, 355). The portrait of the beggar is romantically exaggerated in order to accord with the narrator's admiration for old England. But even the hero is not completely swept off his feet by the beggar: " 'I feel as if I had seen my *Doppelgänger*,' said Searle. 'He reminds me of myself. What am I but a mere figure in the landscape, a wandering minstrel or picker of daisies?' " (XIII, 355). The presence of this fallen figure in the bright landscape thus gives the reader, if not the hero, a glimpse of the other, the darker, side of the English scene. This is supplemented later in the tale, when a more genteel beggar is introduced to provide a contrast to the scholastic cloisters of Oxford. This gentleman beggar—Rawson is his strange name—by his disconcerting presence in the peaceful atmosphere is made to perform a function similar to that of the earlier beggar: "His eyes were weak and bloodshot; his bold nose was sadly compromised, and his reddish beard, largely streaked with grey, bristled under a month's neglect of the razor. In all this rusty forlornness lurked a visible assurance of our friend's having known better days. Obviously he was the victim of some fatal depreciation in the market value of pure gentility" (XIII, 422). The ironic function of this character, however, becomes much more pointed through the conversation between him and Clement Searle:

"My dear Mr. Rawson, American as I am I'm living on charity."

"And I'm exactly not, sir! There it is. I'm dying for the lack of that same. You say you're a pauper, but it takes an American pauper to go bowling about in a Bath-chair. America's an easy country."

"Ah me!" groaned Searle. "Have I come to the most delicious corner of the ancient world to hear the praise of Yankeeland?"

"Delicious corners are very well, and so is the ancient world," said Mr. Rawson; "but one may sit here hungry and shabby, so long as one isn't too shabby, as well as elsewhere. You'll not persuade me that it's not an easier thing to keep afloat yonder than here. I wish *I* were in Yankeeland, that's all!" he added with feeble force. (XIII, 426)

These two glimpses of an England that perhaps even Clement Searle would not admire combine, as in an old masterpiece, to give the reader a proper perspective, if not to shatter the pilgrim's passion. Even he, however, with the insight provided by Rawson's plight, utters a speech that is a virtual death-bed realization: "My friend, you're a dead failure! Be judged! . . . You and I, sir, have *had* no character—that's very plain. We've been weak, sir; as weak as water. Here we are for it—sitting staring in each other's faces and reading our weakness in each other's eyes. We're of no importance whatever, Mr. Rawson!" (XIII, 427). Thus Searle recognizes, as on the previous occasion, another *Doppelgänger*.[14]

This self-realization, of course, does not quite flash upon the hero's consciousness at this juncture; he has known all along the weakness of his own character. But his tendency has been to shirk responsibility and shift the blame to his circumstances, to the much-lamented fact that he was born in the wrong country. Here is his long peroration earlier in the tale:

"I think," he went on with a charming turn and as if striking off his real explanation, "I should have been all right in a world arranged on different lines. . . . I had the love of old forms and pleasant rites, and I found them nowhere—found a world all hard lines and harsh lights, without shade, without composition, as they say of pictures, without the lovely mystery of colour. To furnish colour I melted down the very substance of my own soul. I went about with my brush, touching up and toning down; a very pretty chiaroscuro you'll find in my track! . . . I should have been born here and not there; here my makeshift distinctions would have found things they'd have been true of." (XIII, 357)

Searle's strictures on American culture and its inadequacies are similar to Theobald's, and the views of both the protagonists are echoed by James more directly elsewhere.[15] In the context of the tale, however, we must notice how James underscores the inadequacies of Searle's own character by making him realize toward the end that he has been "as weak as water." Searle's criticism of America, though it is not entirely canceled out by his self-criticism, is thus not the whole point of his story. Soon after the outburst quoted above—"My friend, you're a dead failure!"—Searle makes another meaningful exclamation: "Searle closed his eyes, shivering with a long-drawn tremor which I hardly knew whether to take for an expression of physical or of mental pain. In a moment I saw it was neither. 'Oh my country, my country, my country!' he murmured in a broken voice; and then sat for some time abstracted and lost" (XIII, 428-429). The murmur sounds like the last salute not only of an expatriate but also of a patriot.

"A Passionate Pilgrim," then, is the portrait of an American as an expatriate just as "The Madonna," in part at least, is the portrait of an American as an artist. In both there is an element of sympathy as well as a touch of mild disapproval. Both demand from the reader, for a proper appreciation of the issues involved, an awareness of James's own ambivalence to America and Europe, an ambivalence that seems to be an important element in the psychological make-up of many American artists before and since James. "The Madonna" is less dependent on these external aids to appreciation because it also embodies the universal themes of illusion versus reality and the relation between artistic theory and practice. The element of romance predominates in both, but the saving feature is the author's tendency to expose rather than to endorse the romantic malaise of the hero.

Four Meetings

"The Madonna of the Future" and "A Passionate Pilgrim" are tales of nouvelle scope. "Four Meetings" (1877) is an anecdote, although its length would place it near the borderline of some of James's shortest nouvelles. In the New York Edition it forms part of a volume (XVI) one of whose unifying principles seems to be the brevity of its constituent parts. James makes no reference to "Four Meetings" in the prefaces, perhaps because it belongs among the "poor relations" of the family; but manifestly its place is not among the poorest which James "for this formal appearance in society [cut] without a scruple."[16] At any rate, although we are not, like Ford Madox Ford, "compelled to say that it is unsurpassed in the literature of any language or of any age,"[17] we can still appreciate and admire its simplicity. It opens with a brief introduction by the narrator: "I saw her but four times, though I remember them vividly; she made her impression on me. I thought her very pretty and very interesting—a touching specimen of a type with which I had had other and perhaps less charming associations. I'm sorry to hear of her death, and yet when I think of it why *should* I be? The last time I saw her she was certainly not—! But it will be of interest to take our meetings in order" (XVI, 267). It is a kind of teaser, different from the prologues of the frame tales in that it does not come from a teller other than the main narrator. James employs the same method in a few other tales, such as "The Solution" (1889-90), "The Special Type" (1900), and "The Next Time" (1895). It indicates in advance the attitude of the narrator to the principal character, but we understand his full meaning only after we have finished the piece. Though not quite indispensable, this brief prologue is in perfect harmony with the uncomplicated manner of the body of the tale.

The tale itself is organized on the simplest of designs. The narrator gives a vivid chronological account of each of his four meetings with Caroline Spencer, recreating each with great concision and in a rising order of intensity. The structure is thus very simple and stylized—a succession of four episodes, each with a climax of its own, producing cumulatively an effect of profound pathos at the wasted life of its heroine. In the first of these episodes the narrator begins by a set characterization:

Miss Caroline Spencer was not quite a beauty, but was none the less, in her small odd way, formed to please. Close upon thirty, by every presumption, she was made almost like a little girl and had the complexion of a child. . . . She was "artistic," I suspected, so far as the polar influences of North Verona could allow for such yearnings or could minister to them. Her eyes were perhaps just too round and too inveterately surprised, but her lips had a certain mild decision and her teeth, when she showed them, were charming. . . . She wore a scanty black silk dress. She spoke with slow soft neatness, even without smiles showing the prettiness of her teeth, and she seemed extremely pleased, in fact quite fluttered, at the prospect of my demonstrations. (XVI, 268-269)

Later we glean our own direct impression of the innocent, simple, reticent New Englander and her quiet but passionate ambition to go to Europe. We are amused by her even as the narrator is; her planned preparation for Europe—study, savings, "craze," faith, and so on—is very touching indeed, until we come to the narrator's climactic speech that gives us a dim anticipation of the disappointment in store for her:

You've the great American disease, and you've got it "bad"— the appetite, morbid and monstrous, for colour and form, for the picturesque and the romantic at any price. I don't know whether we come into the world with it—and with the germs implanted and antecedent to experience; rather perhaps we catch it early, almost before developed consciousness—we *feel,* as we look about, that we're going (to save our souls, or at least our senses) to be thrown back on it hard. We're like travellers in the desert—deprived of water and subject to the terrible mirage, the torment of illusion, of the thirst-fever. (XVI, 274-275)

This sounds like an echo of some speeches in "The Madonna" and "A Passionate Pilgrim." In fact, it is the voice of James in his early manner. Its implied skepticism, however, is wasted on the infatuated heroine, who "listened with her rounded eyes. 'The way you express it's too lovely, and I'm sure it will be just like that'" (XVI, 275).

In his account of the second meeting, the narrator again devotes a few sentences to her appearance: "There was no sign of her being older; she was as gravely, decently, demurely pretty as before. If she had struck me then as a thin-stemmed mild-hued flower of Puritanism it may be imagined whether in her present situation this clear bloom was less appealing" (XVI, 278-279). We gather from the conversation that follows that she is as innocent as ever. Her raptures over what the narrator describes to her as "this poor prosaic Havre" give us the measure of her lack of initiation; her complete trust in her cousin alarms the narrator and the reader as well. The interest of the next meeting lies not so much in the revelation of this disaster as in the light it throws on the character of the heroine. Her innocence, we realize, is matched only by her goodness, and the two combine to deprive her of all but her return fare. The narrator's indignation proves ineffectual in the face of her refusal to think ill of her cousin who, it is clear, has completely disarmed her not only by an account of his pecuniary troubles but by the aid of a letter from his wife, the countess. As the narrator puts it, Caroline "positively found it so interesting to be swindled by a flower of that stock—if stock or flower or solitary grain of truth was really concerned in the matter—as practically to have lost the sense of what the forfeiture of her hoard meant for her" (XVI, 292). But Caroline has no idea that she is being swindled. Her last words to the narrator on this occasion are: "Don't be sorry for me. . . . I'm very sure I shall see something of this dear old Europe yet" (XVI, 293).

The irony of this fond hope becomes clear to us when we have our next and last glimpse of Caroline Spencer.

Only five years have gone by since the narrator's last meeting with her, but "she was much older; she looked tired and wasted" (XVI, 298). Without going into detail, I wish to draw attention to just one point. So far, only the innocence of Caroline Spencer has been in evidence; now we see the dignity she has acquired through suffering. One of the best touches in the tale is the narrator's failure to provoke the heroine into voicing her regrets. She remains impenetrable to the end. The most he can bring her to express is contained in a look: "I took from her eyes, as she approached us, a brief but intense appeal—the mute expression, as I felt, conveyed in the hardest little look she had yet addressed me, of her longing to know what, as a man of the world in general and of the French world in particular, I thought of these allied forces now so encamped on the stricken field of her life" (XVI, 310-311). And a little later, as he takes his leave, "Her wan set little face, severely mild and with the question of a moment before now quite cold in it, spoke of the extreme fatigue, but also of something else strange and conceived—whether a desperate patience still, or at least some other desperation, being more than I can say. What was clearest on the whole was that she was glad I was going" (XVI, 312). It is not that the heroine does not realize what has happened, but that she realizes it only too well. Her resignation, however, remains equal to her bitterness.

The matter of this tale, it seems to me, is rich enough to have fed a novel. The spectacle revealed is the waste of a life, and the person involved, on the evidence of the tale itself, is sensitive enough to suggest all sorts of developments. There is nothing in her situation, in other words, that makes it fit *only* for a "short story." Yet the completeness achieved here, as in all other similarly successful cases, looks final enough to render the question of an alternative dimension irrelevant. "Four Meetings" has an obvious thematic affinity with "The Madonna" and "A Passionate Pilgrim"; but, as compared to Theobald and Clement Searle, Caroline Spencer strikes me as more of an individual and less of a type. "The Madonna" and "A Passionate Pilgrim" focus our attention more on the theme; "Four Meetings" more on the character of its heroine. The subject matter of the earlier tales was actually a projection of James's own inner conflicts about Europe, and this is reflected in the very structure of these tales. "Four Meetings" is not completely devoid of the traces of that conflict, but here James has moved on to create one of his many innocent American heroines, whose triumphs touch as well as baffle the reader. There is the peculiarly Jamesian note of ambiguity in the serenity with which Caroline Spencer accepts her destiny. There is also the peculiarly Jamesian feat of compression, in which the experience of a whole lifetime has been rendered in a short, simple tale.

CHAPTER II

Anecdotes

DURING his "sawdust and orange-peel phase" James deliberately concentrated on the writing of tales as opposed to novels.[1] This partiality in favor of shorter lengths continued for a few years after the debacle of *Guy Domville* in 1895, so that between 1888 and 1900 we have the greatest concentration of James's tales, several of which belong to the category of anecdotes. I shall analyze in this chapter three representative constituents of this category.

Europe

Ostensibly "Europe" (1899) may strike one as a variation on the themes of "A Passionate Pilgrim" and "Four Meetings." In "A Passionate Pilgrim" the anglomania of its hero was the reverse side of his alienation from his native land. In "Four Meetings" the emphasis shifts to an innocent New Englander whose catastrophe is caused not so much by the Europe she adores as by her own innocence, which makes her vulnerable and yet ultimately triumphant in a puzzling way. In "Europe" the longing for Europe on the part of the three of its four characters is even more acute than that of Caroline Spencer; its origin too is the same—only Americans, and more especially New Englanders, James seems to imply, could possibly have this intensity of longing for their old home. But the drama here is acted out within the confines of a family, more

closely still within the consciences of the individual
members of that family. Europe becomes a symbol of
liberation, a force that works only with partial success
against the "bland firm antique" Mrs. Rimmle, who herself becomes a symbol of life-denying puritanism. The
three daughters are shown as hopelessly caught between
the two elemental forces of life and death, between Europe
and Mrs. Rimmle.

"Europe" is much shorter than "A Passionate Pilgrim"
and "Four Meetings," but the situation is much more
complex. The narrator of "A Passionate Pilgrim" has to
deal with a character who is rather simple. He depicts the
pathetic hero through a series of similar situations. In
"Four Meetings" again the focus is on one character, all
others being subsidiary. The neatness of the tale, moreover, comes from a process of elimination and the resulting streamlined structure. The heroine of "Four Meetings"
is more complex than Clement Searle, and her character
is revealed progressively, so that there is greater movement
in the tale. The narrator of "Europe" has to deal with
four characters of almost equal importance. Despite their
apparent solidarity, they are in unrecognized mutual
hostility, the mother on one side and the three daughters
on the other; the daughters have to be further distinguished one from the other so as not to form a mere
block of characters. The narrator's sympathy is with the
daughters, but in order to do proper justice to the story
he has to devote even greater attention to the portrayal of
the mother, who, to make the task still more difficult,
is an unsympathetic character. The form of narration
adopted is not a dramatic rendering of all the important
conversations he has with the various members of the
Rimmle family or his own sister-in-law. Furthermore, for
the proper effect, the narrator must also tackle the problem

of geographically and culturally placing his characters. All this material has to be compressed into a short space without more than a minimum loss of all the inherent values of the situation. "Europe," consequently, is a much more concentrated composition. The coach, to use an expressive Jamesian image, is full, and the court in which he has to maneuver its turn very narrow; success lies in achieving that turn without spilling any passenger or displacing any parcel.[2]

The tale opens with a sentence from a conversation among the members of the Rimmle family whom the narrator is visiting: "Our feeling is, you know, that Becky *should* go" (XVI, 341). The conversation is picked up again some five pages later. In the intervening space, the narrator furnishes the necessary background details: the geographical location of his characters, which we later realize is important; the background of the family; a concentrated account of Mrs. Rimmle's own visit to Europe and the resulting crop of mementos and memories upon which her three daughters have been fed ever since; an impression of Mrs. Rimmle; an impression of the three daughters and the features that distinguish one from the other; the context of the conversation from which the opening sentence of the tale comes. This is an impressive amount of data, and the narrator has to exercise an extraordinary degree of control so that each word carries its full significance. The conversation, when resumed, is carried through three pages or so until the end of the first section. It brings out the intensity of the girls' desire to "go" and their inordinate sense of filial duty, their puritanical conscience which is in conflict with that desire. The outcome of the conversation is the decision that Becky and Jane should go while Maria stays with the mother. The narrator informs us how "each of the daughters had tried—heroically, angelically and for the sake of each of her sisters—not to be one of the two" (XVI, 344). After the decision, however, Maria remarks apropos the mother: "I think she's better than Europe!" This produces an exclamation from Becky and Jane, on which the narrator comments: "It was as if they feared she had suddenly turned cynical over the deep domestic drama of their casting of lots. The innocent laugh with which she answered them gave the measure of her cynicism" (XVI, 348). This is a good instance of the economy and subtlety with which the narrator brings out Maria's hidden disappointment and the alarm of her sisters, who see in her remark an insinuation of their betrayal. The feelings of the mother herself are also cautiously conveyed through the familiar channel of the narrator's intuition, thus foreshadowing the subsequent turn of events: "We separated at last, and my eyes met Mrs. Rimmle's as I held for an instant her aged hand. It was doubtless only my fancy that her calm cold look quietly accused me of something. Of what *could* it accuse me? Only, I thought, of thinking" (XVI, 348). The narrator doubts if the old mother will actually let the daughters go, and the doubt is based entirely on an intuitive reading of the mother's character.

In the second section the narrator foreshortens several of his visits to the Rimmles and the conversations with his sister-in-law. It may be questioned why the sister-in-law is necessary, especially in view of the extremely limited space James allows himself in this tale.[3] She contributes to the dramatic texture of the tale. Instead of a direct report of all that the narrator thinks and feels about Mrs. Rimmle and the helplessness of her daughters, we get this necessary information through the narrator's conversations with the *ficelle*. Given the peculiar limitations of the first-person form, the narrator would have to get his information somehow; the alternative of gleaning it from his own direct observation would have been even more space-consuming. Furthermore, through their conversations an opposition is set up between the Brookbridgean and the cosmopolitan view of the situation. The amusement of the story, always important to James, is also enhanced by the introduction of the funny sister-in-law. These points may be illustrated by a conversation in the third section, after she has informed the narrator of Jane Rimmle's refusal to return home with the Hathaways:

I listened eagerly, after which I produced the comment: "Then she simply refused—"

"To budge from Florence? Simply. She had it out there with the poor Hathaways, who felt responsible for her safety, pledged to restore her to her mother's, to her sisters' hands, and showed herself in a light, they mention under their breath, that made their dear old hair stand on end. Do you know what, when they first got back, they said of her—at least it was *his* phrase—to two or three people?"

I thought a moment. "That she had 'tasted blood'?"

My visitor fairly admired me. "How clever of you to guess! It's exactly what he did say. She appeared—she continues to appear, it seems—in a new character."

.   .   .   .   .

I seemed to see it all—to see even the scared Hathaways. "So she *is* alone?"

"She told them, poor thing, it appears, and in a tone they'll never forget, that she was in any case quite old enough to be. She cried—she quite went on—over not having come sooner."

.   .   .   .   .

I burst out laughing. "Magnificent Jane! It's most interesting. Only I feel that I distinctly *should* 'know' her. To my sense, always, I must tell you, she had it in her."

.   .   .   .   .

"You don't know the queerest part. I mean the way it has *most* brought her out."

". . . You don't mean she has taken to drink?"
My visitor had a dignity—and yet had to have a freedom.
"She has taken to flirting."

.   .   .   .   .

". . . But has she means?"
"Means to flirt?"—my friend looked an instant as if she
spoke literally. "I don't understand about the means—though
of course they have something. But I have my impression,"
she went on. "I think that Becky—" It seemed almost too
grave to say.
But *I* had no doubts. "That Becky's backing her?"
She brought it out. "Financing her."
"Stupendous Becky! So that morally then—"
"Becky's quite in sympathy. But isn't it too odd?" my sister-
in-law asked.

.   .   .   .   .

"And what does the old woman say?"
"To Jane's behaviour? Not a word—never speaks of it. She
talks now much less than she used—only seems to wait. But
it's my belief she thinks."
"And—do you mean—knows?"
"Yes, knows she's abandoned. In her silence there she takes
it in." (XVI, 358-361)

Had all this come from the narrator, much of the
excitement, to say the least, would have been lost. Soon
after this conversation the narrator goes to Brookbridge
where at his sister-in-law's house he meets Becky, whom
at first he takes for her mother: "Becky's age was quite
startling; it had made a great stride, though, strangely
enough, irrecoverably seated as she now was in it, she had
a wizened brightness that I had scarcely yet seen in her"
(XVI, 362). He reflects how "Europe," albeit at second
remove, has brought Becky out, both metaphorically and
literally, for it is the first occasion that he meets Becky
outside her mother's drawingroom. During the conversation with Becky he is puzzled to hear that the old Mrs.

Rimmle is "not alive" (XVI, 363), and he pays a visit to the Rimmle house in order to satisfy his curiosity. He finds Mrs. Rimmle "in her usual place. Though wasted and shrunken she still occupied her high-backed chair with a visible theory of erectness, and her intensely aged face— combined with something dauntless that belonged to her very presence and that was effective even in this extremity —might have been that of some immemorial sovereign, of indistinguishable sex, brought forth to be shown to the people in disproof of the rumour of extinction. Mummified and open-eyed she looked at me, but I had no impression that she made me out" (XVI, 365). The visit is brief and the account of it further abbreviated, the narrator concentrating on the malevolently fantastic identification, in the old lady's confused mind, of "Europe" with death. For Jane is dead, and now it is Becky's turn to "go." The narrator comes away thinking he will never again see Becky; some time later he learns about Becky's "departure," her actual death. On his last visit to the Rimmle house, some six months later, he finds "the centenarian mummy" as eternal as ever and Maria looking even older than her mother. Jane is still in Europe.

"Won't Miss Jane come back?"
Oh the headshake she [Maria] gave me! "Never." It positively pictured to me, for the instant, a well-preserved woman, a rich ripe *seconde jeunesse* by the Arno.
"Then that's only to make sure of your finally joining her."
Maria repeated her headshake. "Never." (XVI, 368-369)

Before coming away the narrator has a brief conversation with Mrs. Rimmle:

It was somehow difficult to me to seem to sympathise without hypocrisy, but, so far as a step nearer could do that, I invited communication. "Have you heard where Becky's gone?" the wonderful witch's white lips then extraordinarily asked.

It drew from Maria, as on my previous visit, an uncontrollable groan, and this in turn made me take time to consider. As I considered, however, I had an inspiration. "To Europe?"

I must have adorned it with a strange grimace, but my inspiration had been right. "To Europe," said Mrs. Rimmle. (XVI, 369)

The tale comes to a close with the mother still alive and Maria, it is implied, on her way to Europe–death. The strength of this fine tale derives from the masterly use of images and symbols. The mother assumes a mythical aspect; she becomes a symbol of death. The tale soars into regions of fantasy and terror on the wings of elaborate imagery. The escape of one of the daughters relieves the gloom to a certain extent, but the impression that lasts is of the deadening hold of the "sovereign of indistinguishable sex" over her daughters. The total effect is that of a scathing, though not querulous, condemnation of the witchlike Mrs. Rimmle. That this can be achieved through the agency of a first-person narrator, whose tone remains light without being frivolous and whose point of view remains serious without being solemn, is proof of the wonderful pliability of this time-honored narrative convention.

Brooksmith

"Brooksmith" (1891) is another remarkable specimen of James's ability to establish a character through a sympathetic first-person narrator. The narrator in this case is unhampered by a complicated plot; there is no intricate interlocking of events to serve as a scaffolding, no fully developed scenes. This short tale is straight narration, a character sketch or an essay of the kind that Lamb or Stevenson might have written. It exemplifies the impossibility of erecting good fences between a sketch and a short story. It is not divided into sections, but on closer examination it seems to fall into three structural units. In the first part the narrator evokes the atmosphere of the salon, the "Arcadia" set up by his friend, Oliver Offord, and the important position that the butler, Brooksmith, occupies in it: "I remember vividly every element of the place, down to the intensely Londonish look of the grey opposite houses, in the gap of the white curtains of the high windows, and the exact spot where, on a particular afternoon, I put down my tea-cup for Brooksmith, lingering an instant, to gather it up as if he were plucking a flower. Mr. Offord's drawing-room was indeed Brooksmith's garden, his pruned and tended human parterre, and if we all flourished there and grew well in our places it was largely owing to his supervision" (XVIII, 350). On the specificity of this atmosphere, and on the peculiar position held in it by Brooksmith, depends the efficacy of the rest of the story. So the narrator devotes considerable space, about a third of the whole tale, to this part. The atmosphere, however, is not evoked through fully recreated scenes, but through a careful assemblage of many small illustrative details and snatches of conversation.

The second part of the tale is given to depicting the gradual disintegration of Offord's salon owing to his failing health:

The first day Mr. Offord's door was closed was therefore a dark date in contemporary history. . . . When I took in that our good friend had given up as never before, though only for the occasion, I exclaimed dolefully: "What a difference it will make—and to how many people!"

"I shall be one of them, sir!" said Brooksmith; and that was the beginning of the end. (XVIII, 357)

Brooksmith, we are told, responds to this unfortunate development with a disarming presumption. The narrator could see he was conscious of the decline, almost of the collapse, of our great institution. . . . He had a resigned philo-

sophic sense of what his guests—our guests, as I came to regard
them in our colloquies—would expect. His feeling was that
he wouldn't absolutely have approved of himself as a substitute for Mr. Offord; but he was so saturated with the religion
of habit that he would have made, for our friends, the necessary sacrifice to the divinity. He would take them on a little
further and till they could look about them. I think I saw him
also mentally confronted with the opportunity to deal—for
once in his life—with some of his own dumb preferences, his
limitations of sympathy, *weeding* a little in prospect and returning to a purer tradition. It was not unknown to me that
he considered that toward the end of our host's career a certain
laxity of selection had crept in. (XVIII, 358)

Brooksmith's solicitude for the adherents of the vanishing
salon is touching in view of his own dispossessed future,
of which he is not yet fully aware. The narrator, however,
is now constantly troubled by the question of Brooksmith's
life after Offord's death: "Even my private answer to this
question left me still unsatisfied. No doubt Mr. Offord
would provide for him, but *what* would he provide?—that
was the great point. He couldn't provide society; and
society had become a necessity of Brooksmith's nature"
(XVIII, 359). The narrator has a notion that after Offord's
death he and his friends "for the love of art itself . . . ought
to look to it that such a peculiar faculty and so much
acquired experience shouldn't be wasted. I really think
that if we had caused a few black-edged cards to be struck
off and circulated—'Mr. Brooksmith will continue to receive on the old premises from four to seven; business carried on as usual during the alterations'—the greater number of us would have rallied" (XVIII, 360).

The narrator soon realizes the impracticability of his
plans for setting up Brooksmith. The best he can do is to
try to find him another place and to hope "that he would
be able to give his life a different form—though certainly
not the form, the frequent result of such bereavements, of

his setting up a little shop" (XVIII, 362). The meagerness of the legacy gives the narrator a pause: "Eighty pounds are always eighty pounds, and no one has ever left *me* an equal sum; but, all the same, for Brooksmith, I was disappointed. I don't know what I had expected, but it was almost a shock" (XVIII, 363). To the reader also it comes as a shock, although he has been previously informed, in a casual manner, that Offord "had nothing but his pension and the use for life of the somewhat superannuated house" (XVIII, 351). The shock thus has to do only with the possible impact of the small legacy on Brooksmith's future; no criticism of his late master seems to be implied. Before the visit is over, the narrator makes a consolatory reference to Offord, which "led him to make the speech that has remained with me as the very text of the whole episode":

"Oh sir, it's sad for *you*, very sad indeed, and for a great many gentlemen and ladies; that it is, sir. But for me, sir, it is, if I may say so, still graver even than that: it's just the loss of something that was everything. For me, sir," he went on with rising tears, "he was just *all*, if you know what I mean, sir. You have others, sir, I dare say—not that I would have you understand me to speak of them as in any way tantamount. But you have the pleasures of society, sir; if it's only in talking about him, sir, as I dare say you do freely—for all his blest memory has to fear from it—with gentlemen and ladies who have had the same honour. That's not for me, sir, and I've to keep my associations to myself. Mr. Offord was *my* society, and now, you see, I just haven't any. You go back to conversation, sir, after all, and I go back to my place," Brooksmith stammered, without exaggerated irony or dramatic bitterness, but with a flat unstudied veracity and his hand on the knob of the street-door. He turned it to let me out and then he added: "I just go downstairs, sir, again, and I stay there."

"My poor child," I replied in my emotion, quite as Mr. Offord used to speak, "my dear fellow, leave it to me: *we'll* look after you, we'll all do something for you."

"Ah if you could give me some one *like* him! But there ain't two such in the world," Brooksmith said as we parted. (XVIII, 364-365)

This speech is the best of many good strokes in the tale. It is at once moving and comical. In a minor way it has some of the same urgency of utterance and depth of meaning as the famous outburst of Strether in Gloriani's garden.

After this the narrator gives a concise account of his successive encounters with Brooksmith. On each occasion he finds him in a different job and in less congenial circumstances. The last time he sees him is as a waiter: "I divined moreover that he was only engaged for the evening—he had become a mere waiter, had joined the band of the white-waistcoated who 'go out.' There was something pathetic in this fact—it was a terrible vulgarisation of Brooksmith. It was the mercenary prose of butlerhood; he had given up the struggle for the poetry. . . . However, I supposed he had taken up a precarious branch of his profession because it after all sent him less downstairs" (XVIII, 370-371). The narrator learns at last that Brooksmith has disappeared: "This news was a sharp shock to me, for I had my ideas about his real destination. . . . Somehow and somewhere he had got out of the way altogether, and now I trust that, with characteristic deliberation, he is changing the plates of the immortal gods. . . . He had indeed been spoiled" (XVIII, 371). This last sentence is the essential theme of the tale: the plight of a sensitive servant whom a taste of the society to which he is not born has rendered unfit for the society to which he is. Going beyond that and reading into it the idea of "the unwillingness or inability of society to sustain the artist"[4] is rather farfetched; it ignores the economic disability which intensifies the ironic character of Brooksmith's aspirations. On the other hand, it will not do to read into the tale strictures against a class society. It is a special case: a member of the servant class—who has, to be sure, refined his servant's function to the level of art—after a brief exposure to the amenities of a cultivated circle is unable to accept any other society, whether of his own class or of the upper class, for evidently both lack the sophistication he has seen in Oliver Offord's salon. From the point of view of strict realism, the characterization of Brooksmith is perhaps not entirely flawless. The English butler is something of a myth in literature, if not in life, and James has doubtless romanticized him from his own characteristic concern for aesthetic and social refinements. In any case, butlers are not James's specialty. One may even say with Q. D. Leavis that *"Brooksmith* is a whimsical expression of James's social ideal, and nothing more."[5]

The most important single factor in an anecdote like "Brooksmith" is the careful modulation of the narrator's tone. It is not his gift as a raconteur that is being tapped here so much as the extent of his control over his voice. Without this control, the portrait of Brooksmith might have been impaired by sentimentality; as it is, the portrait, albeit whimsical, is very effective. Another important factor is the right selection of illustrative incident and detail. The actual effect of such a tale should be that, given the space, nothing could be added or subtracted without disturbing the proportions. But since the space is never quite determinable beforehand, the success of the tale lies in creating the impression that its achieved dimension could not have been otherwise.

Greville Fane

A similar impression is created in "Greville Fane" (1892). While writing it, according to his preface, James was aware that this "scant record, to be anything at all, would have to be a minor miracle of foreshortening. For here is exactly an illustrative case: the subject, in this little composition, is 'developmental' enough, while the form has to make the anecdotic concession; and yet who shall say that for the right effect of a small harmony the fusion has failed? We desire doubtless a more detailed notation of the behaviour of the son and daughter, and yet had I believed the right effect missed 'Greville Fane' wouldn't have figured here."[6] The "miracle" is performed in a slightly different manner than in "Europe" and "Brooksmith," for in "Greville Fane" James denies himself almost completely the amenity of illustrating his narrator's insights and observations dramatically; he also forgoes the simplicity of a chronological narrative progression. "Greville Fane" is all summary and report, and the effect of concentration is that much greater.

The "story" element is tenuous. The only real event in the tale is the death of Greville, which takes place off stage. The sequel of that death—the grabbing of her manuscripts by the son and daughter—is disposed of in one quick concluding paragraph. Other events, if they may be so called, such as the marriage of the daughter and the "education" of the son for a novelist's career, mark no turning points in the tale. The entire narrative is, in fact, made up of the narrator's reflections on the life and work of Greville Fane. Consequently, this is a rather unusual piece of composition among James's mature tales. The opening of the tale, however, is quite usual: the narrator starts by establishing the setting for his story. He has been invited to write a brief obituary notice for Greville Fane, who is dying and whom he likes but does not admire. He reaches her house in the neighborhood of Primrose Hill a little after her death, suffers a meeting with her "very tall, very stiff, very cold" daughter, Lady Luard, (XVI, 110) and the son, Leoline, who looks "impudent even in his grief" and whose air is "quite that of his mother's murderer" (XVI, 111). His apprehension that the survivors may already be calculating the proceeds from their mother's unpublished writings is soon confirmed, and he escapes from the unhappy place as soon as possible. Then he writes his little article where he "had to be pointed without being lively" and which "took some doing," and continues to think about Greville Fane: "I'm reluctant to lose that retrospect altogether, and this is a dim little memory of it, a document not to 'serve.' The dear woman had written a hundred stories, but none so curious as her own" (XVI, 112).

This is a familiar Jamesian prologue; but the tale itself is a brief critical-biographical essay. The subject of the "essay" is an inferior novelist; its writer, the narrator, is himself a novelist with superior gifts. The first four pages of his reflections are devoted entirely to comments upon the "art" of Greville Fane. They read like the numerous literary reminiscences of Henry James and could easily be from one of his "partial portraits"; they are delightfully phrased and show uncommon critical sense. The narrator here is more of a critic than a raconteur, more of a reporter than a "dramatist." But there is fictional tension in this part of the tale, and it comes from the contrast between the narrator and Greville. The narrator had at first expected that "her greatness would come out in her conversation" and was not disappointed to find her

only a dull kind woman. This was why I liked her—she rested me so from literature. To myself literature was an irritation, a torment; but Greville Fane slumbered in the intellectual part of it even as a cat on a hearthrug or a Creole in a hammock. She wasn't a woman of genius, but her faculty was so special, so much a gift out of hand, that I've often wondered why she fell below that distinction. This was doubtless because the transaction, in her case, had remained incomplete;

genius always pays for the gift, feels the debt, and she was placidly unconscious of a call. She could invent stories by the yard, but couldn't write a page of English. She went down to her grave without suspecting that though she had contributed volumes to the diversion of her contemporaries she hadn't contributed a sentence to the language. (XVI, 113)

After he has described "the general formula of [her] work" (XVI, 114), her commercial success, and her immense productivity—three novels a year—the narrator adds another touch to the portrait, again through a glimpse of the contrast between his own attitude and hers: "If I hinted at the grand licking into shape that a work of art required she thought it a pretension and a *pose*. She never recognized the 'torment of form'; the furthest she went was to introduce into one of her books (in satire her hand was heavy) a young poet who was always talking about it. I couldn't quite understand her irritation on this score, for she had nothing at stake in the matter" (XVI, 115). These excerpts are illustration enough of the tone and method of the entire tale. The tone is that of an amused critical commentator and the method is largely undramatized narration.

Still, the tale has a human element that lifts it above the level of a literary essay. The limitations of Greville, the bad novelist, are subtly intertwined with those of Greville, the deluded mother. Her innocence in artistic and intellectual matters—which is so deep that the narrator cannot but take an indulgent view of it—is reflected in her ambitious plans for her undeserving children. She wants to train her boy to become a novelist. She has immense confidence in his gift to learn, if not in her own to teach. The boy accepts his mother's principle "that the intending novelist can't begin too early to see life," takes "to cigarettes at ten on the highest literary grounds," and is the object of her "extravagant envy" (XVI, 120). She wants to bring up her daughter "wholly as a *femme du monde*," and spends for that purpose thousands of francs on her education abroad (XVI, 122). The girl, who in her younger years "was only long, very long, like an undecipherable letter," produces at the end of her education the "effect, large and stiff and afterwards eminent in her, of a certain kind of resolution, something as public and important as if a meeting and a chairman had passed it" (XVI, 118). Thus resolved, she succeeds in marrying Sir Baldwin Luard, "a joyless jokeless young man" with "a determination to get on politically that was indicated by his never having been known to commit himself—as regards any proposition whatever—beyond an unchallengeable 'Oh!' " (XVI, 118). This union of kindred spirits makes the mother very happy, for "the connexion was a 'smarter' one than a child of hers could have aspired to form" (XVI, 119). Her happiness is not mitigated by the fact that "my daughter Lady Luard" considers her vulgar and yet suffers "the inky fingers to press an occasional banknote into her palm" (XVI, 119). About her son—"She loved the young imposter with a simple blind benighted love, and of all the heroes of romance who had passed before her eyes he was by far the brightest" (XVI, 127)—she has similar social ambitions although, appropriately in this case, they are not in the direction of marriage into high society. For him "the greatest thing was to live, because that gave you material"; so "her secret dream was that he should have a *liaison* with a countess, and he persuaded her without great difficulty that he had one" (XVI, 128-129).

These ridiculous ambitions of Greville Fane are congruous with her no less ridiculous ideas about literature. The linking of the two completes the comic-pathetic portrait that the author wants to achieve. The products of her affection and expensive care, when they grow up, are horribly selfish creatures. They deplore her vulgarity and low tastes. The daughter particularly is ashamed of her: "I used to figure her children closeted together and putting it to each other with a gaze of dismay: 'Why should she *be* so—and so *fearfully* so [vulgar] when she has the advantage of our society? Shouldn't *we* have taught her better?'" (XVI, 123). The narrator's humane comment upon this matter is: "Indeed she was, poor lady, [vulgar] but it's never fair to read by the light of taste things essentially not written in it. Greville Fane kept through all her riot of absurdity a witless confidence that should have been as safe from criticism as a stutter or a squint" (XVI, 123). At any rate, these go-getters, her children, have no cause to feel superior because it is they who, partly at least, "keep their mother at her desk" (XVI, 124). Their attitude to her is thus established as being callous as well as immoral. But the pathos of her situation is that she is even more blind to their failings as human beings than she is to her own failings as a writer. So she continues to drive "her whimsical pen," to produce "in all places and at all times the same romantic and ridiculous fictions" (XVI, 121), to exercise "an unequalled gift, especially pen in hand, of squeezing big mistakes into small opportunities" (XVI, 122-123), and helplessly to dote on her children to the end, particularly on the fraudulent son with whom—and this is her crowning absurdity—she finally enters into a curious collaboration: "She had now arrived at a definite understanding with him (it was such a comfort!) that *she* would do the form if he would bring home the substance" (XVI, 133).

"Greville Fane" is unique among James's shortest fictions in the compression it achieves through a sensitive and witty first-person narrator, one who makes the value and charm of his narrative rest almost entirely on the truth of his perceptions and the polish of his style. He accomplishes the difficult task of creating sympathy for an absurd character. Greville Fane is completely devoid of awareness, and James evidently did not have much insight into the psychology of what he called "fools." And yet, by employing an artist to deal with this simple case, he chose exactly the right persona.

CHAPTER III

Nouvelles

(ALSO PARABLES)

THE DIFFICULTY of making a fictional hero out of a perfect artist is axiomatic—James himself has acknowledged his awareness of it.[1] It is perhaps only less intricate than the difficulty of giving a similar status to a perfectly good or a perfectly bad man. Such cases have a habit of turning out too good to be true in fiction, if not always in life. James succeeded in overcoming this problem through irony, through an orchestration of the ironic note, particularly in the tales discussed in this chapter. That explains why most of his tales of the "supersubtle fry"[2] are cast in the comic mode. It also explains why the narrators of all these tales are writers and critics who can be plausibly conceived by the reader as managing their narratives with a requisite awareness of the artistic issues involved. This does not contradict my contention that most of the first-person narrators of James are primarily variations of a narrative method, not fully developed characters in their own right. The point is that these deputies, in order to maintain the illusion of autonomy, must always be chosen with due regard to the idiosyncracies of a given situation. A wrong choice of persona invariably produces a false note as, for instance, in the case of "Maud-Evelyn" (1900) where the narrator ruins the effect of the story by her inappropriately frivolous tone.

This is perhaps as good a place as any to emphasize another point that is relevant to all of James's major tales of writers and artists. There is a tendency among critics to concentrate discussion on thematic values in relation to the artistic beliefs and traits of James himself. This is a legitimate concern, justified by what James himself observed in the preface to *The Lesson of the Master:*

Whereas any anecdote about life pure and simple, as it were, proceeds almost as a matter of course from some good jog of fond fancy's elbow, some pencilled note on somebody else's case, so the material for any picture of personal states so specifically complicated as those of my hapless friends in the present volume will have been drawn preponderantly from the depths of the designer's own mind. This, amusingly enough, is what, on the evidence before us, I seem critically, as I say, to gather—that the states represented, the embarrassments and predicaments studied, the tragedies and comedies recorded, can be intelligibly fathered but on his own intimate experience.[3]

However, after a certain point, consideration of the question of *why* James wrote so many tales about writers and artists, and the related question of why so many were written in the 1890s, ought to be confined to biographical studies of James. For the critic, it should be more important to discuss *how* James was able to objectify his self-revelations. It is only then that we can appreciate the narrative technique and the general ironic skill exemplified in these tales. Similarly, we should not forget that the best of these tales point to the moral that the parabolic form, in the hands of a writer like James, is not inimical to a sophisticated modern treatment. They illustrate, moreover, what James spoke of in another connection as his "love of 'a story as a story.'"[4] This predilection of the author saves them from being mere fictional footnotes to his own preoccupations with form. It explains why James

is so concerned with providing an adequate human sub-
stratum in all these tales, a concern that manifests itself
in the numerous subplots, in the minor romances and the
personal involvements of the narrator.

The Next Time

The contrast between the good and the bad writer—and
the enormous disparity between the material rewards of
each—was an element in the anecdote "Greville Fane."
It is the central idea in the nouvelle "The Next Time"
(1895). Jane Highmore with her "generation of triplets"
is an avatar of Greville Fane with her three novels a year.
But in "The Next Time" James adds an interesting complication. Jane Highmore yearns "to be, like Limbert,
but of course only once, an exquisite failure" (XV, 158),
while Limbert wears himself out in a futile effort to "make
a sow's ear of a silk purse!" (XV, 204). Her "fantastic
thirst for quality" (XV, 161) remains unquenched even as
Limbert remains to the end of his career "an undiscourage-
able parent to whom only girls kept being born" (XV, 214).
This antithesis, however, is not as mechanically worked
out as a summary of the tale might suggest. Most of the tale
is devoted to Limbert's side of the dilemma. Mrs. Highmore's failure to be an exquisite failure is more or less
taken for granted and used only as an ironic backdrop for
Ray Limbert's drama.

The narrator begins with a prologue designed to involve
the reader in the ensuing story. Mrs. Highmore approaches
him with a request "to write a notice of her great forth-
coming work" (XV, 157), the ground of her request being
that "I had frightened the public too much for our late
friend [Ray Limbert], but that as she was not starving
this was exactly what her grosser reputation required"
(XV, 161). He is

frankly appalled at what she expects of me. What's she thinking of, poor dear, and what has put it into her head that the
muse of "quality" has ever sat with her for so much as three
minutes? . . . What does she imagine she has left out? What
does she conceive she has put in? She has neither left out nor
put in anything. I shall have to write her an embarrassed note.
The book doesn't exist and there's nothing in life to say about
it. How can there by anything but the same old faithful rush
for it? (XV, 162)

The transition from the prologue to the actual tale is very
smooth, for the first section opens: "This rush had begun
when, early in the seventies, in the interest of her prospective brother-in-law, she approached me on the singular
ground of the unencouraged sentiment I had entertained
for her sister. Pretty pink Maud had cast me out, but I
appear to have passed in the flurried little circle for a
magnanimous youth" (XV, 163).

The narrator is thus bound to the main characters of the
tale by a silken thread. He is a rejected suitor of Maud,
Mrs. Highmore's sister, who later marries Ray Limbert.
This is an incidental connection and, strictly speaking, not
indispensable to his function as a narrator. But it does lend
flavor to the tale: "He [Limbert] saw more even than I
had done in the girl he was engaged to; as time went on I
became conscious that we had both, properly enough, seen
rather more than there was. Our odd situation, that of the
three of us, became perfectly possible from the moment I
recognized how much more patience he had with her than
I should have had. I was happy at not having to supply
this quantity, and she, on her side, found pleasure in being
able to be impertinent to me without incurring the re-
proach of the bad wife" (XV, 166). The point is—as it was
suggested earlier—that James's passion for form is seldom
incompatible with his desire to offer a superior amusement
to the reader. This is but another way of saying that

James's first-person narrators would hardly be the irresistible storytellers they are if they remained rigorously "to the point" throughout their narratives. Their skill, however, lies in maintaining the total effect without ever straying very far from the narrow path.

The rest of the first section tells us how the narrator is favorably impressed first by Limbert's work and then by Limbert himself, how he gets him a correspondent's job with *The Blackport Beacon,* and how the job is lost, thus putting Limbert's marriage with Maud in temporary jeopardy. The narrator gets this news from Maud, and the conversation between the two provides an amusing scene. Limbert's letters are not gossipy enough, and his notice about the narrator's "wretched book . . . was the last straw! He should have treated it superficially" (XV, 172). He had done so but the treatment, in the opinion of the *Beacon,* was not superficial enough. In the next section Limbert resumes work on "The Major Key," his new novel, while Maud patiently waits for the disappearance of her mother's objections to the marriage. This happens when "The Major Key" is accepted by Mrs. Highmore's "pearl of publishers" (XV, 177) for serialization prior to publication; Limbert and Maud are married while the novel is still running.

We had at times some dispute as to whether "The Major Key" was making an impression, but our difference could only be futile so long as we were not agreed as to what an impression consisted of. Several persons wrote to the author and several others asked to be introduced to him: wasn't that an impression? One of the lively "weeklies," snapping at the deadly "monthlies," said the whole thing was "grossly inartistic"— wasn't *that?* . . . The strongest effect doubtless was produced on the publisher when, in its lemon-coloured volumes, like a little dish of three custards, the book was at last served cold: he never got his money back and so far as I know has never got it back to this day. "The Major Key" was rather a great performance than a great success. (XV, 178-179)

During the next four or five years Limbert produces two unprofitable masterpieces while his family grows by three children. Mrs. Highmore keeps pouring advice into Limbert's ears about "how a reputation might be with a little gumption . . . 'worked.' Save when she occasionally bore testimony to her desire to do, as Limbert did, something some day for her own very self, I never heard her speak of the literary motive as if it were distinguishable from the pecuniary. . . . To listen to her you would have thought the profession of letters a wonderful game of bluff" (XV, 181). This section contains no fully developed scene, but the impression of domestic pressures, which will soon drive Limbert into a long and resolute defiance of his genius, is created synoptically:

Within doors and without Limbert's life was overhung by an awful region that figured in his conversation, comprehensively and with unpremeditated art, as Upstairs. It was Upstairs that the thunder gathered, that Mrs. Stannace kept her accounts and her state, that Mrs. Limbert had her babies and her headaches, that the bells for ever jangled at the maids, that everything imperative in short took place—everything that he had somehow, pen in hand, to meet, to deal with and dispose of, in the little room on the garden-level. I don't think he liked to go Upstairs, but no special burst of confidence was needed to make me feel that a terrible deal of service went. (XV, 182)

In the third section we learn that Limbert has accepted an editorial position and, what is more, has decided to woo the public if that will enable him to balance his accounts. The narrator welds Limbert's several remarks on the subject into a long cynical speech:

We've sat prating here of "success," heaven help us, like chanting monks in a cloister, hugging the sweet delusion that it lies somewhere in the work itself, in the expression, as you said, of one's subject or the intensification, as somebody else somewhere says, of one's note. . . . What *is* "success" anyhow? When a book's right it's right—shame to it surely if it isn't. When it sells it sells—it brings money like potatoes or beer. . . . Success be hanged!—I want to sell. It's a question of life and death. I must study the way. I've studied too much the other way—I know the other way now, every inch of it. I must cultivate the market—it's a science like another. . . . I haven't been obvious—I must *be* obvious. I haven't been popular— I must *be* popular. It's another art—or perhaps it isn't an art at all. It's something else; one must find out *what* it is. It is something awfully queer?—you blush!—something barely decent? All the greater incentive to curiosity! . . . Of course, I've everything to unlearn; but what's life, as Jane Highmore says, but a lesson? I must get all I can, all she can give me, from Jane. She can't explain herself much; she's all intuition; her processes are obscure; it's the spirit that swoops down and catches her up. But I must study her reverently in her works. Yes, you've defied me before, but now my loins are girded: I declare I'll *read* one of them—I really will; I'll put it through if I perish! (XV, 187-188)

In accordance with this system, Limbert takes all manner of precautions, but unhappily for him the new book, which he has consciously written down to the public, turns out to be yet another masterpiece: "It was, no doubt, like the old letters to the *Beacon,* the worst he could do; but the perversity of the effort, even though heroic, had been frustrated by the purity of the gift" (XV, 194). The whole of the fourth section is given to a typically Jamesian scene, in which an artificial excitement is imparted to the process whereby the narrator learns of Limbert's dismissal from the magazine. Later in the scene, however, he prophesies to Jane Highmore that for Limbert there will never be any success. He also puts down the moral of the parable:

"Que voulez-vous?" I went on; "you can't make a sow's ear of a silk purse! It's grievous indeed if you like—there are people who can't be vulgar for trying. *He* can't—it wouldn't come off,

I promise you, even once. It takes more than trying—it comes by grace. It happens not to be given to Limbert to fall. He belongs to the heights—he breathes there, he lives there, and it's accordingly to the heights I must ascend," I said as I took leave of my conductress, "to carry him this wretched news from where *we* move!" (XV, 204)

This is followed by the last section, in which the reader's interest is sustained by the narrator's now serious tone. Limbert continues to nurse hopes for "the next time" as he retreats to the country: "He had found a quieter corner than any corner of the great world, and a damp old house at tenpence a year, which beside leaving him all his margin to educate his children, would allow of the supreme luxury of his frankly presenting himself as a poor man" (XV, 208). At the same time, he keeps adding to the number of his "fine miscarriages" (XV, 208). This section gives greater attention to some of the painful consequences of his commercial failure, but it is done without any sentimental inflection in the narrator's tone:

She [Mrs. Limbert] had her burdens, dear lady: after the removal from London and a considerable interval she twice again became a mother. Mrs. Stannace too, in a more restricted sense, exhibited afresh, in relation to the home she had abandoned, the same exemplary character. In her poverty of guarantees at Stanhope Gardens [Mrs. Highmore's place] there had been least of all, it appeared, a proviso that she shouldn't resentfully revert again from Goneril to Regan. She came down to the goose-green like Lear himself, with fewer knights, or at least baronets, and the joint household was at last patched up. It fell to pieces and was put together on various occasions before Ray Limbert died. He was ridden to the end by the superstition that he had broken up Mrs. Stannace's original home on pretences that had proved hollow, and that if he hadn't given Maud what she might have had he could at least give her back her mother. I was always sure that a sense of the compensations he owed was half the motive of the

dogged pride with which he tried to wake up the libraries.
(XV, 209)

More attention is also paid to Mrs. Limbert's ultimate
acceptance of her husband's genius: "I believe that in these
final years she would almost have been ashamed of him if
he had suddenly gone into editions" (XV, 212). As a result
of the effect of all these background figures and details,
Limbert's case is sufficiently humanized and the tale is
saved from being a bare parabolic exemplification of un-
appreciated genius. As the final twist in the tale, Limbert
is shown as having completely renounced his futile efforts
to cultivate the public. He goes to work on his last book

in quiet mystery, without revelations even to his wife. . . . The
great thing was that he was immensely interested and was
pleased with the omens. I got a strange stirring sense that
he had not consulted the usual ones and indeed that he had
floated away into a grand indifference, into a reckless consciousness of art. The voice of the market had suddenly grown
faint and far: he had come back at the last, as people so often
do, to one of the moods, the sincerities of his prime. . . . What
had happened, I was afterwards satisfied, was that he had quite
forgotten whether he generally sold or not. He had merely
waked up one morning again in the country of the blue and
had stayed there with a good conscience and a great idea. He
stayed till death knocked at the gate, for the pen dropped
from his hand only at the moment when, from sudden failure
of the heart, his eyes, as he sank back in his chair, closed for
ever. "Derogation" is a splendid fragment; it evidently would
have been one of his high successes. I am not prepared to say
it would have waked up the libraries. (XV, 215-216)

In the end he regains even his good conscience, and his
triumph over the public is thus shown to be complete.

The tone of the tale generally remains that of high
comedy, but it does not impair the seriousness of the
author's intention. Furthermore, the chief source of comic

mirth is not the hero himself, even though the exagger-
atedly protracted defiance of his genius, which itself is
exaggerated, has its comic aspect. The joke essentially is
on "the broad-backed public. . . . Such a study as that of
Ray Limbert's so prolonged, so intensified, but so vain
continuance in hope (hope of successfully growing in his
temperate garden some specimen of the rank exotic
whose leaves are rustling cheques) is in essence a 'story
about the public,' only wearing a little the reduced face
by reason of the too huge scale, for direct portrayals, of the
monstrous countenance itself."[5] This "monstrous countenance" is telescoped in Mrs. Highmore whose "fond con-
sumers . . . wagged their great collective tail artlessly for
more" (XV, 160), in Mr. Highmore who "took his stand
on accomplished work and, turning up his coattails,
warmed his rear with a good conscience at the neat book-
case in which the generations of triplets were chronologi-
cally arranged" (XV, 176), in *The Blackport Beacon* whose
appetite for the chatty is insatiable, in Mr. Bousefield the
editor who for all his pretensions prefers the "screaming
sketches" of Minnie Meadows, and in the circulating libraries whose sleep Limbert tries in vain to disturb.

The Death of the Lion

In regard to James's penchant for contrasts—a point
noticed in "Greville Fane" and "The Next Time"—I
should briefly mention first "The Private Life" (1892),
where the contrast determines the entire structure of the
tale. In the preface James discusses the genesis of the tale
and concludes: "One's harmless formula for the poetic
employment of this pair of conceits couldn't go further
than 'Play them against each other'—the ingenuity of
which small game 'The Private Life' reflects as it can."[6]
The conceits are antithetical, so that by playing them

against each other James achieves the balance of an extended dramatized epigram. Clare Vawdrey, the eminent writer, is really two men[7]—as the narrator tells his accomplice in the game, Blanche Adney, "One goes out, the other stays home. One's the genius, the other's the bourgeois, and it's only the bourgeois whom we persnoally know" (XVII, 244). Lord Mellifont, the eminent man of affairs (although he paints too), in Blanche Adney's words, "isn't even whole" (XVII, 245)—he literally disappears the moment he is alone.

The tale is suitably divided into two sections. In the first the narrator makes the discovery about Clare Vawdrey, in the second about Lord Mellifont. The first discovery, however, is made directly by him, and there is some appropriateness in this, for he himself is a writer (though we are not told whether he has an alternate identity). The second discovery is conveyed to the narrator by Blanche Adney, an actress; there is appropriateness in this too, for Lord Mellifont after all is an actor on the vast stage of public affairs. The epigram is thus transformed into a brilliant piece of drama. Other elements are introduced, which contribute to the epigrammatical structure of the story and add to the entertainment of the reader. The narrator's account of his discovery is matched by Blanche Adney's account of hers; she wants to see the "real" Clare Vawdrey; the narrator on his side is equally eager to "see" for himself the nonexisting Lord Mellifont when he is alone with himself. Both try, and another variation is introduced here: Blanche Adney succeeds in seeing the real Vawdrey while the narrator is balked in his efforts to surprise Lord Mellifont in his solitude by the unexpected appearance of Lady Mellifont, in whose eyes he sees "the confession of her own curiosity and the dread of the consequence of mine" (XVII, 261).

"The Private Life" is thus all cleverness and sleight of hand insofar as its execution goes. It is a kind of joke as well as a kind of truth. But a brilliant joke or epigram should not be explicated; it should only be heard. It would be wrong to deduce from "The Private Life" that every man of genius, according to James, is as fortunately endowed as Clare Vawdrey with two peacefully coexisting selves. The man of public affairs is another matter, and in his case it may be nearer the truth to suggest that James wanted to represent in Lord Mellifont a typical case.

At any rate, "The Death of the Lion" (1894) is a powerful refutation of any complacent notion about the "private life" of a genius and its invulnerability. Here again, no doubt, the case is considerably exaggerated in order to make the intended point; and the effect of exaggeration, as in most of these tales, is comedy bordering on fantasy or, if you like, fantasy bordering on comedy. The story is told, as in the case of "The Author of Beltraffio," by an earnest disciple of the hero. The focal point is the process of artistic disintegration that sets in once the privacy of Neil Paraday is invaded by the hordes of publicity mongers and, as a consequence, he is raised to the dubious status of the "poor foredoomed monarch of the jungle."[8] The lion is doomed the moment he is dragged out of the privacy of his den. We cannot say that he is lured out of that sanctum, since the moral of the fable is his helplessness once the process is under way. The devoted services of the narrator, who has a vision of the horrible end from the beginning, also prove ineffectual, for he, a poor honest scribe, is nothing as opposed to the "blind violent force" represented by Mrs. Weeks Wimbush, "wife of the boundless brewer and proprietress of the universal menagerie" (XV, 123).

The organization of the tale is very effective. The narrator begins with a tantalizing mention of "a change of heart," which "must have begun when I received my manuscript back from Mr. Pinhorn" (XV, 99). Then he gives an extremely funny and concentrated account of the way he got the assignment to do an article on Neil Paraday. This brief retrospect presents a satirical picture of the newspaper world represented by Mr. Pinhorn, with its "reverberations" represented by Miss Braby, Lord Crouchley, and Mrs. Bounder. A complete anecdote in itself, it gives the reader an inkling of the fatal exposure awaiting the hero. Toward the end of the section, speaking of the sudden dispatch with which Mr. Pinhorn had "bundled me off," the narrator remarks: "It was a pure case of professional *flair*—he had smelt the coming glory as an animal smells its distant prey" (XV, 102). We should notice the bestial imagery that recurs throughout the tale; both the hunters and the hunted are repeatedly pictured as animals or as keepers of animals.

The second section opens with a warning of the type quite common to Jamesian narrators: "I may as well say at once that this little record pretends in no degree to be a picture either of my introduction to Mr. Paraday or of certain proximate steps and stages. . . . These meagre notes are essentially private, so that if they see the light the insidious forces that, as my story itself shows, make at present for publicity will simply have overmastered my precautions. The curtain fell lately enough on the lamentable drama" (XV, 103). These remarks indicate how the narrator weaves his spell, giving at the same time an idea of what the story is to "show." The rest of this section, even briefer than the first, tells how the narrator's article—"a little finicking feverish study of my author's talent"—was rejected, for Mr. Pinhorn wanted "the genuine article, the revealing and reverberating sketch to the promise of which, and of which alone, I owed my squandered privilege" (XV, 105). The narrator now also enlightens us as to what he meant in the preceding section about his change of heart: "There had been a big brush of wings, the flash of an opaline robe, and then, with a great cool stir of the air, the sense of an angel's having swooped down and caught me to his bosom. . . . With my manuscript back on my hands I understood the phenomenon better, and the reflexions I made on it are what I meant, at the beginning of this anecdote, by my change of heart" (XV, 105).

Thus we are prepared for the appearance of the "genuine article," done by someone else of course, in *The Empire*. But before seeing this article the narrator has a brief session with the master, who reads out to him the written plan of his next book: "The idea he now communicated had all the freshness, the flushed fairness, of the conception untouched and untried: it was Venus rising from the sea and before the airs had blown upon her" (XV, 106). A short conversation follows in which the narrator expresses his concern about the menace to Neil Paraday's privacy. Ironically enough, the danger manifests itself just then in the form of a visitor whose identity is revealed in the next section. Meanwhile, the narrator happens to notice the article in *The Empire*, which gives rise to grim musings:

The big blundering newspaper had discovered him, and now he was proclaimed and anointed and crowned. . . . A national glory was needed, and it was an immense convenience he was there. What all this meant rolled over me, and I fear I grew a little faint—it meant so much more than I could say "yea" to on the spot. In a flash, somehow, all was different; the tremendous wave I speak of had swept something away. It had knocked down, I suppose, my little customary altar, my twinkling tapers and my flowers, and had reared itself into the

likeness of a temple vast and bare. When Neil Paraday should
come out of the house he would come out a contemporary.
That was what had happened: the poor man was to be
squeezed into his horrible age. I felt as if he had been over-
taken on the crest of the hill and brought back to the city.
A little more and he would have dipped into the short cut
to posterity and escaped. (XV, 110-111)

Here again we see how the narrator's intuitive powers
are being tapped in order to anticipate the subsequent
turn of events. The narrator here has a rather precarious
objective basis for his dark prophecies, but the next two
sections justify his apprehensions. Neil Paraday comes out
of the house "exactly as if he had been in custody, for
beside him walked a stout man with a big black beard,
who, save that he wore spectacles, might have been a police-
man, and in whom at a second glance I recognized the
highest contemporary enterprise" (XV, 112). Paraday's
captor is Mr. Morrow—the ominous name points to what
is in store for the hero—the representative of no less than
thirty-seven journals, holding a special commission from
The Tatler, "whose most prominent department, 'Smatter
and Chatter'—I dare say you've often enjoyed it—attracts
such attention" (XV, 113). Paraday sinks to a bench "at
once detached and confounded" (XV, 113), while Mr.
Morrow goes on blandly, pocketing "the whole poor place
while Paraday and I were wool-gathering" (XV, 114), talking of Guy Walshingham and Dora Forbes, confusing his
listeners about the real sex of these two celebrities and
ultimately sending the poor frightened master back into
the house. This fifth section is brilliantly comic. Mr. Morrow is horrified by the prospect of having to listen to anything so irrelevant to his purpose as the author's works;
he had come only for the "surroundings" which he has
well enough in hand to publish "a charming chatty fa-

miliar account of Mr. Paraday's 'Home-life,' " and to send it "on the wings of the thirty-seven influential journals, . . . to use Mr. Morrow's own expression, right around the globe" (XV, 121).

These five sections constitute, structurally, the first part of the tale. Here the prey is discovered; the actual killing is to be done by the lionizing London society, led by the expert keeper of lions and lambs, Mrs. Wimbush.[9] The general tone of the tale is firmly established in these fast-moving sections. The narrator's point of view, clear from the outset, becomes thoroughly defined by the time we see him in the full exercise of his irony with Mr. Morrow. In the sixth section, therefore, we see "the king of the beasts of the year" in London, circulating "in person to a measure that the libraries might well have envied" (XV, 122). The narrator is determined to protect him, but he has reckoned without Mrs. Wimbush, who is always making "appointments with him [Paraday] to discuss the best means of economising his time and protecting his privacy" (XV, 125).

In the seventh section we have a companion scene to the earlier one with Mr. Morrow. Here, however, the narrator's ingenuity is better employed, for his gospel of seeking the author "in his works as God in nature" (XV, 133) is addressed to the more receptive ears of an innocent American girl, Fanny Hurter. Her name notwithstanding, she is presented with affectionate irony; the narrator's success in weaning her away from Neil Paraday ironically contrasts with his failure on the real front, where the more formidable and fatal antagonist, Mrs. Wimbush, ultimately triumphs. In the eighth section we get further instances of the narrator's failure to protect Paraday. Paraday has been caught by a young painter, Mr. Rumble, according to whom "to figure in his show [the narrator

likens his studio to a circus] was not so much a consequence as a cause of immortality" (XV, 136). No sooner
is he out of this than he is "stuffed by Mrs. Wimbush into
the mouth of another cannon," another painter who is "to
show how far *he* could make him go" (XV, 136). The
narrator frets and fumes in vain over the editors of maga-
zines who make Paraday "grind their axes by contributing
his views on vital topics and taking part in the periodical
prattle about the future of fiction" (XV, 137). It is suggested that Paraday "surrendered himself much more liberally than I surrendered him," for "how could he have
heard a mere dirge in the bells of his accession?" (XV,
137-138).

The climactic stage in the battle between the narrator
and Mrs. Wimbush is reached over her plans for Paraday
to visit her country house, Prestidge. It is on the cards, as
James would say, that the narrator should be worsted in
this conclusive bout, and the lion is taken away to Prestidge where the narrator soon joins him. This section,
a good specimen of Jamesian foreshortening, is a concentrated account of all that leads up to the collapse of
Paraday. Paraday's own lack of resistance to the forces be-
setting him is neither stressed nor suggested with undue
irony, the whole point being his utter helplessness in the
circumstances: the "lion" has been tamed. ——

In the ninth, and penultimate, section the narrator
varies his method by an epistolary interlude—he quotes
extensively from his letters to Fanny Hurter, with whom—
this is just an incidental cog in James's "machinery of
entertainment"—he is in love.[10] This gives a dramatic
on-the-spot tone to his report from Prestidge, where he
feels his "own flesh sore from the brass nails in Neil Paraday's social harness" (XV, 140). As a piece of ironic reporting, this section and the next, into which it carries over,

are superb. The narrator incisively sketches all the lion hunters at Prestidge—the Princess who "is a massive lady with the organisation of an athlete and the confusion of tongues of a *valet de place*" (XV, 141), Lady Augusta Minch, Lord Dorimont, Miss Collop alias Guy Walshingham, Dora Forbes, the mustached male author of "Obsessions," and so on. Their colossal indifference to the master's writings is caricatured: "Every one's asking every one about it [Paraday's latest book] all day, and every one's telling every one where they put it last. I'm sure it's rather smudgy about the twentieth page" (XV, 141). Paraday's manuscript plan of his new book has been lent to Mrs. Wimbush who gave it to Lady Augusta Minch who gave it to Lord Dorimont who thinks he must have left it in the train. Paraday has fallen ill, having caught a chill during the party's visit to the neighboring Bigwood, the seat of the Duke. He lies neglected upstairs while Mrs. Wimbush and her crew are occupied with Guy Walshingham: *"Le roy est mort—vive le roy"* (XV, 150). Mrs. Wimbush is in fact "fundamentally disappointed in him. This was not the kind of performance for which she had invited him to Prestidge, let alone invited the Princess. I must add that none of the generous acts marking her patronage of intellectual and other merit have done so much for her reputation as her lending Neil Paraday the most beautiful of her numerous homes to die in" (XV, 152-153).

We notice a change in the narrator's tone in the last two sections, similar to the change in tone in the later part of "The Next Time." It becomes informed with righteous indignation as the end of the hero draws near. The gradation is appropriate to the purpose of the tale, which is to portray sarcastically forces that are not merely ridiculous but also monstrous. The only overdone touch is the brief deathbed scene, with the master murmuring his last wish to the narrator:

"That thing I read you that morning, you know."
"In your garden that dreadful day? Yes!"
"Won't it do as it is?"
"It would have been a glorious book."
"It *is* a glorious book," Neil Paraday murmured. "Print it as it stands—beautifully."
"Beautifully!" I passionately promised. (XV, 153-154)

The irony of the situation of course is that Paraday does not know of the loss of the fragment; but this detail could have been easily spared, for it is incongruous with the tone of the rest of the tale.

"The Death of the Lion" is among James's greatest tales in view of its sustained irony. The author works through a variety of oppositions and contrasts—between the narrator and Mr. Morrow, between the indestructible Mrs. Wimbush and the simple Fanny Hurter, between the helplessness of Paraday and the ferocity of his hunters, between Paraday, the bewildered victim of his admirers, and Guy Walshingham and Dora Forbes, the more than willing aspirants to lionhood. The chief merit of the tale is that it is not held down by the seriousness of its thematic elements—the hazards of success or the criminal disregard for an artist's anonymity or the absurdity of the social snobs whose admiration for an artist is so often completely devoid of any interest in his work. These motifs are properly absorbed in the fictive medium. To say that it is a parable is but another way of saying that it is a great tale wherein a universal truth has been given an appropriate fictional garb.

The Figure in the Carpet

The narrator of "The Private Life" is described by Blanche Adney—his lively colleague in the tale—as "a searcher of hearts—that frivolous thing an observer" (XVII, 233). Adapting this, I may call the narrator of "The Figure in the Carpet" (1896) a searcher of minds— that frivolous thing, a critic. In this case, however, the search is also directed to the narrator's own deficiencies. This is not to suggest that he is a straight autobiographical narrator. Instead he, unlike the other narrators of the tales about artists, is an ironic center of revelation; he also belongs to the tribe of critics James is satirizing in the tale. The ironic tone of this tale is thus considerably enhanced by the dual function of the narrator. Apart from "A Light Man" (1869) and "The Aspern Papers" (1888), "The Figure" is the only tale in which James employs this kind of narrator. In the two earlier tales, however, the intention is more unambiguous.

A close scrutiny of the text will bear out this contention. We learn at the very outset that the narrator is a young reviewer who "had done a few things and earned a few pence," but whose competence as a critic is questionable. His wit is highly developed but this quality is not quite in character; he owes it to his narrator's function. James himself was conscious of the anomaly, for he refers in the preface to "the aspiring young analyst whose report we read and to whom, I ruefully grant, I have ventured to impute a developed wit."[11] James's ruefulness, I think, stems from the fact that he has imputed to the young analyst a trait which but for his role as first-person narrator he would not have. If we imagine for a moment that this tale is told by an impersonal narrator—ignoring the various other dislocations it would cause—the wit would be aimed at the actual narrator as much as at his partners, George Corvick and Gwendolen Erme, and it would proceed from the impersonal narrator, that is, from the author himself. The reader must therefore adjust himself to the ambiguous position of the narrator so as not to accept him as an ideal critic. There *is* no ideal critic in the tale: "The question that accordingly comes up, the issue of the affair, can be but whether the very secret of perception hasn't been lost. That is the situation, and 'The Figure in the Carpet' exhibits a small group of well-meaning persons engaged in a test. The reader is, on the evidence, left to conclude."[12]

I have already mentioned that the narrator is a young reviewer with limited critical experience. The next thing we notice is the level of his critical perceptions. His friend Corvick has just requested him to do a review of Vereker's latest novel for *The Middle*—Corvick himself would have done it but for a summons from his intended, Gwendolen Erme:

"Of course you'll be all right, you know." Seeing I was a trifle vague he added: "I mean you won't be silly."

"Silly—about Vereker! Why what do I ever find him but awfully clever?"

"Well, what's that but silly? What on earth does 'awfully clever' mean? For God's sake try to get *at* him. Don't let him suffer by our arrangement. Speak of him, you know, if you can, as *I* should have spoken of him."

I wondered an instant. "You mean as far and away the biggest of the lot—that sort of thing?"

Corvick almost groaned. "Oh you know, I don't put them back to back that way; it's the infancy of art! But he gives me a pleasure so rare; the sense of"—he mused a little—"something or other."

I wondered again. "The sense, pray, of what?"

"My dear man, that's just what I want *you* to say!" (XV, 221)

It is true that in this passage, as in the rest of the tale, the narrator is made to feign ignorance and obtuseness partly in order to enhance the comic value of the narrative. At the same time, however, he is also made to expose both

his own and his friends' critical shallowness. Thanks to
his employment as a Jamesian narrator in a tale cast in
the comic mode, he is not a fool or a completely unconscious humorist; but thanks to the thematic intention of
James, he is not a great literary critic. The reader is likely
to miss the comic vibrations of the tale if he takes the
narrator too severely to task for what may be called his
functional stupidities, but he will also miss the point of
the tale if he takes the narrator or his friends for ideal
critics. Thus after his little article has appeared in *The
Middle*, all the narrator thinks of is that it "was a basis
on which I could meet the great man" (XV, 222). Later
at Bridges (whose owner, Lady Jane, reminds us of Mrs.
Wimbush of "The Death of the Lion") his conversation
with Hugh Vereker is one long ironic glance at his own
critical obtuseness. To begin with, the very degree of his
shock on learning that in Vereker's opinion his article was
"the usual twaddle" (XV, 226) is a comment on his complacent immaturity. Later when the master makes amends
for this unintended insult, we see in the narrator's reactions a consistent failure to get the point. Of course, the
dialogue is deliberately set up to state the central idea of
the story dramatically as well as comically. But this does
not controvert the point that the narrator is made to
represent himself as lacking the critical perception demanded by Vereker-James. The narrator wants Vereker
to assist the critic. The retort to that is: "Assist him? What
else have I done with every stroke of my pen? I've shouted
my intention in his great blank face!" (XV, 231). The
narrator suggests that since the master has talked of the
initiated, there should be initiation. The retort is: "What
else in heaven's name is criticism supposed to be?" (XV,
231). The narrator blushes at this and takes "refuge in
repeating that his account of his silver lining was poor in

something or other that a plain man knows things by."
The retort to that is: "Besides, the critic just *isn't* a plain
man: if he were, pray, what would he be doing in his
neighbour's garden?" (XV, 232). The narrator wants to
know if the secret is "a kind of esoteric message," and the
master's answer, perhaps the severest so far, is: "Ah my
dear fellow, it can't be described in cheap journalese!"
(XV, 233). The narrator comes out finally with the question, "Is it something in the style or something in the
thought?" And the master, after some hesitation, answers:
"Well, you've a heart in your body. Is that an element of
form or an element of feeling? What I contend that nobody
has ever mentioned in my work is the organ of life" (XV,
233-234). At the end of this colloquy the master's final
advice to his disciple is: "Give it up—give it up!" (XV,
235). The same advice is repeated a few pages later on the
occasion of another meeting (XV, 240). The narrator does
in fact take it, for at the end of "a maddening month" he
renounces his "ridiculous attempt. . . . The buried treasure
was a bad joke, the general intention a monstrous *pose*"
(XV, 236).

From this point on, the narrator begins to depend on
the chance of coming by the secret through George Corvick, whom he has already told of his conversation with
Vereker. His curiosity, in other words, loses whatever
critical motivation it had and becomes a journalist's
hunger for news. Now that he has demonstrated his own
lack of perception, he can address himself more exclusively
to his function as a narrator and report how others go
about the task of discovering Vereker's "secret." These
others, however, are no better equipped to understand
Vereker's art. George Corvick may have "done more
things than I, and earned more pence" (XV, 219), but he
too is no more than a reviewer; the only apparent advan-

tage he has over the narrator is that he is in love with Gwendolen Erme so that "poor Vereker's inner meaning gave them endless occasions to put and to keep their young heads together" (XV, 243). The narrator imagines them as absorbed in a game of chess with Hugh Vereker. From him the image comes approvingly (XV, 245), but the reader might well respond that critical activity is not a game of chess between the critic and the author. The point of the story seems to be that the whole quest of "the figure in the carpet" proceeds along lines that are almost fatuous— the inquirers approach it as they would a puzzle, and it is *not* a puzzle.

A few pages later the narrator again in a self-congratulatory way uses the image of a game: "For the few persons, at any rate, abnormal or not, with whom my anecdote is concerned, literature was a game of skill, and skill meant courage, and courage meant honour, and honour meant passion, meant life" (XV, 250). Abstracted from context this sentence gives no idea of its ironic implications, for even if we concede that criticism can be adequately pictured as such a game, the narrator and his friends are hardly the right kind of players. F. O. Matthiessen makes this mistake of ignoring the total context of the tale when he says: "In it ["The Figure in the Carpet"] the ideal readers are those for whom 'literature was a game of skill,' since 'skill meant courage . . . meant life.'"[13] The fact of the matter is that there are no ideal readers in the story. The narrator gives up after a month of feverish scrutiny of the author's works; it is clearly hinted that Corvick persists because of the greater opportunities it affords him of being close to Gwendolen Erme; Gwendolen's interest is even more frivolous, for in Corvick's words "she wants to set a trap" (XV, 245). These readers are not meant to strike us as anything more than "a small group of well-meaning persons."

What, then, should we make of Corvick's triumphant "Eureka" from Bombay and his subsequent assertion that he has had his discovery verified by Vereker himself? The narrator accepts this claim as true and believes that Corvick passed the secret on to Gwendolen before his death. But the question is, should we believe it? If we do, the entire meaning of the tale is eclipsed. The onus for the failure of the narrator to grasp Vereker's "exquisite scheme" gets shifted to the series of arbitrary deaths which seem to clutter the pages of "The Figure in the Carpet." In other words, we have to take these deaths far more seriously than what is warranted by the tone of the narration and the intention of the author. Corvick in that case is to be accepted as having passed the "test" in which the author shows "a small group of well-meaning persons engaged"; he becomes an embodiment of the "very secret of perception" whose loss James wanted to demonstrate and whose reinstatement was "the lively impulse, at the root of . . . this ironic or fantastic stroke."[14] But the point of the story is to show the absence of critical faculty, not the presence of an arbitrary fate and its dealings "with a man's avidity" (XV, 260).

As a matter of fact, there is a hint in the tale that Corvick did not discover any secret and that his claim is just a clever trick to patch up his relations with Gwendolen and hasten her into marriage. His death, followed by those of Vereker and his wife, enables Gwendolen to perpetuate his fraud and keep the narrator and the reader on tenterhooks until the conclusion of the episode. Before leaving for Bombay, Corvick startles the narrator by telling him that he is "not a bit engaged to her [Gwendolen], you know!" (XV, 249). The narrator draws an inference from this unexpected declaration "that the girl might in some way have estranged him" (XV, 249). Later when Corvick writes to Gwendolen that he will tell her the secret after their marriage, her reaction is: "It's tantamount to saying —isn't it?—that I must marry him straight off!" (XV, 256). A little later the narrator asks Gwendolen if "she was under an engagement," to which her answer is, "Of course I am! . . . Didn't you know it?" The narrator goes on to remark: "At bottom I was troubled by the disparity of the two accounts; but after a little I felt Corvick's to be the one I least doubted" (XV, 257). A few pages later the narrator states that he "subsequently grew sure that at the time he [Corvick] went to India, at the time of his great news from Bombay, there had been no positive pledge between them whatever. There had been none at the moment she was affirming to me the very opposite" (XV, 262). From all of this it seems fair to infer that, given Gwendolen's extraordinary eagerness to have the secret, Corvick was only trying to trick her into marriage through a false claim.

Of course, the hint is shrouded in vagueness, but had it been made clearer the narrator could not have persisted in his fond hope of getting at the secret through Gwendolen. Gwendolen, we notice, is not terribly upset by her husband's sudden death, and the narrator remarks that "it never would have occurred to me moreover to suppose she could come to feel the possession of a technical tip, of a piece of literary experience, a counterpoise to her grief. Strange to say, none the less, I couldn't help believing after I had seen her a few times that I caught a glimpse of some such oddity." And then he hastens "to add that there had been other things I couldn't help believing, or at least imagining" (XV, 264). A glimpse of these other things is given when the narrator impatiently remarks at her refusal to part with Corvick's secret: "I know what to think then. It's nothing!" (XV, 266). Gwendolen's not betraying Corvick's ignorance is understandable, for such an act would have to be accompanied by an admission that she herself had been duped. Furthermore, it would have precluded the final turn of the screw which comes with the narrator's discovery that Drayton Deane, whom Gwendolen marries and leaves a widower, is not even aware of the existence of the secret. The narrator's last words are: "I may say that to-day as victims of unappeased desire there isn't a pin to choose between us. The poor man's state is almost my consolation; there are really moments when I feel it to be quite my revenge" (XV, 277). The "revenge" is the vaguest of the hints that the narrator perhaps has finally understood Corvick's trick.

Without some such explanation, the actual intention of the story is likely to be misunderstood. It may be objected that the author's mystification is not worth the trouble, that he could have made the point more explicit without any damage to the effectiveness of the tale. As it is, the tale has not always been correctly understood or adequately appreciated. Its title has been given wide currency in serious critical terminology, but the tale itself has not been given its due as the most ironic of James's stories of writers and artists. I have already referred to Matthiessen's misreading. R. P. Blackmur succeeds in avoiding that mistake, for he notices that "a frenzied curiosity is not passion," which is all that the narrator and his friends are shown as having.[15] But Blackmur also fails to take full advantage of his perception. His final word on the tale seems to contradict the intention embodied in the text as well as in the preface: "James may have meant more for it—his preface suggests that he did—but it would seem actually, as written, to mean no more than that there is a figure in the carpet if you can imagine it for yourself; it is not there to discover. It is rather like Kafka, *manqué*, the exasperation of the mystery without the presence of mystery, or a troubled conscience without any evidence of guilt."[16] I think this represents impatience with the comic-ironic-detective mode of the tale. It is a Jamesian parody of one kind of criticism, the kind that James castigates more directly in his essay entitled "Criticism": "The vulgarity, the crudity, the stupidity which this cherished combination of the offhand review and of our wonderful system of publicity have put into circulation on so vast a scale may be represented . . . as an unprecedented invention for darkening counsel. The bewildered spirit may ask itself, without speedy answer, What is the function in the life of man of such a periodicity of platitude and irrelevance?"[17]

Of all the interpretations of "The Figure," the one least acceptable is that of Perry D. Westbrook. He maintains: "Both on the surface and in its implications the fable is a warning to the critics not to take a self-important author too seriously. . . . The critics in the story are mere dupes; the novelist is a poseur, a fraud."[18] The novelist's seriousness about his intention is doubtless exaggerated, but that accords with the total ironic tone of the story; it does not entitle us to take his so-called critics more seriously than their treatment in the tale warrants. Westbrook is the only critic to point out that "Corvick has only pretended to find the figure in the carpet in order to win the girl,"[19] but he has not made proper use of this insight.

Another interesting comment is by Edouard Roditi, who compares "The Figure" with Oscar Wilde's *Portrait of Mr. W. H.* Roditi's complaint is that James "never describes, for his readers, any of Vereker's works, never quotes anything, never gives us any hint of the critical and analytical methods which his characters follow in their quest of the hidden meaning of Vereker's work. The reader thus never develops any real interest in a problem which remains so vague that we never share the enthusiasm and despairs of the characters nor follow them in their quest."[20] James does not do any of these things because they are not to his purpose. The excellence of Vereker's works has to be taken on trust. The main emphasis of the tale, I have tried to show, is on how we should go about the task of interpreting the works of such a writer. And the moral of it is that the methods pursued by his three admirers do not signify a genuine adult interest in Vereker's works: their methods are not the right ones.

CHAPTER IV

The Turns of the Screw

THE NARRATOR of "The Figure in the Carpet" has a dual role, and the failure to notice this has led to a partial distortion of the meaning of that tale. We are confronted with a somewhat similar situation in "The Turn of the Screw" (1898), where the governess, apart from being a narrator, is a more than normally active participant in the action of the tale. In the battle of articles that has raged over the interpretation of "The Turn of the Screw," several combatants, particularly those often designated as Freudians, either have attached almost no importance to the governess' role as a narrator or have taken her for a false center of narration.[1] They have tended to misinterpret some of the generic traits that the governess shares with the rest of James's first-person narrators. Because of this failure to study the complex interrelation between these generic traits and the distinctly individual characteristics of the governess, they have mistaken her main function as an unconscious revelation of her own psychopathological state of mind.

Thus Edmund Wilson, the most persistent exponent of the Freudian interpretation of the tale, was "inclined to conclude from analogy that the story is primarily intended as a characterization of the governess."[2] In 1948, under pressure from the evidence supplied by James's *Notebooks*,

Wilson conceded that "James's conscious intention, in *The Turn of the Screw,* was to write a *bona fide* ghost story," but he was at the same time "led to conclude that, in *The Turn of the Screw,* not merely is the governess self-deceived, but that James is self-deceived about her."[3] Mistrust of an author's expressed intention in favor of the critic's own thesis can go no further. In his latest (1959) statement, however, Wilson withdraws his previous concessions to alternative interpretations of the tale, brushes aside all refutations of his own theory, and states: "Since writing the above, I have become convinced that James knew exactly what he was doing and that he intended the governess to be suffering from delusions."[4]

The fundamental care in any analysis of "The Turn of the Screw" would seem to be a correct understanding of its narrator's role. The mere fact that she is a first-person narrator does not entitle us to conclude that she is also the main subject of the story or that the intention of the story is primarily to portray her. Nor should it lead us to reject her reliability as a witness. We have seen in the first-person narratives analyzed so far that the narrator, with the exception of the one in "The Figure in the Carpet," is used primarily as a method of telling the story. The method is variously employed according to each tale's theme, scope, and predesigned point of emphasis. These variations manifest themselves in the structure of the individual tales, in the degree and nature of the narrator's functional involvement in the action, in his point of view, in his general mode of apprehension. In none of these tales is the narrator either autobiographical (in the sense that the story is primarily *his* story) or unreliable. Furthermore, the narrators of these tales have frequent intuitions which evidently have not aroused suspicion in the mind of any critic with regard to their reliability. These intuitions are both a means of foreshadowing the subsequent events and a device to achieve economy in presentation. The governess of "The Turn of the Screw," I submit, despite her comparatively greater involvement in the action of the narrative and her consequent importance as a character discussable in her own right, does not abandon her function as a narrator. On the contrary, an understanding of her character cannot be divorced from an understanding of her role as narrator, without falsifying the whole meaning of the tale. As a narrator she is no different, in many essential respects, from the narrators of the tales mentioned above. Whatever differences there are stem from the nature of the narrative—and the underlying theme—with which she is called upon to deal.

It is important to establish the governess' reliability as a witness in the context of James's practice in his other first-person tales. We have already seen that, except for "The Figure in the Carpet," the narrators discussed so far are unambiguously reliable. Even the narrator of "The Figure" is unreliable only in that his approach to Hugh Vereker's works is meant to strike us as being critically deficient, not because his facts are incorrect or distorted to suit his own purposes. This is reflected in the tone of the tale itself and corroborated by the *Notebooks* and the preface.[5] Let us now take a few tales that I have not yet examined. The narrator of "A Light Man" (1869) reveals himself cynically in the process of telling the story, but James makes no attempt to create an ambiguous impression by concealing his cynicism. The tale is cast in the form of a diary, and its tone is similar to that of Iago's soliloquies. Furthermore, the intention of the author with regard to the narrator-hero is clearly indicated in the choice of an epigraph from Browning's "A Light Woman":

And I—what I seem to my friend, you see—
  What I soon shall seem to his love, you guess.
What I seem to myself, do you ask of me?
  No hero, I confess. (M, XXV, 211)

James never again used exactly this kind of narrator. But a similar cynical self-revelation is attempted by the narrator of "The Aspern Papers" (1888), where the intention of the author is unmistakably reflected in the very tone of the narrative and its denouement. Edmund Wilson says, "In the case of *The Aspern Papers,* there is no uncertainty whatever as to what we are to think of the narrator: the author is quite clear that the papers were none of the journalist's business and that the rebuff he received served him right."[6] Wilson, however, makes too much of the fact that in the New York Edition James placed "The Turn of the Screw" "not among the ghost stories but between *The Aspern Papers* and *The Liar.*"[7] It is true that all the other ghostly tales in the canon—except "The Great Good Place," which is not quite "ghostly"—are collected in Volume XVII, but the same volume also contains "The Birthplace" and "Julia Bride," which are not ghost stories. In the preface to this volume James speaks of his "desire, amid these collocations, to place, *so far as possible,* like with like."[8] May we not say that, in view of its length, James did not find it possible to group "The Turn of the Screw" with the other ghostly tales? For the same reason, perhaps, he could not place "Daisy Miller," included in Volume XVIII, among his international tales, most of which are collected in Volumes XIII and XIV.

According to my reading, there are no other first-person tales in which James uses the narrator as an ironic self-revealer. Edmund Wilson mentions "The Path of Duty" (1884) and "The Friends of the Friends" (1896).[9] "The

Path of Duty" is a simple enough story; it is narrated by a woman who, impelled by mixed motives, leads Ambrose Tester and Lady Vandeleur to "the path of duty." The irony of the tale, and of its title, is completely unambiguous, and it is as clear to the narrator as it should be to the reader. Take, for instance, the last few sentences of the tale:

Yes, they [Ambrose Tester and Lady Vandeleur] are certainly in felicity, they have trod the clouds together, they have soared into the blue, and they wear in their faces the glory of those altitudes. They encourage, they cheer, inspire, sustain each other; remind each other that they have chosen the better part. Of course they have to meet for this purpose, and their interviews are filled, I am sure, with its sanctity. He holds up his head, as a man who on a very critical occasion behaved like a perfect gentleman. It is only poor Joscelind that droops. Haven't I explained to you now why she doesn't understand? (M, XXV, 175-176)

The point of the tale is that the path of duty, although it was meant to separate them, has brought Ambrose Tester and Lady Vandeleur even closer, much to the bafflement of poor Joscelind (Mrs. Tester) and to the suggested discomfiture of the narrator herself. Wilson concedes that "we are quite clear as we finish the story, as to what role the narrator has acutally played."[10] To this one may add only that the narrator, despite her role, is not the primary subject of the tale. At any rate, since there is no ambiguity in "The Path of Duty," I fail to understand how it supports Wilson's thesis that there *is* ambiguity in "The Turn of the Screw." If anything, it should lead one to think by analogy that, had an ambiguity been intended in "The Turn of the Screw," it would have been made at least as clear as it is in "The Path of Duty."

"The Friends of the Friends," again, is quite an unambiguous tale; the "ambiguity" concerning the ghost is clearly meant to emphasize the jealousy of the narrator. The reader, in other words, is left in no doubt that the narrator "—ghost or no ghost—is rejecting the man."[11] Furthermore, the intention of the tale is also indicated, in the prologue, by the first narrator: "I've read with the liveliest wonder the statement they [the pages that constitute the actual story] so circumstantially make and done my best to swallow the prodigy they leave to be inferred" (XVII, 323). Again, while introducing the narrative, the first narrator remarks: "She writes sometimes of herself, sometimes of others, sometimes of the combination. It's under this last rubric that she's usually most vivid" (XVII, 323). This remark shows that "The Friends of the Friends" also is not primarily a characterization of the narrator, who is functioning at the most both as narrator and as participant.

This somewhat rapid survey of James's practice in his other first-person narratives suggests the idea that, wherever James employs an ironic center of narration, he is careful to leave the reader in no doubt about his intention. It seems reasonable to expect that he would have done the same for "The Turn of the Screw," had his intention been to present the governess as an unreliable witness.[12] The importance that should be given to a writer's intention in evaluating his work is, of course, a controversial issue. One may only partly agree with René Wellek and Austin Warren when they say that the "meaning of a work of art is not exhausted by, or even equivalent to, its intention."[13] But certainly an excessive emphasis on the author's intention leads to exclusive reliance on historical readings, psychoanalytical interpretations, biographical investigations, conjectures, and so on. At the same time, however, a check has to be exercised on one's own ingenuities of interpretation, particularly when they seem to run counter to the author's intention in the work itself. When I refer to James's intention here, I mean his intention as reflected in "The Turn of the Screw." Furthermore, in the context of this controversy, it should be clear that the point at issue is the very subject of the tale. So even the externally expressed, conscious intention of James is perhaps not so irrelevant as it may be in normal circumstances. The external evidence of the *Notebooks* and the prefaces has already been sufficiently stressed by the anti-Freudians, who have also focused attention on the Freudians' numerous distortions of this evidence.[14] I shall confine my attention in the subsequent discussion largely to the internal evidence of the text, bearing in mind that the governess is acting both as a typical Jamesian narrator and as an individual Jamesian character, and that she is not employed as an ironic center of revelation.

The prologue to the tale, more than any other of James's prologues, is integrally related to the main body of the tale; it is also more elaborate than any other. The first narrator performs the usual duty of setting the stage. He mentions the context that led to Douglas' remark: "I quite agree—in regard to Griffin's ghost, or whatever it was—that its appearing first to the little boy, at so tender an age, adds a particular touch. But it's not the first occurrence of its charming kind that I know to have been concerned with a child. If the child gives the effect another turn of the screw, what do you say to *two* children—?" (XII, 147-148). Surely we cannot brush aside this hint, which gives us the general idea that the ensuing tale is to be about two haunted children. This is how Douglas' auditors take his hint, and this is how we should take it.

The first narrator is also engaged in creating a proper mood for the reception of the governess' narrative. While reading his account of the curiosity aroused by Douglas' announcement, we identify ourselves with the receptive attitude of the suppositious company gathered round the fire on that Christmas Eve. We become attuned to the idea of reading a tale that is "beyond everything" for "general uncanny ugliness and horror and pain" (XII, 148). This is the second function of the prologue.

The third, and probably most important, function performed by the prologue is to establish in the reader's mind an initial image of the governess' personality. This is done through the medium of Douglas, according to whom the governess "was a most charming person. . . . She was the most agreeable woman I've ever known in her position; she'd have been worthy of any whatever" (XII, 149). Now Douglas, during his brief appearance in the prologue, strikes us as a fairly sympathetic person; so does the first narrator. Thus there is no reason to suggest, as Wilson does, that "it is a not infrequent trick of James's to introduce sinister characters with descriptions that at first sound flattering."[15] As a matter of evidence, in no Jamesian prologue-tale is our impression of the second narrator in conflict with the impression given by the first narrator. Of course, in "The Turn of the Screw" the initial impression about the governess does not come straight from the first narrator. We may wonder why James introduces Douglas at all, but the question, carried to its logical limit, would lead us to ask why James prefixes a prologue at all. Why, moreover, does James make Douglas send for the manuscript, thus causing an "unnecessary" delay in the launching of the drama? In other words, such questions are merely hair-splitting irrelevancies.[16] The fact remains that we have no basis for discrediting the testimony of Douglas in regard to the governess.

Finally, in addition to establishing the "authority" of

the governess,[17] the prologue also telescopes certain preliminary details about the background of the narrative. As the first narrator points out, "It appeared that the narrative he [Douglas] had promised to read us really required for a proper intelligence a few words of prologue" (XII, 152). James exercises a great deal of deliberation and control in the choice of these details; he gives only those which contribute to a proper understanding of the governess' narrative without destroying its suspense. So we get a condensed account of the parentage of the governess, of her meeting and instantaneous infatuation with her handsome employer, of the conditions accompanying her job, of the death of her predecessor, and so on. Through these details James is also creating the kind of inevitability proper to a powerful ghost story. But for the fact that she was "the youngest of several daughters of a poor country parson," the governess might not have so readily fallen in love with her employer; nor would she have been impressed by the fact "that he put the whole thing to her as a favour, an obligation he should gratefully incur" (XII, 152, 153). But for her infatuation, the young and inexperienced governess would not have accepted the job with its forbidding conditions; nor would she have clung so resolutely to their observance. Again, but for these strange conditions the subsequent events at Bly would not have been so intensely horrible, nor her behavior so abnormally conscientious.

The prologue, then, properly considered, should dispel many doubts about the primary subject of the tale, about the reliability of the governess as a witness, and about her sanity as a character.[18]

The tale itself may be divided, for the sake of convenience, into four parts, each consisting of six sections. In the first part, the governess brings her narrative to the point where she has been exposed to both the ghosts; in the second, we get the process of reasoning, supported by outside events, whereby she convinces herself that the children are corrupted; in the third, we get a picture of her awkward relations with the children and a further confirmation of her earlier conviction—this phase culminates in the decision to communicate with her employer; in the fourth, we see first her failure with Flora and then her "success" with Miles.

The governess begins her narrative with the adeptness we would expect of her, not as a governess but as a Jamesian narrator. James, it will be conceded, is fully aware of the effect he wants to create on the reader through the medium of the governess. It is not surprising that he should make her choose such details, have such impressions, throw such hints as will contribute, by a complex magic of their own, to the atmosphere suitable for a tale of the supernatural. Thus, the governess' initial state of mind is conveyed through "a little see-saw of the right throbs and the wrong" (XII, 158). Her first impression of the house, for instance, is an illustration of the "right throbs": "I remember as a thoroughly pleasant impression the broad clear front, its open windows and fresh curtains and the pair of maids looking out; I remember the lawn and the bright flowers and the crunch of my wheels on the gravel and the clustered tree-tops over which the rooks circled and cawed in the golden sky" (XII, 158). This sunny picture is obviously meant to provide a contrast with the subsequent shady events that take place at Bly. By the same token, the following reminiscence of the governess foreshadows later events: "There had been a moment when I believed I recognised, faint and far, the cry of a child; there had been another when I found myself just consciously starting as at the passage, before my door, of a light footstep. But these fancies were not marked enough not to be thrown off, and it is only in the light, or the gloom, I should rather say, of other and subsequent matters that they now come back to me" (XII, 160).

But the most suggestive premonition of horror is contained in a passage where the governess gives us an illustration of her "wrong" throbs. Earlier we had the governess' first impression of the exterior of the house; now we get her first impression of its interior. The two combine to spotlight the hiatus between appearance and reality.[19]

But as my little conductress, with her hair of gold and her frock of blue, danced before me round corners and pattered down passages, I had the view of a castle of romance inhabited by a rosy sprite, such a place as would somehow, for diversion of the young idea, take all colour out of story-books and fairy-tales. Wasn't it just a story-book over which I had fallen a-doze and a-dream? No; it was a big ugly antique but convenient house, embodying a few features of a building still older, half-displaced and half-utilized, in which I had the fancy of our being almost as lost as a handful of passengers in a great drifting ship. Well, I was strangely at the helm!

These "throbs," I believe, are not here to reveal the governess' emotional instability or morbidity. In terms of verisimilitude, they do not violate our sense of how a twenty-year-old Victorian girl should feel during her first few hours in a huge unfamiliar house. Apart from that, their real function is to create the right atmosphere and to plant the right suggestions.

After the reactions of the governess in the opening section, we come to the first of the objective turns in the tale—the letter from Miles's school. Accompanying the letter is the uncle's injunction: "Read him, please; deal with him; but mind you don't report. Not a word. I'm off!" (XII, 165). The governess' perturbation at being

saddled with an unexpected responsibility on the very
second day of her arrival at Bly is perfectly credible; so is
her decision to speak to Mrs. Grose about it. We must
remember also that she has not yet seen Miles. So in her
conversation with Mrs. Grose (who is illiterate), the governess understandably puts her own apprehensions in the
plainest possible terms so as to watch the housekeeper's
reaction. At this stage, in other words, she is not investing
the letter "on no evidence at all, with a significance somehow ominous";[20] she is only seeking the necessary reassur-
ance. She persists in her inquiries because of her suspicion
that Mrs. Grose is concealing something, "especially as,
toward evening, I began to fancy she rather sought to
avoid me" (XII, 168). The correctness of the governess'
intuition is borne out by the piecemeal manner in which
Mrs. Grose surrenders what she knows of Miss Jessel and
Quint. Her hesitation about telling the new governess
everything all at once is plausible: she does not want to
frighten the young woman. This would be the explanation
for the protracted cross-examination of the housekeeper by
the governess on the level of verisimilitude. But on the level
of narrative method, the continual exchange between the
two women is the familiar Jamesian practice of dramatizing
the process whereby the narrator gradually arrives at his
data. Thus, when the governess first questions her about
Miss Jessel, Mrs. Grose is evasive:

But the next day, as the hour for my drive approached, I
cropped up in another place. "What was the lady who was
here before?"
    "The last governess? She was also young and pretty—almost
as young and almost as pretty, Miss, even as you."
    "Ah then I hope her youth and her beauty helped her!" I
recollect throwing off. "He seems to like us young and pretty!"
    "Oh he *did*," Mrs. Grose assented: "It was the way he liked

every one!" She had no sooner spoken indeed than she caught herself up. "I mean that's *his* way—the master's."

I was struck. "But of whom did you speak first?"

She looked blank, but she coloured. "Why of *him*."

"Of the master?"

"Of who else?"

There was so obviously no one else that the next moment I had lost my impression of her having accidentally said more than she meant; and I merely asked what I wanted to know. (XII, 168-169)

The point to be gathered from this passage is that it contains the first veiled reference to the liaison between Quint and Miss Jessel. Mrs. Grose is at first under the impression that the governess knows something about it— her "Oh he *did*." Then she catches herself up, and is able to transfer her reference to the master, without being detected because the governess knows nothing about Quint. Again, this is but another instance of the way James deepens the mystery, by dropping hints whose meaning is revealed retrospectively. Through the emphasis on the governess' apprehensions, James is also preparing us for the heightened impact of her spontaneous liking for Miles: "Everything but a sort of passion of tenderness for him was swept away by his presence. What I then and there took him to my heart for was something divine that I have never found to the same degree in any child— his indescribable little air of knowing nothing in the world but love" (XII, 171). This emphasis on the unearthly beauty of Miles, in its turn, is meant to accentuate the horror of the governess, and of the reader through her, when she later realizes that it is a mere camouflage. For the present, it serves to motivate her decision to take no action on the incriminating letter. The governess is, however, made to explain this decision as if to forestall possible objections to its correctness:

What I look back at with amazement is the situation I accepted. I had undertaken, with my companion, to see it out, and I was under a charm apparently that could smooth away the extent and the far and difficult connexions of such an effort. I was lifted aloft on a great wave of infatuation and pity. I found it simple, in my ignorance, my confusion and perhaps my conceit, to assume that I could deal with a boy whose education for the world was all on the point of beginning. I am unable even to remember at this day what proposal I framed for the end of his holidays and the resumption of his studies. (XII, 172-173)

Perhaps a more ordinary governess in this position might have adopted a different course of action. But, in that case, James would have written a different story. James made her take this decision, which is consistent with her character, because he wanted his tale to take the course it does. It becomes quite clear later in this section that the governess is also motivated by a desire to impress her employer. It must be stressed, as Heilman also has done, that the governess does not repress her love for her employer.[21] On the contrary, James makes her discuss it in order to justify her desperate observance of the employer's injunction not to bother him about anything. Take, for instance, the following passage:

It was a pleasure at these moments to feel myself tranquil and justified; doubtless perhaps also to reflect that by my discretion, my quiet good sense and general high propriety, I was giving pleasure—if he ever thought of it!—to the person to whose pressure I had yielded. What I was doing was what he had earnestly hoped and directly asked of me, and that I *could,* after all, do it proved even a greater joy than I had expected. . . . One of the thoughts that, as I don't in the least shrink now from noting, used to be with me in these wanderings was that it would be as charming as a charming story suddenly to meet some one. Some one would appear there at the turn of a path and would stand before me and smile and approve. I didn't ask more than that—I only asked that he should *know;* and the only way to be sure he knew would be to see it, and the kind light of it, in his handsome face.[22] (XII, 174-175)

It is, ironically enough, when she is thinking of the master one day that the governess is first visited by what she later knows was Quint's ghost. Like the poet of *The Ancient Mariner,* James does not describe the supernatural horor directly; he reflects it through a description of the strangely changed surroundings.

The place moreover, in the strangest way in the world, had on the instant and by the very fact of its appearance become a solitude. . . . It was as if, while I took in, what I did take in, all the rest of the scene had been stricken with death. I can hear again, as I write, the intense hush in which the sounds of the evening dropped. The rooks stopped cawing in the golden sky and the friendly hour lost for the unspeakable minute all its voice. (XII, 176)

We recognize in this passage the echo of an earlier one in which "the rooks circled and cawed in the golden sky." It continues to reverberate until we come to the point where the governess sees the apparition for the second time: "The terrace and the whole place, the lawn and the garden beyond it, all I could see of the park, were empty with a great emptiness" (XII, 185). We should bear in mind that the governess at this stage does not know that she is face to face with a ghost, but the author does. So he makes the governess record her impressions in such a way as to prepare the ground for the later revelation:

He remained but a few seconds—long enough to convince me he also saw and recognised; but it was as if I had been looking at him for years and had known him always. Something, however, happened this time that had not happened before; his stare into my face, through the glass and across the room, was as deep and hard as then, but it quitted me for a moment during which I could still watch it, see it fix successively several other things. On the spot there came to me the added shock of a certitude that it was not for me he had come. He had come for some one else. (XII, 184)

Objections can be raised to everything that the governess intuitively perceives in the story. For example, it may be asked, why her certitude here? I have already mentioned that James's narrators, as a rule, are endowed with a fine intuitive awareness. Besides, in the subsequent pages, the governess does after all try to verify her certitude; and unaware at this point that her visitor is a visitant, she would not be as repelled by her certitude as some of us might be because of our knowledge, thanks to the prologue, that the stranger is a ghost. The real explanation, the one that leads us to the technical core of James's method in this case, is that James repeatedly employs the intuitions of the governess to maintain suspense and to deepen the mystery. The alternative method of providing unassailable evidence for whatever happens would have defeated this purpose.

In the next section the narrative moves at a breathless speed to the point where Mrs. Grose says, "Yes. Mr. Quint's dead" (XII, 192). Essentially, this section is the familiar Jamesian dramatization of disclosure, in this case the process by which the governess discovers that she has seen a ghost. Enough has already been written about the description of Quint given by the governess, the description that enables Mrs. Grose to identify him. Edmund Wilson, for instance, acknowledged this point as the one major flaw in his hallucination theory.[23] Recently, however, he has accepted a farfetched explanation of even this anomaly: "As for the explanation of the governess's describing correctly the person of Peter Quint, it is so clear that—though slily contrived—one wonders how one could ever have missed it; yet it had never, so far as I know, been brought out before the publication, in *American Literature* of May, 1957, of a paper by John Silver called "A Note on the Freudian Reading of 'The Turn of the Screw.'" The governess, Mr. Silver suggests, had learned about Quint's appearance from the people in the village with whom we know she had talked and who had presumably also told her of the manner of Quint's death."[24] On turning to Silver's article, we find that he has taken inordinate pains to provide this prop to Wilson's tottering theory, one of his arguments being that "in Chapter IV, we learn that the village 'through the park and by the good road' is only twenty minutes away, thus allowing convenient intercourse between Bly and the village."[25] He connects this "evidence" with this piece of conversation between the governess and Mrs. Grose:

> "Was he a gentleman?"
> I found I had no need to think. "No." . . .
> "Then nobody about the place? Nobody from the village?"
> "Nobody—nobody. I didn't tell you, but I made sure."
> (XII, 188-189)

This connection produces Silver's conclusion that "the governess lets drop that she has actually *been to the village to check*."[26] In the context of the tale, however, the governess' remark, "I didn't tell you, but I made sure," can only mean that she has thought it over, perhaps even made inquiries, and found that nobody had been seen entering the house. I think that there is no need to belabor Silver's examination further, except to point out that his pursuit of fictional characters beyond the confines of the given text is not legitimate. In any case, it is not the same thing as a close scrutiny of the text, and is perilously close to the kind of critical conjectures represented by the notorious curiosity regarding Lady Macbeth's children. It seems likely that both Wilson and Silver, if they pressed their investigation along this line, could come out with the theory that the governess' male visitant was some clever impersonator from the village "only twenty minutes away." One may ask with Elmer Edgar Stoll, "Is this not the now timeworn fallacy of confounding art and reality? It is like inquiring into the previous history of Falstaff or Hamlet, of the heroines or the Macbeths, who (of course), except as very meagerly furnished by the dramatist, have none."[27]

In the sixth section the governess formulates her strategy. She turns to the housekeeper for clarification, for sympathy and support—which is natural, I suppose, in a haunted woman. At the same time, she keeps a firm hold on her own intuition that the ghost wants to appear to the children. This, according to our understanding of the subject James has in mind and according to the technique he is employing, is the only way of carrying the tale further. The governess does not have any suspicion at this point that the children are in league with the ghost—she herself has not yet been exposed to the second ghost. So "something within me said that by offering myself bravely as the sole subject of such experience, by accepting, by inviting, by surmounting it all, I should serve as an expiatory victim and guard the tranquility of the rest of the household. The children in especial I should thus fence about and absolutely save" (XII, 195). A few pages later she says, "I was a screen—I was to stand before them" (XII, 199). Here also James remembers to motivate her decision adequately by making her think of the master: "I now saw that I had been asked for a service admirable and difficult; and there would be a greatness in letting it be seen—oh in the right quarter!—that I could succeed where many another girl might have failed" (XII, 199).

The additional information she gathers from Mrs. Grose in this section is important, since it supports her subsequent realization that the children had been corrupted by the dead servants. It is from Mrs. Grose that she gets the details, vague as they are, of Quint's death; their conversation is not rendered dramatically, but this is no reason for Silver to imagine that the governess went about gathering these details in the village.[28] The ghost of Miss Jessel is also introduced, in this section, after an interval in which the governess watches the children "in a stifled suspense, a disguised tension, that might well, had it continued too long, have turned to something like madness" (XII, 199). There is a perceptible variation in the way the governess is exposed to Miss Jessel's ghost. The variation, for one thing, avoids monotony, and, for another, it accords with the fact that the governess has already been initiated into her "dreadful liability" to visitations (XII, 193).

In the second part of the tale, the governess reasons herself, and the reader, on the basis of some objective evidence, into a conviction that the children are still under the influence of "their false friends."[29] In the seventh section she reports her experience by the lake to Mrs. Grose. We should remember that on this occasion she is more upset for two reasons: she knows she has seen a ghost, and she suspects that Flora too has seen it and has tried to hide the fact from her. Hence, her description of Miss Jessel is different from that of Quint, less physical in detail: "Another person—this time; but a figure of quite as unmistakeable horror and evil: a woman in black, pale and dreadful—with such an air also, and such a face!—on the other side of the lake. I was there with the child—quiet for the hour; and in the midst of it she came" (XII, 203-204). By not letting this scene run too close to the earlier one about Quint, James also avoids repetition.

In the previous section, the governess had been "haunted with the shadow of something she [Mrs. Grose] had not told me"; it now turns out that she was correct. Mrs. Grose now makes some dim remarks about the liaison between Quint and Miss Jessel, although she still says nothing about the children's involvement in it (see XII, 207-208). This vagueness, and dilatoriness, is again designed not so much by the poor housekeeper as by the clever James, who remains consistent in his refusal to specify overtly the nature of the evil at Bly. However, it is implied that Miss Jessel had a deeper reason, not just her vacation, for leaving the house:

"Yet you had then your idea—"
"Of her real reason for leaving? Oh yes—as to that. She couldn't have stayed. Fancy it here—for a governess! And afterwards I imagined—and I still imagine. And what I imagine is dreadful." (XII, 208)

This may be an oblique hint that Miss Jessel was pregnant before she left Bly, and that she either died in childbirth or committed suicide. In any case, the vagueness only intensifies the impression that the general atmosphere in which the children had been brought up was corrupt in many ways.

Although the governess pronounces in this section her theory about the children's secret communication with the ghosts, she is not yet completely sure. James could not allow her this certainty at this stage. He has still to "knead the subject of my young friend's, the suppositious narrator's, mystification thick."[30] So we have her turning it over and over in her own mind and with Mrs. Grose: "To gaze into the depths of blue of the child's eyes and pronounce their loveliness a trick of premature cunning was to be guilty of a cynicism in preference to which I naturally preferred to abjure my judgement and, so far as might be, my agitation" (XII, 210). Meanwhile, she must get all she can from Mrs. Grose: "She had told me, bit by bit, under pressure, a great deal; but a small shifty spot on the wrong side of it all still sometimes brushed my brow like the wing of a bat" (XII, 211). After this conversation Mrs. Grose has nothing more to add to the past history of Bly; hence her role becomes even more exclusively that of a *ficelle*.

In the next section, we have an account of the governess' harrowing uncertainty about her secret suspicions, for "the immediate charm of my companions was a beguilement still effective even under the shadow of the possibility that it was studied" (XII, 218). The shadow hangs over her relations with the children: "Sometimes perhaps indeed (when I dropped into coarseness) I came across traces of little understandings between them by which one of them should keep me occupied while the other slipped away. There is a naïf side, I suppose, in all diplomacy; but if my pupils practised upon me it was surely with the minimum of grossness" (XII, 220). The profusion of cautious words in the language of the governess should be noticed; she is evidently in no hurry to jump to conclusions.

Before going on with her account of the next apparition, the governess allows herself a ruminatory pause, which is very effective: "I find that I really hang back; but I must take my horrid plunge. In going on with the record of what was hideous at Bly I not only challenge the most liberal faith—for which I little care; but (and this is another matter) I renew what I myself suffered, I again push my dreadful way through it to the end. There came suddenly an hour after which, as I look back, the business seems to me to have been all pure suffering; but I have at least reached the heart of it, and the straightest road out is doubtless to advance" (XII, 220). This is one of the strokes in the narrative that go to make it "an *amusette* to catch those not easily caught (the 'fun' of the capture of the merely witless being ever but small), the jaded, the disillusioned, the fastidious."[31] There is one important change in the response of the governess to the apparition:

He was absolutely, on this occasion, a living detestable dangerous presence. But that was not the wonder of wonders; I reserve this distinction for quite another circumstance: the circumstance that dread had unmistakeably quitted me and that there was nothing in me unable to meet and measure him.

I had plenty of anguish after that extraordinary moment, but I had, thank God, no terror. . . . It was the dead silence of our long gaze at such close quarters that gave the whole horror, huge as it was, its only note of the unnatural. If I had met a murderer in such a place and at such an hour we still at least would have spoken. Something would have passed, in life, between us; if nothing had passed one of us would have moved. The moment was so prolonged that it would have taken but little more to make me doubt if even *I* were in life. I can't express what followed it save by saying that the silence itself—which was indeed in a manner an attestation of my strength—became the element into which I saw the figure disappear; in which I definitely saw it turn, as I might have seen the low wretch to which it had once belonged turn on receipt of an order, and pass, with my eyes on the villainous back that no hunch could have more disfigured, straight down the staircase and into the darkness in which the next bend was lost. (XII, 222-223)

It is passages like these, and there are several of them, that combine to lift the tale far above the crudeness of an ordinary thriller. And, if I may be allowed the repetition, the power of these passages comes ultimately from the author of the tale; it will not do to explain it away by suggesting that the "anxious, fearful, possessive, domineering, hysterical and compulsive" governess is only trying to mask her own perfidy, morbidity, or insanity.[32]

We get in the passage quoted above a foretaste of the kind of struggle in which the governess is to be thrown, after her lingering doubts have been dispelled by the events and reflections recorded in sections ten through thirteen. The events, if we choose to look at them from one cursory angle, have an ostensibly innocuous surface; in this case, the reflections of the governess are bound to appear unwarranted and unconvincing. In the tenth section she returns to her room after the encounter with Quint's apparition and finds Flora's bed empty. In the context of her recent adventure it is highly disturbing. We must also bear in mind that it was "horribly late" in the night and that she had left Flora in "the perfection of childish rest" (XII, 221). Her initial scare is therefore perfectly justified. The explanation of Flora, despite its plausibility, is disconcerting and uncanny, provided we do not lose sight of her tender age, the time of the night, the governess' state of mind, and, above all, the general drift of the tale. No wonder the governess "in the state of her nerves . . . absolutely believed she lied" (XII, 225). A few nights later—in the interval she has had another brush, this time with Miss Jessel's ghost—she wakes up again to find Flora's bed empty. The child is at the window and is "disturbed neither by my re-illumination nor by the haste I made to get into slippers and into a wrap. Hidden, protected, absorbed, she evidently rested on the sill—the casement opened forward—and gave herself up" (XII, 228). This last is, of course, her intuition, but it is borne out by what the governess sees, to her consternation, from the window of another room. She sees Miles in the garden below, looking "not so much straight at me as at something that was apparently above me. There was clearly another person above me—there was a person on the tower" (XII, 229). This again is an intuition, but it is supported by the evasive explanation offered by Miles of his and his sister's strange midnight escapade. His explanation, like Flora's on the previous occasion, has the eerie tone of being too plausible to proceed from the unaided intelligence of a mere child. It is not surprising, therefore, that the governess should formulate the conclusion that she had earlier forbidden herself to entertain: "The four, depend upon it, perpetually meet. If on either of these last nights you had been with either child you'd clearly have understood." She goes on to tell Mrs. Grose, "Their more than earthly beauty, their absolutely unnatural goodness [is] a game. . . . It's a policy and a fraud!" (XII, 236, 237). In the interest of his theme, it may be suggested, James had to give his narrator this lucid realization; and he could not have chosen a more effective way, or a more opportune moment, for doing it. The contrast between the apparent innocence and the real contamination of the children—a contrast that is the keynote of the terror produced by "The Turn of the Screw"—is thus clinched at almost exactly the middle point of the tale.

The governess' knowledge of the reality and her continued failure to recognize its ugly face in the appearance —it is this dilemma that causes the anguish she feels in the third part of the tale. Her relations with the children, throughout this phase, are painfully awkward. This is recorded in her various assertions in section thirteen. These assertions should not be taken, along lines recommended by any oversimplified psychological apparatus, as an indication of the hollowness of her case. Studied in the context of James's technique and subject (a less acceptable name for both would be "intention"), they are necessary for the very progress of the tale. Another complicating factor now, for the governess, is that her eyes are temporarily sealed. There is no accounting for this phenomenon on the rational level: the ghost appears when and to whom it will. But on the fictional level there *is* an explanation, that James wants to deepen the mystification of the governess—and through her the reader's—so as to emphasize her struggle with the demons. Hence, also, the insistence on the children's secret communion with the evil spirits in the presence of the governess: "There were times of our being together when I would have been ready to swear that, literally, in my presence, but with my direct sense of it closed, they had visitors who were known and were welcome. . . . The little wretches denied it with all the added volume of their sociability and their tenderness, just in the crystal depths of which—like the flash of a fish in a stream—the mockery of their advantage peeped up" (XII, 244-245).

By making the ghosts temporarily invisible to the governess, James adds to the ghostly atmosphere, and without an inexpert or indiscriminate piling up of the palpable but ineffectual horrors: "the strange dizzy lift or swim (I try for terms!) into a stillness, a pause of all life, that had nothing to do with the more or less noise we at the moment might be engaged in making and that I could hear through any intensified mirth or quickened recitation or louder strum of the piano. Then it was that the others, the outsiders, were there" (XII, 245-246). Still another way in which the governess is harassed by the children is by "being plied with the supposition that he [the uncle] might at any moment be among us. It was exactly as if our young friends knew how almost more awkward than anything else that might be for me" (XII, 247). The children write letters addressed to their uncle, but the governess "carried out the spirit of the pledge given not to appeal to him when I let our young friends understand that their own letters were but charming literary exercises. They were too beautiful to be posted" (XII, 247). Edmund Wilson has distorted these details to suit his thesis: "But the children become uneasy: they wonder when their uncle is coming, and they try to communicate with him—but the governess suppresses their letters."[33] The governess' statement, on the other hand, makes it quite clear that she did not secretly suppress the letters—she "let our young friends understand that their own letters were but charming literary exercises." Similarly, Wilson condenses the complex conversation between the governess and Miles, recorded in section fourteen, into one misleading sentence that makes a travesty of the text: "The boy finally asks her frankly when she is going to send him to school, intimates that if he had not been so fond of her, he would have complained to his uncle long ago, declares that he will do so at once."[34] What actually happens is far from this. When Miles suddenly asks her when he is going back to school (XII, 249), the alternative before her is either to betray knowledge of his expulsion from the school or to evade the question. She hesitates for a while and then chooses the second alternative—to adopt the first would mean bringing everything out in the open, for which both she and the author are not yet prepared. She is not prepared for it because in her mind the subject of Miles's expulsion is inextricably linked with the dreadful subject of the evil visitants. The author does not want to bring about a showdown at this juncture because he wants to carry the tale further: the possibilities of mystification and terror are not yet fully exhausted.

So the conversation hovers perilously close above the still unmentioned subject not only of the expulsion but of the ghosts. The entire scene is indeed haunted by the shadow of the unspoken. Miles seems to want to learn whether the governess knows of his expulsion from the school. The governess hems and haws because she does not know whether she should confront Miles with an open accusation; at the same time she is angling for some sort of confession about what he did at the school to merit dismissal. Furthermore, unless we abstract this conversation from the preceding context, the questions and answers of Miles are quite disturbing in their precocity and tone. (See XII, 249-252.)

The following section, fifteen, throws light on the full implications of this conversation as the governess grasps them: "He had got out of me that there was something I was much afraid of, and that he should probably be able to make use of my fear to gain, for his own purpose, more freedom. My fear was of having to deal with the intolerable question of the grounds of his dismissal from school, since that was really the question of the horrors gathered behind" (XII, 254). Frightened by Miles's "sudden revelation of a consciousness and a plan," she is seized with the impulse to "give the whole thing up—turn my back and bolt" (XII, 255). However, on entering the schoolroom, she finds her eyes "in a flash . . . unsealed. In the presence of what I saw I reeled straight back upon resistance" (XII, 256). The unsealing of her eyes at this point serves as a timely reminder, to her and to us, of the nature of the struggle in which she is involved. Her personal motives for running away fade—she reels "straight back upon resistance" against the evil visitants in order to save the children's souls.

In the next section, the governess informs Mrs. Grose of her latest encounter with Miss Jessel's ghost. In doing so, she takes the liberty of verbalizing, for the benefit of Mrs. Grose, what passed mutely between her and the apparition. When the poor unimaginative Mrs. Grose asks her in utter stupefaction, "Do you mean she spoke?", the governess replies, "It came to that" (XII, 259). It is not surprising that Mrs. Grose should ignore the meaning of this qualification, which obviously in the context means, "It amounted to that." But it is amazing that Oscar Cargill should take it to prove that the governess is "a demonstrable pathological liar," his point being that we know the ghost of Miss Jessel was absolutely quiet.[35] Incidentally, Cargill's essay is an assemblage of the boldest, and the most untenable, assertions and conjectures with regard to James's intention, sources, and text that I have come across in the whole body of Jamesian criticism. For instance, he concludes his theory that one of James's "real" sources for "The Turn of the Screw" was "The Case of Miss Lucy R." in *Studien über Hysterie* by Breuer and Freud (1895): "But perhaps the most interesting revelation that James thought of the governess' story as a psychoneurotic case history is the fact (to which the governess constantly refers and which James surely meant the acute reader to note) that her all-important interview took place in 'Harley Street'—the conventional 'physicians' row' of fiction dealing with London."[36] The argument is, at least for one reader, too fantastic to permit further comment.

The conversation between the governess and Miles in section seventeen is the next stage in her approach to the final catastrophe. In its general tone of eeriness it is a more terrible echo of the governess' two earlier conversations with Miles, more terrible because of the way it proceeds and because of the mysterious intervention that puts an end to it:

"Dear little Miles, dear little Miles, if you *knew* how I want to help you! It's only that, it's nothing but that, and I'd rather die than give you pain or do you a wrong—I'd rather die than hurt a hair of you. Dear little Miles"—oh I brought it out now even if I *should* go too far—"I just want you to help me to save you!" But I knew in a moment after this that I had gone too far. The answer to my appeal was instantaneous, but it came in the form of an extraordinary blast and chill, a gust of frozen air and a shake of the room as great as if, in the wild wind, the casement had crashed in. (XII, 267)

The conversation also illuminates the theme of the tale, which, it becomes increasingly clear, is the struggle of the governess against the evil forces that have the children in thrall.

The final part of the tale is remarkable for its combination of accelerated pace and reflective tone. Things happen in rapid succession; at the same time, we are aware of a weariness in the governess' voice, a weariness presaging the tragic end. I shall not dwell upon the first half of this part, in which the governess gives up Flora as irretrievably lost and sends her away with Mrs. Grose to the employer. This is the climax of the tale as far as Flora is concerned. It should be noticed that throughout the tale James has kept the governess', and through her the reader's, concern for Miles a shade deeper than that for Flora. Thus the effect of the climactic scene—covering the last three sections—is considerably heightened through the departure of Mrs. Grose and Flora. The governess is now face to face with Miles, alone, except of course for the hovering presence of Quint. The importance of this isolation is suggested through the apprehensive reflections of the governess: "No hour of my stay in fact was so assailed with apprehensions as that of my coming down to learn that the carriage containing Mrs. Grose and my younger pupil had already rolled out of the gates. Now I *was*, I said to myself, face to face with the elements, and for much of the rest of the day, while I fought my weakness, I could consider that I had been supremely rash" (XII, 293). Thus her hopes of saving Miles—hopes that are her motive for pursuing the issue—are appropriately tempered by her premonitions: "I wandered . . . all over the place and looked, I have no doubt, as if I were ready for an onset. So, for the benefit of whom it might concern, I paraded with a sick heart" (XII, 293-294).

While waiting for Miles in the dining room, she is reminded of the occasion when she had seen Quint's ghost outside the window: "Here at present I felt afresh— for I had felt it again and again—how my equilibrium depended on the success of my rigid will, the will to shut my eyes as tight as possible to the truth that what I had to deal with was, revoltingly, against nature. I could only get on at all by taking 'nature' into my confidence and my account, by treating my monstrous ordeal as a push in a direction unusual, of course, and unpleasant, but demanding after all, for a fair front, only another turn of the screw of ordinary human virtue" (XII, 295). Here it is not the governess cleverly seeking to disarm us of our possible objections to her relentless pursuit of the matter with Miles; it is the author deliberately seeking to foreshadow the end of the tale and to intensify its tragic-ironic impact. The conversation that ensues between the governess and Miles proceeds quietly, until Miles says, "Well—so we're alone!" (XII, 297). After this, the irony becomes more and more direct and painful. The governess keeps coming closer to the point at which she may be able to give the last pull to the, by now, thin veil between her and Miles. But she is still held back by reservations. It is this element, along with other factors such as the narrative style and arrangement of the tale, that gives the desired irresistibility to the governess' account. Had the point of the tale been to expose the baselessness of her suppositions and suspicions, the author would have made the governess do away with her doubts more expeditiously, made her suppress them, or, better still, not have endowed her with so many. On the contrary, he employs these doubts for the double purpose of characterizing the governess as a veracious reporter and of maintaining the suspense of the tale right up to the end.

Thus, the emphasized elation of the governess at Miles's initial confession (about the letter he had stolen) is soon followed by her qualms about the wisdom of conducting her inquiry any further: "He almost smiled at me in the desolation of his surrender, which was indeed practically, by this time, so complete that I ought to have left it there" (XII, 306). It is true that if she had left it there, "The Turn of the Screw" would have been a less terrible tale than it is. The responsibility, in other words, for carrying it to the bitter end rests with James. Again, we have the governess' temporary drop into confusion when Miles tells her that, at school, he said "things" to the few he liked: "Those he liked? I seemed to float not into clearness, but into a darker obscure, and within a minute there had come to me out of my very pity the appalling alarm of his being perhaps innocent. It was for the instant confounding and bottomless, for if he *were* innocent what then on earth was I?" (XII, 307). The Freudians would perhaps rejoin, "A pathological liar," and not stay for a further question. Taken in the context of the method so far, this is yet another stroke by which James keeps us tensely attentive and uncertain. The uncertainty, however, is removed when at the governess' question, "What *were* these things?" the ghost of Quint reappears, evidently to prevent Miles's confession from going any further: "For there again, against the glass, as if to blight his confession and stay his answer, was the hideous author of our woe— the white face of damnation" (XII, 308). Furthermore, Miles's conjecture about the identity of the ghost that is now invisible to him—he mentions first Miss Jessel, then Peter Quint—is the last irrefutable confirmation of the governess' position that the children's innocence is a mere mask. How else would he know what the governess is referring to? His rage at the governess is quite understandable. He is bewildered at the sudden sealing of his eyes and the consequent cessation of aid from the evil source. Besides, he knows what the governess is hinting at and is infuriated at her refusal to be forthright. Still another explanation is the one given by Heilman: "The climax of his disease . . . is his malevolent cry to the governess—'you devil!' It is his final transvaluation of values: she who would be his savior has become for him a demon."[37]

The death of Miles, painful as it is, should not be allowed to sidetrack us into disbelieving or damning the governess, for we would be missing the whole point of the tale. The death is the culminating turn of the Jamesian screw. Even as the governess thinks, exultingly, of the boy's liberation, she realizes "what it truly was that I held. We were alone with the quiet day, and his little heart, dispossessed, had stopped" (XII, 309). Her tragedy is that, with the best of intentions, she fails to save either Flora or Miles. The conclusion of the tale is thus profoundly pessimistic: evil emerges triumphant. There is, however, another way of looking at the final outcome: Are we justified in equating "saving" with the saving of Miles's life? Of course, even if our answer to this question is no, the tale does not gain the optimism represented by a "happy" ending. But, then, how many of James's endings are happy in the conventional sense?

I have tried to show that the text of "The Turn of the Screw," even if we ignore all external evidence, does not warrant any speculations about the actual intention of James, about the reliability of the governess, or about the reality of the ghosts. The governess, with all her deep involvement in the action, is a typical Jamesian first-person narrator, whose record and reflections—that is, the objective phenomena she reports and the conclusions she draws from them—are demonstrably meant to be taken as true.[38] Her intuitive faculty is more highly developed than that of any other Jamesian narrator, except perhaps the narrator of *The Sacred Fount*, because without that James could not have worked the spell and the suspense he so remarkably has. The nature of the subject has a determining influence on the persona James projects in this tale. The same explanation applies to the occasional assertions of the governess. There is nothing, in short, in the tone of the tale, or in its various details, to support the contention that the governess is a pathological case study or that she is an ironic center of narration. If in the foregoing analysis Edmund Wilson has figured prominently, it is because he seems to me to have violated both the text and the larger context more flagrantly and more persistently than any adherent of his theory. In conclusion, I should like to repeat with R. B. Heilman "that a great deal of unnecessary mystery has been made of the apparent ambiguity of the story. Actually, most of it is a by-product of James's method."[39] The one minor modification that may be added to this statement is that the ambiguity is a product of an unfortunate failure to understand James's method, for the method itself is not inherently ambiguous. With the aid of this method he quickened the dross of the conventional ghost story into a terrifying yarn of the supernatural, comparable in power and meaning to *The Ancient Mariner*. If *The Ancient Mariner* is the greatest literary ballad in English, "The Turn of the Screw" has a claim to being the greatest literary ghost story. This description, far from constricting the deeper meanings of the tale, should perhaps be the only point of departure for a fruitful probe into those deeper meanings.

PART TWO

THE AUTHOR
HIMSELF

CHAPTER V

Three Early Tales

THE TITLE used for this part of the book, "The Author Himself," may surprise some readers: this was intentional. To make matters worse, I am going to insist on the omniscience, if not the omnipresence, of the author in the tales discussed here. This insistence, lest it look perverse or heretical, needs some explanation. It is meant to emphasize my dissatisfaction with the prevalent casual use of "point of view" in connection with James's method. The expression has been frozen into an opaque formula, which is often used to evade, or to simplify, the task of examining James's narrative devices in all their intricacy. Having made a ritualistic bow to James's mastery of the point of view, most Jamesians tend to make a beeline for other, more popular, concerns, be they thematic or philosophical or biographical. In this rush the total meaning of the work in question is sometimes reduced to a misleadingly oversimplified statement. Although I have no quarrel with the legitimacy of these concerns, I suggest that a nod to James for his point-of-view technique does little justice to the complex way in which it actually works in his individual pieces. Thus, starting with an examination of three of his early tales, I have tried to show how in his major tales James was able to refine the omniscient-narrator convention and subject it to a rigorous artistic discipline.

A Tragedy of Error

The earliest work of a great writer can be an irresistible hunting ground to the critic who is looking for anticipations and foreshadowings of his author's later work. There is a tendency either to read too much into it, with the beguiling aid of hindsight, or to subject it to a condescending, almost invidious, comparison with the maturer work of the same author. To a certain extent, perhaps, both tendencies are inescapable, and an awareness of their existence is likely to produce an excessive cautiousness. This apprehension is all the more acute as one approaches the very first published tale of Henry James in order to analyze it and to discover some of its intrinsic merits.

"A Tragedy of Error" appeared anonymously in *The Continental Monthly* of February 1864; it remained unidentified for almost a century until Leon Edel discovered and established it conclusively as James's first published tale.[1] It is told by an omniscient narrator, and the focus of my discussion will be on the nature and method of this narrator. However, because the tale may not be widely known, a brief sketch of its plot may precede the discussion. Madame Hortense Bernier is upset by a letter announcing her husband's unexpected arrival in H—, a French seaport town, where in his absence she has taken a lover, Vicomte Louis de Mayrau. She fears, despite facile assurances to the contrary from her less disturbed lover, that it will be impossible to conceal the love affair. So without taking the lover into her confidence, she resorts to a desperate remedy: she makes a deal with a mercenary ferryman to drown the unsuspecting husband when he disembarks; her husband is lame and cannot swim. Eventually she is baffled in her plan by the lover's deciding to meet M. Bernier aboard the steamer—it happens in such a way that she cannot prevent it. As a result, the lover is mistaken by the ferryman as his intended victim. The story ends with Madame Bernier's "great cry" as she sees "a figure emerge from below the terrace, and come limping towards her with outstretched arms" (p. 317).

The tale opens in a melodramatic manner: "A low English phaeton was drawn up before the door of the post office of a French seaport town. In it was seated a lady, with her veil down and her parasol held closely over her face. My story begins with a gentleman coming out of the office and handing her a letter" (p. 295). Thus the omniscient narrator unabashedly reveals his manipulating hand in the first paragraph. It may be pointed out, however, that James is never shy of occasionally using the authorial "I" in his fiction. He makes a similar appearance in the opening paragraph of *The Ambassadors:* "The principle I have just mentioned as operating . . ." (XXI, 3).[2] The important thing to note is the point at which James picks up his narrative in "A Tragedy"—the arrival of the husband's letter. After this the reader is not given a summarized account of Madame Bernier's relations either with her husband or with her lover. Our curiosity about the contents of the letter is soon satisfied. Neither the lady nor her lover is described directly. That there is something suspicious in their being together is indicated indirectly: "This couple seemed to be full of interest for the passers by, most of whom stared hard and exchanged significant glances" (p. 295). The lady's reaction to the letter is also reflected indirectly: "Such persons as were looking on at the moment saw the lady turn very pale as her eyes fell on the direction of the letter" (p. 295). One notices also the adroitness with which the first glimpse of the lover's character is given: "Her attitude was almost that of unconsciousness, and he could see that her eyes were closed. Having satisfied himself of this, he hastily possessed himself of the letter, and read as follows" (p. 295). The letter reflects the husband's innocence and his unsuspecting jubilation at the prospect of a reunion. The irony of this is of course very obvious, indeed far more obvious than it would be on similar occasions in the later James.

The conversation, as the lovers drive to Madame Bernier's home, is skillfully managed so as to foreshadow later events and to maintain the reader's suspense. The foreshadowing is done by the dense imagery of the conversation, which also suggests the pompous hollowness of the lover: "In life we are afloat on a tumultuous sea; we are all struggling toward some *terra firma* of wealth or love or leisure. The roaring of the waves we kick up about us and the spray we dash into our eyes deafen and blind us to the sayings and doings of our fellows. Provided we climb high and dry, what do we care for them?" (p. 297). Throughout this conversation there is almost no authorial comment, and the reader is left completely free to form an impression of the speakers. The suspense is intensified by the fact that, as the lovers draw close to their destination, the reader sees through the insincerity of the lover. The character of the wife is another matter; she is the central figure in the drama and the author is particularly keen to prolong the reader's uncertainty about her. She tells her lover that she has "half a mind to drown myself literally," but the discerning reader can see that the other half of her mind is probably occupied with another plan.

We do not get a fuller glimpse of this other, and more terrible, half until we reach the second and longest section in the tale. The author dramatizes the agitation of his heroine by posting the maid Josephine at the keyhole of her lady's boudoir: "This is what she saw" (p. 300). Through this simple device, the description of Madame

Bernier as she takes brandy by the glassful and looks constantly at the sea, arming herself in her decision, is transformed into a scene of power. The brief colloquy between the maid and the cook is also an effective and economical choral comment.

The second section is designed to dramatize the terrible character of Madame Bernier. She leaves the house resolved and pale; it is clear she has renounced the idea of suicide, since she leaves instructions for her lover to await her return. We do not know the purpose of her excursion into the "crowded region, chiefly the residence of fishermen and boatmen," but "if for any reason a passer by had happened to notice her, he could not have helped being struck by the contained intensity with which she scrutinized every figure she met" (p. 301). James's use of the hypothetical spectator is a significant compositional device whereby he is able to maintain the indirection or objectivity of his presentation. This is the guise under which the omniscient narrator speaks quite frequently in the later work of James. In a sense, it is a substitute for the intuitions and the speculative commentary of the first-person narrator.

To go back to the story, soon the wife finds what she is looking for, and the process of her discovery is again dramatized through a vivid inset scene in which she witnesses a boatman's brutality. The functional significance of this scene is not only to indicate the character of the boatman, but also to suggest the heroine's unerring sense for spotting the most suitable person for the job she has in mind. The calculated way in which she makes her pact with the boatman is an admirable achievement of the narrator's art and gives a full picture of the woman's character. The boatman himself is finely characterized. We notice that the narrator is restrained throughout and concentrates in his occasional editorial remarks not on Madame Bernier but on the boatman. Nonetheless, there are a few places in which he exercises his time-honored right to interpolate a brief "philosophical" opinion: "We say a countenance is 'lit up' by a smile; and indeed that momentary flicker does the office of a candle in a dark room. It sheds a ray upon the dim upholstery of our souls. . . . Ah me! the faces which wear either nakedness or rags; whose repose is stagnation, whose activity vice; ignorant at their worst, infamous at their best!" (p. 304). In the context, however, even this outburst is designed partly to suggest the way Madame Bernier's mind is working—she is sizing up her man for the proposal and thinking of the contrast between the ferryman as he looks to her now and as he did with "a certain rascally gleam" in his eyes while offering his services to her a little while before. The most amusing of these interpolations, however, is the footnote that James adds by way of authenticating his remark that Madame Bernier's prettiness helps her with the boatman: "I am told that there was no resisting her smile; and that she had at her command, in moments of grief, a certain look of despair which filled even the roughest hearts with sympathy, and won over the kindest to the cruel game" (p. 314). It is amusing because of the young author's scrupulous desire to keep his own ironical comments out of the main narrative and his inability to suppress them altogether. The boatman's cynical irony toward the close of the section is another skillful touch:

"Shall I trust you?"

"Am I not trusting you? It is well for you that I do not allow myself to think of the venture I am making."

"Perhaps we're even there. We neither of us can afford to make account of certain possibilities. Still, I'll trust you, to. . . . *Tiens!*" added the boatman, "here we are near the quay." Then with a mock-solemn touch of his cap, "Will Madame still visit the cemetery?"

"Come, quick, let me land," said Madame Bernier, impatiently.

"We *have* been among the dead, after a fashion," persisted the boatman, as he gave her his hand. (pp. 314-315)

The next two sections are appropriately brief, taken up as they are with the externals of the denouement. In the third section again we see the author in a stance which disappears in James's later work: "Though I have judged best, hitherto, often from an exaggerated fear of trenching on the ground of fiction, to tell you what this poor lady did and said, rather than what she thought, I may disclose what passed in her mind now" (p. 316). What he tells is rather rudimentary. If we accept the narrator's authority, our heroine has no qualms about the trap she has set for her husband; her thoughts are entirely occupied by her lover, who—she has learned—has gone somewhere else to pass the night. It may be remarked that in the author's fidelity to what his heroine does and says, and in his not directing his omniscience to her thoughts, lies whatever strength this early tale has. The glimpse that he does give of her thoughts is enough to suggest that he is not yet competent enough to divine the heroine's mind in more than a naive elementary way. Furthermore, his objectivity provides sufficient evidence for the reader to deduce the heroine's thoughts from her actions. Paradoxically, however, this is also the weakness of the tale, for it fails to present the situation of the woman in all its psychological complexity.

Leon Edel in his perceptive comments on the tale says that its "plot is somewhat creaky and we are asked to assume that the lover, who is not lame, also cannot swim."[3] But the tale makes no such demand. We are told, of course, that the lover takes the husband's place in the boat, but beyond that the narrative is silent. To imagine that the lover was actually drowned is not necessary in order to appreciate the "tragedy" of Madame Bernier; at any rate it involves us into pursuing the tale beyond the point that concludes it. Furthermore, the "tragedy" of the title undoubtedly has an ironic intention which remains independent of the equivocal suggestion about the fate of the lover. The only other comment on the tale I know of is a brief note by Robert L. Gale, whose ostensible purpose is to adduce additional proof for James's authorship "by comparing the figurative and near-figurative language of the story with that of James's later and known fiction."[4] The proof is, however, redundant in view of Edel's conclusive evidence. The comparison itself, though supported by statistics of sorts, is essentially forced and of a kind that seems to postulate speciously the dictum that in the beginning of every author is his end. For example, Gale remarks: "It is curious that the word *floating*, which is used in James's later works so often that it becomes almost a mannerism, should appear in his very first image."[5] It seems to me no more curious than the constant occurrence in James's later work of any other word, such as "is," that also occurs in "A Tragedy of Error."

During the ten years after "A Tragedy of Error," James published nine other omniscient-narrator tales. Almost all of them exhibit the characteristics observed in "A Tragedy" to varying degrees, and almost none of them surpasses it in the restraint and objectivity of the narrative voice. "The Story of a Year" (1865), for example, opens in a manner similar to "A Tragedy": "My story begins as a great many stories have begun within the last three years, and indeed as a great many have ended; for, when the hero is dispatched, does not the romance come to a stop?"[6]

As we read a little further, we notice that the narrator is far more relaxed than the one in the earlier tale: "Good reader, this narrative is averse to retrospect"; "I have no intention of following Lieutenant Ford to the seat of war"; "Alack, my poor heroine had no pride!"; "But as I can find no words delicate and fine enough to describe the multifold changes of Nature, so, too, I must be content to give you the spiritual facts in gross"; "Heaven forbid that I should cross that virgin threshold—for the present!"[7] One reason for this garrulous bonhomie may be that James is dealing here with a more complex situation and does not yet have the requisite mastery over his material; consequently he seeks to slur over some of the difficult moments by a rather naive admission of his inability to render them. It has been pointed out that James had "material enough here for a novel but he brought it into the scope of twenty-five pages."[8] Had this been done with success, James, we can imagine, would have been proud of the performance. As it is, the tale remains important only for its historical interest.[9]

The common formal characteristics of these earliest James tales may be summarized in this way: the omniscient narrator is in constant good-humored communication with the reader, a habit that is sometimes overdone, as in "The Story of a Year"; he exercises his omniscience quite liberally, almost indiscriminately; the narrative is a mixture, not always well measured enough to produce the right kind of balance, of straight characterization, illustrative dramatic scenes, and authorial analysis. According to Cornelia Pulsifer Kelley, the basic flaw in most of these tales is James's failure to "reconcile artistry and analysis."[10] It may be described as a failure to use the omniscient narrator effectively. The plot is not always so constructed as to avoid jolts; the clearest illustration of such a jolt is to be found in "The Story of a Masterpiece" (1868), where the author interrupts the main story to give an unnecessarily detailed account of an earlier episode in the heroine's past.[11] The style of these early tales is simple and lively, although the imagery tends to be either purely decorative or plainly allegorical. It may be remarked in conclusion that James achieves a greater measure of artistic success in tales which are limited in scope and essentially anecdotic in form, for example in "A Tragedy of Error," "A Day of Days" (1866), and "The Romance of Certain Old Clothes" (1868).

Madame de Mauves

"Madame de Mauves" (1874) marks the first important turning point in James's employment of the omniscient narrator. For the first time we get a potentially important Jamesian character—the American innocent abroad—combined with a method that later becomes central—the choice and use of a central consciousness to reflect the narrative. James described it as "experimentally international";[12] he might, with justification, have described it also as formally experimental. It has all the groping characteristics, the tentativeness, of an early technical experiment.

The tale, in the familiar manner of James's longer tales, is divided into several sections. It does not, like some of the early tales, open with a formal announcement by the narrator to the effect that his story has begun and that it concerns this or that period or character. This in itself is a minor advance in the direction of sophistication. The author takes a couple of sentences to set the scene before introducing his hero, Longmore, upon whom he comments briefly: "Though not in the least a cynic he was what one may call a disappointed observer, and he never chose the right-hand road without beginning to suspect after an

hour's wayfaring that the left would have been the better"
(XIII, 215-216). The process of this young man's encounter
with his old acquaintance Mrs. Draper, brief as it is, could
have been dispensed with, for the introduction of the little
daughter Maggie does not contribute anything of value to
the story. The important thing, however, is that the reader
gets his first glimpse of Madame de Mauves through the
eyes of Longmore: "What chiefly struck Longmore in her
face was the union of a pair of beautifully gentle, almost
languid grey eyes with a mouth that was all expression and
intention" (XIII, 217). Longmore's infatuation with Madame de Mauves is hinted through his conversation with
Mrs. Draper. Mrs. Draper, we soon see, has been introduced
in order to avoid any authorial interruption in the narrative and to cut short the process of Longmore's discovery of
Madame de Mauves's marital misalliance. Even before
he receives Mrs. Draper's explanatory letter, Longmore
knows that Madame de Mauves is unhappy; on his second
chance encounter with the heroine, he finds "it natural to
guess that this same husband was the source" of her un-
happiness (XIII, 220). Mrs. Draper's letter, which is
reproduced in the tale, confirms this guess: "It's the
miserable story of an American born neither to submit
basely nor to rebel crookedly marrying a shining sinful
Frenchman who believes a woman must do one or the
other of those things" (XIII, 222). The reader, of course,
does not yet know how to take this view of the matter, but
he soon learns that it is essentially correct even though it
comes from Mrs. Draper, a minor figure, one of those
numerous Jamesian women roaming around in Europe,
"having left her husband in Wall Street" (XIII, 217).

The confirmation comes from the long authorial aside
contained in the second section, the longest section in the
tale. It is true that the narrator is not as awkward here as

he is in "The Story of a Masterpiece." But how far is the aside a mere duplication of the details already given and the purpose already served by Mrs. Draper's letter? We hear only the omniscient narrator's voice as he spells out the impression already given of the background of Madame de Mauves's marriage. The information is perhaps necessary for a proper understanding of the Euphemia phase of Madame de Mauves, and indeed of the failure of her marriage and her own responsibility for it. But it remains an interpolation by the author, which could have been avoided by dramatizing all these details through a fuller use of Mrs. Draper, the *ficelle*. The reader's curiosity about Longmore's own gradual understanding of the heroine's domestic complications is thus considerably dulled by the advantage he is given over Longmore so early in the tale. On the other hand, this advantage becomes the source of ironic tension between the superior knowledge of the reader and the comparative ignorance of Longmore, as we shall see. It may also be mentioned that this part of the tale is irresistibly interesting in itself because of its wit and apt characterization; the old grandmother with her advice to the bewildered Euphemia at the threshold of marriage is particularly well portrayed. Nonetheless, it remains an episode complete in itself and is not adequately merged into the structure of the tale.

After the second section, we are less interested in the unfolding of Madame de Mauves's unhappy married life through the developing awareness of Longmore. But we are interested in watching the growth of his own love for Madame de Mauves and in seeing how she will meet this new complication. The earlier phase of the relationship is suitably foreshortened and considerably veiled by Longmore's speculations regarding her French relatives—although his mind is made up about them too definitely to permit any new revelation. The reader, for his part, has already been exposed to these personages, so that further glimpses of them seem repetitive. One such glimpse is given through an account of Madame Clairin's short married life. In the context of the whole tale, of course, this detail falls into proper place: it is an ironic contrast to the final outcome of her brother's marriage. Madame Clairin's husband, an outsider to aristocracy, blows out his brains; her sister-in-law, also an outsider, remains inexorably firm, with the result that M. de Mauves has to blow out his brains. But this piece of information about Madame Clairin, coming straight from the omniscient narrator, remains incongruous with the predominant narrative method of the tale.

Madame Clairin's designs on Longmore, and his awareness of them, drive him closer to Madame de Mauves. A decisive stage in his love for the heroine is reached when he decides not to join his friend Webster in Brussels. The author suggests his motive with restraint, without a parenthetical hint to the reader. Longmore's view of M. de Mauves remains essentially the same as at the beginning: "He knew that M. de Mauves was both cynical and shallow; these things were stamped on his eyes, his nose, his mouth, his voice, his gesture, his step" (XIII, 247). The author's own attitude to Longmore's oversimplified view is not overtly expressed, but there is some evidence of a reluctance to grant total approval. By the time this section comes to a close, Longmore has been represented as having understood vaguely the nature of the relationship between M. de Mauves and his wife, although he "would have given much to be able to . . . make out the game she was playing" (XIII, 257). The reader, however, is more curious to make out the game Longmore is playing.

In the next section Longmore has his first frank talk with Madame de Mauves. She gives him evasive answers and urges him to join his friend in Brussels: "Longmore was asking himself with an agitation of his own in the unspoken words whether all this meant that he was in love" (XIII, 261). The reader, already alerted, knows that he is; but the reticence of the author on this point is noteworthy. Madame de Mauves's side of the affair is given directly: "An emotional friendship she had not desired. . . . She liked him extremely, she felt in him the living force of something to which, when she made up her girlish mind that a needy nobleman was the ripest fruit of time, she had done too scant justice" (XIII, 261). Again it is important that the narrator does not say explicitly whether Madame de Mauves loves Longmore or not; the reader can soon guess that her sentiment is clouded by her more rigid conscience. Meanwhile, we see Longmore caught in a significant conversation with M. de Mauves, who exhibits the first traces of an uneasy conscience, reflected perversely in his desire to see his wife conveniently compromised by a liaison with Longmore. He does not put it quite as bluntly as this, but Longmore draws the necessary inference while writing to Mrs. Draper: "The Count at any rate would have enjoyed the comfort of believing his wife as bad a case as himself, and you'll hardly believe me when I assure you he goes about intimating to gentlemen whom he thinks it may concern that it would be a convenience to him if they should make love to Madame de Mauves" (XIII, 269). The recourse to this epistolary expedient, for the second time in the tale, is indicative of the author's dependence on outmoded devices. This particular letter does no more than make explicit the suggestions already contained in the preceding pages; it betrays an unnecessary mistrust of the reader's

ability to grasp those suggestions and draw his own in-
ferences.

In Paris, Longmore gets his long-desired proof of M.
de Mauves's infidelity. He returns to Saint-Germain
"conscious of no distinct desire to 'make love' to her"
(XIII, 274). It turns out that his accidental discovery of
M. de Mauves's liaison with another woman has coincided
with a similar discovery on Madame de Mauves's part.
This occasions a greater frankness between the two, but
their conversation is not handled with great subtlety or
restraint. The speeches are too long and sententious, and
the exchange is not as dramatic as it could be. Once again,
as we hear Madame de Mauves telling Longmore about
her "world," we have a sense of repetitiousness, since we
have already learned about her world and the delusions
which led her into it. The core of the scene, however, is
sound. Madame de Mauves expounds her "philosophy"
in the same breath that she denies possessing any: "I
believe, Mr. Longmore . . . that I've nothing on earth
but a conscience—it's a good time to tell you so—nothing
but a dogged obstinate clinging conscience. . . . I don't
speak in vanity, for I believe that if my conscience may
prevent me from doing anything very base it will effectually prevent me also from doing anything very fine"
(XIII, 281). The reader realizes the irony of this statement
at the end of the tale: something "very fine" on Madame
de Mauves's part would perhaps have been to relent and
thereby prevent her husband's suicide. Longmore demon-
strates the intensity of his passion and the failure of his
understanding simultaneously, when he suggests that in
his case "the unaccommodating organ we speak of might
be blinded and gagged a while, in a really good cause, if
not turned out of doors. In yours—is it absolutely beyond
being 'squared'?" (XIII, 281). Madame de Mauves makes

"no concession to his tone. 'Don't laugh at your conscience,' she answered gravely; 'that's the only blasphemy I know'" (XIII, 282). This is a foretaste of the rigidity of her attitude and Longmore's bewilderment at it—the note on which the tale is to end. The conversation is brought to an abrupt close by the unexpected appearance of M. de Mauves, who is a little sarcastic about Longmore's return. Longmore observes that the husband's presence "had checked her disposition to talk" and wonders "if matters were none the less plainly at a crisis between them . . . what it was on her part that prevented some practical protest or some rupture" (XIII, 283). Once again he "relapsed with aching impotence into the sense of her being somehow beyond him, unattainable, immeasurable by his own fretful logic" (XIII, 283-284). The section ends with a brief exchange between Longmore and Madame Clairin, whose innuendoes culminate in a crude frontal attack: "Don't pretend to tell me . . . that you're not in love with that pretty woman" (XIII, 285).

The next section is a virtual continuation of this conversation between Longmore and Madame Clairin, separated though the two meetings are by several days during which he remains in "a constant fear that . . . the magic of her magnanimity might convert M. de Mauves" (XIII, 286). This contrasts with the actual cause of the husband's conversion, which is not the magic of her magnanimity but the pressure of her severity. Madame Clairin puts Longmore in an embarrassing position by making him listen to the details of her sister-in-law's domestic tangles. She acts as the mouthpiece of her family, even as on an earlier occasion her grandmother had done. She comments upon Madame de Mauves's failure to retain her husband's affections and upon her lack of taste and tact; she dips "into the family annals" (XIII, 290); she acts, in her own words, "scientifically" in order to "see my brother free to do as he chooses; to see his wife contented" (XIII, 291). The climax of this uncomfortable exchange is reached when Longmore, caught between his nicety and his curiosity, listens to Madame Clairin's report of what M. de Mauves proposed to his wife in his last interview with her, the report ending with her words: "And now, monsieur . . . we count on you!" (XIII, 293). The proposed arrangement appalls Longmore, not because he himself has never thought of it but because of the cynicism, lucidity, and absence of any scruples with which it is made. What Madame Clairin and M. de Mauves propose is, of course, a crude externalization of the desires buried under his own squeamish conscience. It must be mentioned that a recognition of the correspondence between his inarticulate desires and the proposal made to him, as well as a recognition of the differences between the two, is left to the reader.

This scene precipitates the conflict in Longmore's mind by clarifying the terms of that conflict. In the next section we see him alone, torn by several considerations most of which are aptly summed up by one of the numerous questions he puts to himself: "Why should his first—his last—glimpse of positive happiness be so indissolubly linked with renunciation?" (XIII, 299). The backdrop for his inner conflict is provided by his ramble through the forest into an unfamiliar region, where in the garden of a country inn "his heart . . . gradually checked its pulses and left him looking at life with rather a more level gaze" (XIII, 298). He looks enviously at the happy artist and his companion and seems "afloat on the sea of ineffectual longing" (XIII, 304), listens skeptically to the landlady's view of the relationship between the two, and walks back to Saint-Germain "with less philosophic resignation to any event and more of the urgent egotism of the passion pronounced by philosophers the supremely selfish one," thinking "that he was somehow only a graver equivalent of the young lover and the rustling Claudine was a lighter sketch of Madame de Mauves" (XIII, 305, 306). His dream, after he sinks into a quiet sleep in the forest, is too vivid to be anything more than "a striking allegory" (XIII, 308). It is an early anticipation of the numerous illuminating moments that occur again and again in the major novels and tales of James, moments that often change the course of the principal characters' lives in *The Portrait of a Lady, The Ambassadors, The Wings of the Dove, The Golden Bowl,* "The Altar of the Dead," "The Jolly Corner," and so on.

Sheltered temporarily "in his quickened conviction that the only sound policy in life is to grasp unsparingly at happiness," Longmore returns that evening to Madame de Mauves, "wondering with a strange mixture of dread and desire whether Madame Clairin had repeated to her sister-in-law what she had said to him," and "lost in a painful confusion of hopes and ambiguities" (XIII, 308). This last important meeting is the most difficult part of the narrative; for, with less restraint and psychological deftness, it could have easily exploded into crude melodrama. As it is, it is probably the best episode in the whole tale. The intensity of the encounter comes from the distance that now seems to separate Longmore from Madame de Mauves: he has thought himself into a position where he is prepared to "grasp unsparingly at happiness"; she evidently has stiffened herself further into a position where in her eyes the only honorable course for him is to go away "out of the fulness of your own wisdom and the excellence of your own taste" (XIII, 314). The subtlety comes from the author's ability to represent convincingly the process by which Longmore finally surrenders to Madame de Mauves's point of view. It is also the most painful scene from Longmore's side of the case; and here again we have to appreciate the author's success in putting the pain across to the reader without detracting anything from the dignity or credibility of Longmore's renunciation. However, there is one striking flaw even in this remarkable section: it ends not conclusively but arbitrarily with Madame Clairin's sudden intrusion. Her appearance could have been structurally more effective if it had ended Longmore's resistance to Madame de Mauves's appeal. Instead, it only induces him to feel "an immense answering desire not to do anything then that might seem probable or *prevu* to this lady" (XIII, 316). Longmore, instead of saying good-bye, bids only good-night to Madame de Mauves, thus needlessly carrying his conflict further.

As a result of this error of execution, the opening paragraphs of the last section have an anticlimactic impact on the reader, who gains no new insight by having to read how "little by little her perfect meaning sank into his mind and soothed it with a sense of opportunity which somehow stifled his sense of loss" (XIII, 317). What now passes through Longmore's mind is repetitious. The conflict is stretched slightly beyond the dramatically right moment, which would have been in the previous scene. His last encounter with M. de Mauves in Paris is also an unnecessary foreshadowing of the end: "It glimmered upon him odiously M. de Mauves might grow ashamed of his political compact with his wife, and he felt how far more tolerable it would be in future to think of him as always impertinent than to think of him as occasionally contrite" (XIII, 323). Similarly his last meeting with Madame de Mauves strikes one as a concession to sentimentality; both her wishing him "all the happiness you deserve" and the author's remark about "something of infinite value . . . floating past him" (XIII, 326) could have been avoided with much gain to the total effect of their separation.

In the last few pages of the tale, the author gives us the baffled response of M. de Mauves to Longmore's withdrawal from the scene. It is understandable that James would have wanted to round off his narrative neatly, but it does seem to end the story on the trite note that some people will live unhappily ever after. Finally, one may be puzzled by "a certain ambiguity in the moral evaluation of the heroine's conduct."[13] The reader is not quite sure about how the author meant him to judge the heroine's unbending, unforgiving rigidity. Behind the individual episode, of course, there also lurks the familiar ambivalence of James toward the civilized immorality of the Old World and the austere self-reliance of the New. The ambiguity is not lessened by the fact that the ultimate source of Longmore's information, about M. de Mauves's efforts to win his wife's pardon and his suicide on failing to do so, is Madame Clairin. Longmore, however, apparently accepts the veracity of this information. Otherwise his "feeling of wonder, of uncertainty, of awe" would not be quite comprehensible; the reader has to be content with a similar feeling.

"Madame de Mauves," then, has faults. But in it James is more successful than he has been so far in portraying a complex situation involving complex characters. The general tone of the tale is psychological rather than romantic. It is told by an omniscient narrator who tries hard to restrict his omniscience to one character for the greater part of the narrative, exercises restraint in his occasional narratorial comments, and shows a great deal of respect for the reader's privilege—if not his ability—to form his own judgments. The sociological and philosophical aspects of the theme are important in view of their frequent recurrence in James's subsequent works. One has only to think of the numerous American and European characters—Daisy Miller, Winterbourne, Bessie Alden, Isabel Archer, Gilbert Osmond, Ralph Touchett, Strether, Milly, Kate, and so on—whom Longmore, Euphemia Mauves, M. de Mauves, and Madame Clairin anticipate, to realize this tale's place in the development of James's fictional studies in international contrasts. One need not be reminded of James's continual creation of heroes and heroines who sacrifice their personal happiness at some high altar. If these aspects have not been much dwelt upon here, it is only because they are better known and more often discussed than the technical aspects are.

Benvolio

"A Tragedy of Error" is a good early example of an anecdote from among James's omniscient-narrator tales; "Madame de Mauves" is a successful early nouvelle. In "Benvolio" (1875) we have the earliest of his parables told by an omniscient narrator and cast in the dimensions of a nouvelle. Excluded from the New York Edition, it has never been given the detailed examination it deserves, for it has immense biographical and thematic significance as well as intrinsic narrative charm and excellence of execution.

The first striking feature of "Benvolio" is its fairy-tale character, indicated amusingly enough in the opening paragraph: "Once upon a time (as if he had lived in a fairy-tale) there was a very interesting young man. This is not a fairy-tale, and yet our young man was in some respects as pretty a fellow as any fairy prince" (M, XXIV, 303). The rest of the tale conforms to the essential pattern of a fairy tale. The characters have suggestively allegorical names—Benvolio, Countess, Scholastica—but no local habitation. The diplomatic appointment which the Countess, in order to get the hero away from Scholastica, presents to him, "on a great sheet of parchment, from which the royal seal dangled by a blue ribbon" (M, XXIV, 360), is at the court of Illyria.[14] Scholastica herself is dispatched by the scheming Countess to "an island on the other side of the globe," to the Antipodes. Benvolio's resemblance to a fairy prince is underlined in his physical appearance: "Benvolio was slim and fair, with clustering locks, remarkably fine eyes, and such a frank, expressive smile that on the journey through life it was almost as serviceable to its owner as the magic key, or the enchanted ring, or the wishing-cap, or any other bauble of necromantic properties" (M, XXIV, 303-304). The Countess is "rich, extremely pretty, and free to do as she listed. She was passionately fond of pleasure and admiration, and they gushed forth at her feet in unceasing streams. . . . She represented felicity, gaiety, success; she was made to charm, to play a part, to exert a sway" (M, XXIV, 311-312). Scholastica, living with her blind father in a house which "looked like a convent or a prison" (M, XXIV, 322), is a "quiet garden-nymph" (M, XXIV, 323), and the deepening of her smile is "like the broadening ripple of a lake" (M, XXIV, 333). Indeed, the whole course of the tale is so like a fairy tale that in the concluding paragraph the author-narrator regrets his having "said at the beginning of my story that it was not to be a fairy-tale," and he ends the tale with the apology: "But excuse me; I am writing as if it *were* a fairy-tale!" (M, XXIV, 362).

Since, however, it *is* a fairy tale, the constant presence, not to speak of the omniscience, of the authorial "I" is not at all anomalous or obtrusive. On the contrary, it gives

the story the appeal and simplicity of an oral narrative
without the author's having to establish his own identity
as a witness. Thus the convention of the omniscient narrator is employed in such a manner as to comprehend the
advantages of a first-person narrator without any of its
encumbrances. The informality of the omniscient narrator succeeds in establishing a kind of rapport with the
reader, essential in a fairy tale.

Like most fairy tales, "Benvolio" is also a parable, with
a moral. Benvolio's "magic ring" is his "poetic imagination" (M, XXIV, 304); and, as the narrator delightfully
puts it, "if we may call a spade a spade, why should we
not call such a person as Benvolio a poet?" (M, XXIV,
305). Unlike the later "poets" of James's creation—and
also unlike an earlier one, the artist of "The Madonna
of the Future"—Benvolio is young and perhaps because
of that "a tissue of contradictions" (M, XXIV, 304). In
substance, however, these contradictions seem to make of
him two distinctly different men, like Clare Vawdrey of
"The Private Life"; "It was as if the souls of two very different men had been placed together to make the voyage
of life in the same boat, and had agreed for convenience's
sake to take the helm in alternation. The helm, with Benvolio, was always the imagination; but in his different
moods it worked very differently" (M, XXIV, 305). The
alternations of his moods are reflected in his manner, dress,
conversation, and even his dwelling place: "At home he
lived in two chambers. One was an immense room, hung
with pictures, lined with books, draped with rugs and
tapestries. . . . The other, his sleeping-room, was almost
as bare as a monastic cell" (M, XXIV, 306). He receives
his friends and entertains them "at boisterous, many-
voiced suppers" (M, XXIV, 307) in the sumptuous room,
but he does his poetic scribbling in the monastic cell.

Benvolio is like Clare Vawdrey, but with an important difference: Vawdrey has achieved a successful solution in his separation of the artist and the social animal in him; his real self in never involved in his mundane activities. Benvolio, on the other hand, has apparently achieved no such solution, for "his fancy was a weathercock, and faced east or west as the wind blew" (M, XXIV, 306). The moral of his vacillation between the Countess and Scholastica is his failure to achieve a workable harmony, not between romance and realism,[15] but between the rival claims of the world and of the muse.

The Countess, representing the world, "charmed him, excited him, interested him; but . . . she failed to satisfy him" (M, XXIV, 315). Benvolio, with the help of his abundant imagination, does her "more than justice" (M, XXIV, 315) when he tells her in an eloquent outburst: "You represent the world and everything that the world can give, and you represent them at their best—in their most generous, most graceful, most inspiring form. If a man were a revolutionist, you would reconcile him to society.[16] You are a divine embodiment of all the amenities, the refinements, the complexities of life. You are the flower of urbanity, of culture, of tradition!" (M, XXIV, 318-319). This poetic tribute is quite in character, but the reader knows from what he has been told by the author that she does not wholly deserve it. The Countess herself is percipient enough to see this, for she gives him a gentle snub: "You have too much imagination!" (M, XXIV, 319). The point is that the Countess is not to be identified with the world at its best, unless of course we put a rather cynical limitation on the world's best. The fact that Benvolio sees the Countess in such a rosy light suggests the excess of his imagination and the cause of his failure to come to terms with the world. So there is an ambivalent play upon the value of the Countess, although the ambivalence finally disappears because the author's own point of view is distinctly differentiated from the hero's.

Scholastica represents the muse in isolation from the world. Benvolio's greater intellectual affinity with Scholastica is reflected in the care with which the author renders the relationship. The Countess is presented directly by the omniscient narrator, Scholastica indirectly and hence more dramatically through the gradually developing awareness of Benvolio. Apart from providing variation, the more detailed rendering of Benvolio's attachment to Scholastica suggests a deeper involvement of the poet with the muse. However, the muselike aspect of Scholastica is a little complicated by the introduction of her blind father, the professor, whose bookish interests seem to be shared by his daughter and ironically treated by the author: "The old man had never heard of his [Benvolio's] verses; he read nothing that had been published later than the sixth century; and nowadays he could read only with his daughter's eyes" (M, XXIV, 329). Thus the opposition to the Countess is provided not by the muse alone but by abstract learning, which fails to satisfy Benvolio the poet completely: "the dusky world of fact" pulls him in one direction, "an El Dorado of thought" in another (M, XXIV, 332). Another difference, however, is that the Countess—who "had his book on her table, but he once noticed that half the leaves were uncut"[17] (M, XXIV, 324)—is not really in love with Benvolio, while Scholastica—her volume of Benvolio's verses had a "well-thumbed air" (M, XXIV, 329)—is not only in love but also in complete intellectual sympathy with him: "Scholastica gazed at him, but she understood him too" (M, XXIV, 335). A clear proof of this understanding is conveyed in what she tells him about his function as a poet. We must notice that while the blind professor, ignorant of Benvolio's talent, is struck by his "great aptitude for philosophical research" (M, XXIV, 341), Scholastica regards him primarily as a poet: "No . . . a poet ought to run all risks—even that one which for a poet is perhaps most cruel. But he ought to escape them all!"[18] (M, XXIV, 341).

Nonetheless, Benvolio identifies Scholastica too much with abstract science and suddenly finds himself "thinking of her as a neat little mechanical toy, wound up to turn pages and write a pretty hand, but with neither a head nor a heart that was capable of human ailments" (M, XXIV, 336). He turns once again to the Countess with renewed ardor, writes a play—"this was the proper mission of his faculties, he cried to himself—the study of warm human passions, the painting of rich dramatic pictures, not the dry chopping of logic" (M, XXIV, 337)—starts another, but soon begins to wonder "what in the name of mystery had suddenly become of his inspiration, and why the witticisms in his play and his comedy had begun to seem as mechanical as the cracking of the post-boy's whip" (M, XXIV, 339). Thus his fluctuation continues: "It was a life of alternation and contrast, and it really demanded a vigorous and elastic temperament. Sometimes his own seemed to him quite inadequate to the occasion—he felt fevered, bewildered, exhausted. But when it came to the point of choosing one thing or the other, it was impossible to give up either his wordly habits or his studious aspirations" (M, XXIV, 342-343). Benvolio's indecision is conveyed in this way: "Scholastica gave him some tea, and her tea, for mysterious reasons, was delicious; better, strange to say, than that of the Countess, who, however, it must be added, recovered her ground in coffee" (M, XXIV,

343-344). In the end the Countess manipulates a separation between Benvolio and Scholastica—not until after the reader has been given a hint that the "easy, fruitful, complex life [of Benvolio] might have lasted for ever" in spite of, or rather because of, his vacillation (M, XXIV, 358). Benvolio does not quite believe the Countess' promise that "if he would trust her, he should never miss that pale-eyed little governess . . . but he appears to have been guilty of letting himself be persuaded without belief" (M, XXIV, 361). After some time, however, Benvolio breaks with the Countess completely, telling her: " 'Don't you see . . . can't you imagine, that I cared for you only by contrast? You took the trouble to kill the contrast, and with it you killed everything else. For a constancy I prefer this!' And he tapped his poetic brow. He never saw the Countess again" (M, XXIV, 362).

The tale does not come to an end on this inconclusive point. In the last brief paragraph the author tells us that "if Benvolio missed Scholastica, he missed the Countess also, and led an extremely fretful and unproductive life, until one day he sailed for the Antipodes and brought Scholastica home. After this he began to produce again; only, many people said that his poetry had become dismally dull" (M, XXIV, 362). This completes the parabolic meaning of the tale: a poet, in order to do full justice to his poetic genius and temperament, must achieve a balance between the world and the closet, for both are indispensable to the proper fruition of his genius. The moral, however, like that of any literary parable well told, is contained within the total structure and texture of the tale. It has been implied that the general character of the tale is symbolic, even though the symbols are closer to being allegorical. But allegory is not as jejune or thin a thing as it is sometimes assumed to be, particularly if its correspondences do not stick out woodenly. "Benvolio" succeeds because its allegorical elements are not allowed to stiffen into a mechanical device for conveying too obvious a moral.

CHAPTER VI

Nouvelles

BETWEEN "Madame de Mauves" (1874) and "The Pupil" (1891), James published nearly a dozen omniscient-narrator nouvelles. The best of these, with the exception of the "The Liar" (1888) and "The Lesson of the Master" (1888), are marked by that *"emphasised* internationalism" of which he speaks in the preface to *Lady Barberina*[1] and which more or less fades from the productions of his major phase. Of the tales in Volume XIV of the New York Edition, James remarks that "in a whole group of tales I here collect the principle of illustration has on the other hand quite definitely been that the idea could *not* have expressed itself without the narrower application of international terms."[2] We notice the relaxation of this emphasis most clearly in "A London Life" (1888), which significantly enough was not grouped by James with any of the numerous international tales in the canon, an anomaly that he takes many words to explain in the relevant preface: "What here concerns us is that 'A London Life' breaks down altogether, I have had to recognize, as a contribution to my comprehensive picture of bewildered Americanism. I fail to make out to-day why I need have conceived my three principal persons as sharers in that particular bewilderment."[3] Speaking of the purpose of the tale, he remarks: "It wasn't after all of the prime, of the very most prime, intention of the tale in question that the persons concerned in them [*sic*] should have had this, that, or the other land of birth; but that the central situation should really be rendered."[4] Our own experience of the tale would bear out the soundness of James's discernment.

The Pupil

The effectiveness of "The Pupil" also is largely independent of its international ramifications or setting. The Moreens no doubt are an amusing "band of [American] gipsies," even as Pemberton is a young American with "four years at Yale in which he had richly supposed himself to be reacting against a Puritan strain" (XI, 519). But the intense drama produced by their coming together has its real source elsewhere, in the combined consciousness of Pemberton and his pupil, Morgan Moreen. It is quite significant that James in the preface does not "pretend really to have 'done' them [the Moreens]; all I have given in 'The Pupil' is little Morgan's troubled vision of them as reflected in the vision, also troubled enough, of his devoted friend."[5] The real focus of the tale, then, is the interreflected "troubled vision" of the two friends, not the shiftlessness of the American "migratory tribe" (XI, 523).

This calls for another brief reference to "A London Life" in order to clarify the nature of the connection between that tale and "The Pupil." Laura Wing, we may recall, is the central character in "A London Life," whose somewhat hypersensitive reaction to her Londonized sister's moral depravity forms the focus of narration. James sticks to this focus except for a few pages wherein he contrives an interview between Lady Davenant and Wendover, behind Laura's back. With characteristically severe self-criticism, James does "penance" in the preface for this "lapse from artistic dignity."[6] Even without this lapse "A London Life" would not be as good as "The Pupil," it seems to me, because of its general facile manner and its heroine's inferior sensibility. The moral squalor she recoils from is actually a few shades blacker than that which repels Morgan and Pemberton in "The Pupil." But her motives remain considerably prudential; hence our view of her agony is a little tempered by Lady Davenant's attitude, "a Regency attitude," in F. R. Leavis' phrase. Leavis goes on to point out: "James's own attitude has enough of her [Lady Davenant] in it to produce the witty and satirical treatment in which *A London Life* relates closely to *What Maisie Knew*."[7] Here, however, I part company with Leavis, who seems to me to be largely correct in what he implies about "A London Life" but quite mistaken in his insistence that *What Maisie Knew* is a "high-spirited" comedy.[8] He reads in "A London Life," "The Pupil," and *What Maisie Knew* a descending order of "moral horror" and an ascending order of comedy: "The things that Maisie hears and sees are much of the order of those which horrified Laura in 'A London Life,' but *What Maisie Knew*, in tone, is even more removed from the earliest of the three stories than *The Pupil* is."[9] To me, on the contrary, these three pieces show an ascending order of moral horror, with the comedy becoming increasingly more grim and indistinguishable from tragedy, particularly because of the contributive intensity of pathos and satire in "The Pupil" and *Maisie*. The following analysis will, I hope, support my contention in regard to "The Pupil."

The eight sections of "The Pupil" fall roughly into two parts. In the first we are shown the process of Pemberton's coming to understand the Moreens and his own increasingly awkward position among them. In the second part we are shown the effect of the family's mendacity on the sensitive mind of Morgan as seen and felt by Pemberton, now from the vantage point of close intimacy. The first part culminates in a "scene" between Pemberton and the two Morgans, after which he sees "fully for the first time where he was." Simultaneous with this perception is the other, that "he couldn't at the pinch bear to leave the child" (XI, 533). The second part culminates in the terrible final scene, in which Morgan collapses under the violent shock of the family's public exposure and the no less violent upset at the prospect of escape with his devoted friend. In the first part the mendacious Moreens strike Pemberton, and through him the reader, as ridiculous but not quite vile or immoral. If the story had ended with the fourth section, I would have no hesitation in accepting Leavis' opinion that "in *The Pupil* we no longer have the note of horror. . . . Except for not paying their bills the Moreens are intensely respectable."[10] In the second part, however, the Moreens' irresponsibility reveals its sinister side—because of its tragic effect on their son, it becomes highly culpable. Thus, in spite of its surface smoothness, the tale comes close to being a powerful condemnation of the parents.

The most important element in the first section is the skill with which James establishes the duality of Pemberton's motivation in accepting the tutorship. Initially the mercenary motive is there, even though there is a disturbing insinuation in Morgan's "mocking foreign ejaculation, 'Oh la-la!'" at Mrs. Moreen's assurance, "All that will be quite regular." Other hints from the boy follow until we come to this passage:

"You're very witty," Pemberton remarked to the child—a proposition his mother echoed with enthusiasm, declaring Morgan's sallies to be the delight of the house.

The boy paid no heed to this; he only enquired abruptly of

the visitor, who was surprised afterwards that he hadn't struck him as offensively forward: "Do you *want* very much to come?"

"Can you doubt it after such a description of what I shall hear?" Pemberton replied. Yet he didn't want to come at all; he was coming because he had to go somewhere, thanks to the collapse of his fortune at the end of a year abroad spent on the system of putting his scant patrimony into a single full wave of experience. He had had his full wave but couldn't pay the score at his inn. Moreover he had caught in the boy's eyes the glimpse of a far-off appeal. (XI, 515)

The second, and potentially stronger, motive that persuades Pemberton to take the job is "the glimpse of a far-off appeal." It is a case of friendship at first sight. The entire interview is too compact for a summary or for a clear picture through excerpted quotations. Brief as it is, it involves our attention completely through its meaningful suggestions about the prospects of Pemberton, about the tension between Mrs. Moreen and Morgan, about the mixed reactions produced in the tutor's mind by the precocious boy and his mobile "small satiric face" (XI, 514), and so on.

The second section begins with a picture of the impression produced by the rest of the Moreen family on Pemberton. Covering just one long paragraph, it is a masterpiece of collective ironic portraiture. Take, for instance, this account of Mr. Moreen's response to Pemberton's curiosity about salary: "The young man had endeavoured to keep these stammerings modest, and Mr. Moreen made it no secret that *he* found them wanting in 'style.' He further mentioned that he aspired to be intimate with his children, to be their best friend, and that he was always looking out for them. That was what he went off for, to London and other places—to look out; and this vigilance was the theory of life, as well as the real occupation, of the whole family. They all looked out, for they were very frank on the subject of its being necessary" (XI, 517-518). And thus it goes on till we realize that Pemberton must have obtained no more light on the subject of his salary than he had from Mrs. Moreen on the earlier occasion. After this, however, the narrative plunges us into a generalized account of Pemberton's view of the family and particularly his view of the difference between the rest of the family and Morgan Moreen. Here the author employs the interesting device of going ahead in time and projecting what Pemberton later thought of the whole experience. The impression is almost as if Pemberton were reminiscing in his own voice:

Indeed the whole mystic volume in which the boy had been amateurishly bound demanded some practice in translation. To-day, after a considerable interval, there is something phantasmagoric, like a prismatic reflexion or a serial novel, in Pemberton's memory of the queerness of the Moreens. If it were not for a few tangible tokens—a lock of Morgan's hair cut by his own hand, and the half-dozen letters received from him when they were disjoined—the whole episode and the figures peopling it would seem too inconsequent for anything but dreamland. (XI, 518-519)

We also get in this section the first disturbing glimpse of the Moreens' desire to get rid of the child:

They passed him over to the new members of their circle very much as if wishing to force some charity of adoption on so free an agent and get rid of their own charge. They were delighted when they saw Morgan take so to his kind playfellow, and could think of no higher praise for the young man. It was strange how they contrived to reconcile the appearance, and indeed the essential fact, of adoring the child with their eagerness to wash their hands of him. Did they want to get rid of him before he should find them out? (XI, 522)

At this stage Pemberton does not know that the boy has already found them out, since Morgan's only reported comment so far on his family is about their much-mixed language, for which his term is "Ultramoreen" (XI, 520). But the next section, however, embodies a very brief scene, which embarrasses Pemberton because of his distaste at having to hear Morgan's aspersions against the family. Later he is to think "of that clumsy moment on the beach at Nice as the dawn of an understanding that had broadened" (XI, 526). In this scene Morgan comes very close to unmasking his parents openly. Pemberton is conscientious enough to pretend that he does not understand Morgan's insinuation and thus to prevent the child from going any further. Here again the author anticipates Pemberton's later insights: "He did understand fully before long, but he made a fight even with himself before he confessed it. He thought it the oddest thing to have a struggle with the child about. He wondered he didn't hate the hope of the Moreens for bringing the struggle on. But by the time it began any such sentiment for that scion was closed to him" (XI, 527). These deliberate gaps in chronological order suggest the confidence of the writer that he can engage the interest of the reader on a principle of organization higher than mere suspense. The scene, meanwhile, has served its purpose of illuminating the fast-developing attachment between teacher and pupil. The last few lines, for instance, give a physical image of their bond in opposition to the rest of the Moreens:

"Well, at any rate you'll hang on to the last."

"To the last?"

"Till you're fairly beaten."

"*You* ought to be fairly beaten!" cried the young man, drawing him closer. (XI, 527)

The irony of this tender passage, with its "last" and "beaten," flashes on the reader fully at the end of the tale. I have already referred to the brief climactic scene in the next section; the rest of it is a summarized account, preceding that scene, of Pemberton's peregrinations with Morgan in Paris, where the Moreens are now living in indigent circumstances. During these wanderings Pemberton "used sometimes to wonder what people would think they were—to fancy they were looked askance at as if it might be a suspected case of kidnapping" (XI, 530). This foreshadows his later idea that they "ought to go off and live somewhere together" (XI, 545) and Morgan's still later fancy that they should escape[11] (XI, 570). By the close of this section Pemberton has no illusions left about the Moreens or about the fact of his having "simply given himself away to a band of adventurers" (XI, 533). If in spite of this he cannot give up his unpaying tutorship, it is because he is too attached to the boy. At the same time, he is tortured by "the problem of how far it was excusable to discuss the turpitude of parents with a child of twelve, of thirteen, of fourteen" (XI, 535). The duration of this torture is thus casually mentioned—Morgan was eleven at the beginning of the tale. The climax is reached when the boy once again breaks out and, ignoring his tutor's evasions, tells him with precocious pompousness, "I'm not afraid of the stern reality" (XI, 537). Pemberton persists in his scruples about betraying his employers to their son, but Morgan's overburdened mind finds an outlet in his "suddenly leaning his arms on the table, burying his head in them, and bursting into tears" (XI, 538). It is under this pressure that Pemberton threatens to leave them unless he is paid, and also to tell Morgan the reason for his leaving. The Moreens react reprehensibly to this threat, not because they cannot pay him but because they seem to attach no importance to "his superstition of delicacy" (XI, 538). In the remarkably ironic scene, following the threat, between Pemberton and Mrs. Moreen, she pockets with unseemly hurry the fifty francs she has brought him and accepts without any qualms his condition for staying on: "You may tell him any horror you like!" (XI, 543). It is in this scene that the Moreens cease to be comic figures.

Pemberton of course, in keeping with his innate delicacy, takes no advantage of the "permission" given by Mrs. Moreen, but a couple of days later the boy himself returns to the awkward subject. On this occasion they do look at the facts together, and Pemberton gets the full measure of the boy's knowledge: "When he tried to figure to himself the morning twilight of childhood, so as to deal with it safely, he saw it was never fixed, never arrested, that ignorance, at the instant he touched it, was already flushing faintly into knowledge, that there was nothing that at a given moment you could say an intelligent child didn't know" (XI, 547). This, in a way, is the point of the story: how much a child knows and how intensely he reacts to this knowledge.[12] Springing from the experience of the deeply involved Pemberton, and not from the abstract philosophizing pen of his creator, such a generalization can be safely incorporated into the text of the tale without fear of its being stigmatized as a bald moral lesson. Had it come sooner or later in the tale, it might have been less inevitable; it is the precise moment of its occurrence which gives it the force it has. The boy's anguish, which is the most important source of the tale's energy, is reflected in such utterances as: "I don't know what they live on, or how they live, or *why* they live! What have they got and how did they get it? . . . Who are they, anyway, and what are they? I've thought of all that—I've thought of a lot of things" (XI, 549). This gives the tale a tone different from, and more urgent than, that of a high-spirited comedy.

The point can be reinforced by comparison with a brief excerpt from "A London Life." Laura is with her brother-in-law, inquiring about her sister who has eloped: "She only sat there looking at him while he leaned against the chimney smoking a short cigar. There was a silence during which she felt a heat of irrational anger at the thought that a little ignorant red-faced jockey should have the luck to be in the right as against her flesh and blood" (X, 425). The irony of this notion and the fact that it is directed against Laura herself are quite unmistakable. Morgan too is constantly shown thinking of his "flesh and blood," but the nature of his preoccupation is different. He is so critical of their moral slovenliness that we are always in sympathy with the agony he undergoes; the "agony" of Laura is always close to being laughable. It is only fair to add that this effect seems to be clearly intended by James in "A London Life."

It should also be noted that Morgan, in spite of his torment, is not at all sentimentalized in the tale: he is shown as being too intelligent and mature to pose as a martyr; and Pemberton's reflections about him are singularly free of exaggerated sentimentality. His case is allowed to move us on its own merits. His death, for instance, is properly led up to. His weak heart is mentioned in the first section, and in this we have an ironic foreshadowing of the final catastrophe:

"You *do* keep something back. Oh you're not straight—*I* am!"

"How am I not straight?"

"Oh you've got your idea!"

"My idea?"

"Why that I probably shan't make old—make older—bones, and that you can stick it out till I'm removed."

"You *are* too clever to live!" Pemberton repeated.

"I call it a mean idea," Morgan pursued. "But I shall punish you by the way I hang on."

"Look out or I'll poison you!" Pemberton laughed. (XI, 551)

Pemberton can laugh because this idea has probably never occurred to him. Furthermore, he has learned to treat Morgan as an equal with whom he can indulge in adult repartee. The pleasantry of this conversation, nonetheless, barely conceals the tragic irony which explodes in the end like a carefully laid timebomb.

We may skip the next section, in which the two friends are separated by Pemberton's acceptance of another tutorship in London, and examine the last scene. For some time Pemberton has been serving his second term with the Moreens, now again in Paris—waiting "in a queer confusion of yearning and alarm for the catastrophe which was held to hang over the house of Moreen" (XI, 572). He and Morgan return from a walk one day to find that "the storm had come—they were all seeking refuge. The hatches were down, Paula and Amy were invisible . . . and Ulick appeared to have jumped overboard" (XI, 574). The elder Moreens, "not prostrate but . . . horribly white," now appeal to Pemberton "to induce his young charge to follow him into some modest retreat" (XI, 575). The boy, in whose eyes Pemberton has just seen "tears of a new and untasted bitterness" (XI, 575), is thrilled for a moment with the prospect of going away, only to sink to a sudden death. The effect of this on the parents is noteworthy:

"He couldn't stand it with his weak organ," said Pemberton —"The shock, the whole scene, the violent emotion."

"But I thought he *wanted* to go to you!" wailed Mrs. Moreen.

"I *told* you he didn't, my dear," her husband made answer.

Mr. Moreen was trembling all over and was in his way as deeply affected as his wife. But after the very first he took his bereavement as a man of the world. (XI, 577)

The impression one gathers from their brief remarks—an impression that would be less terrifying were it conveyed in more words—seems to be that the Moreens are inwardly relieved at this unexpected resolution, albeit partial, of their tangle. But it is unnecessary to lay too much stress on this reading of their reaction to Morgan's death in order to appreciate the irony of the tale's conclusion. Death, unless it is treated with casual dispatch, as in E. M. Forster's novels, is always a challenging matter for a writer. James more often than not avoids death scenes or else fails to keep them free of unintentional melodrama as, for instance, in the case of *Roderick Hudson, The American,* "Daisy Miller," and "The Modern Warning." It is all the more remarkable that he succeeds so well in depicting the scenes involving the death of children in three of his tales—"The Author of Beltraffio," "The Pupil," and "The Turn of the Screw." In all three cases, death comes to the children inevitably, not arbitrarily, and leaves the reader profoundly moved.

The Birthplace

If the ironic vibrations of "The Pupil" border on the tragic, those of "The Birthplace" (1903) border on the comic. The issues involved in both tales are deeply serious. Morgan Moreen is sacrificed by his insensitive status-seeking parents at the altar of a depraved social ideal; the pathos of his death is sharpened into tragic intensity because of his agonizing disapproval of all his parents stand for. Morris Gedge is saved from being sacrificed at an equally debased altar by the supreme defense of his scathing irony. This preserves his integrity and sanity, and preserves also through no "fault" of his—and thereby hangs the ironic "success" of his defense—his job. The *donnée* of "The Birthplace," according to the preface, had struck James as "the perfect theme of a *nouvelle*,"[13] although it is interesting to note that in his *Notebooks* James speaks of it as an anecdote "arrangeable, workable—for 6000 words."[14] The masterly execution of this theme has given us one of his best nouvelles, perfect in structure and perfect in tone; it is no wonder that James decided to "leave 'The Birthplace' to plead its own cause."[15]

The first three sections of the tale build up Morris Gedge's gradual awareness of the false priestly role he is expected to perform at the shrine of the great Poet. The closer he gets in his devotion to the Poet—a devotion that takes the form of "nightly prowls" (XVII, 151) during which he is "really with *Him*" (XVII, 157)—the farther he gets from the attitude of the gaping worshipers and the unperceiving overseers. As a narrative unit these three sections accelerate the action of the tale to a point where Gedge begins to see himself, in the fourth section, as "on his way to become two different persons, the public and the private" (XVII, 161). The discrepancy between his two selves has now begun to rankle in his mind to such a degree that he must discuss with his wife "the *morality* of their positions" (XVII, 163). The discussion leaves him completely isolated, for Mrs. Gedge is possessed of a moral sense totally at the mercy of prudence. In the fifth section he gets the opportunity to give vent to his real feelings about the shrine—its emptiness, its worshipers, its managers—and to dissociate himself from the stupidity and fraud of the whole show. His appreciative audience is provided by the stray American couple who have been there before, in the time of his very different predecessors, the Putchins. This marks the first important turning point in the tale and divides it roughly into two halves. After this, his mind is at rest in proportion to the relief given by his honest outburst. But the "sweet aftertaste of his freedom" (XVII, 182) is reflected in his subsequent performance as the warden of the Place; and, in the sixth section, the nemesis appears in the impressive form of Mr. Grant-Jackson, who warns him firmly against the consequences of his continued indiscretions. In his response we first catch—though his wife does not—the tones of his supreme irony. In the final section we see the ironist in full stride, once again in the appreciative company of his American friends. The climax is clinched by the second visit of Mr. Grant-Jackson, who has now come to reward him. The irony has fallen flat on both the worshipers and the managers of the Birthplace.

This harmony of structure is achieved by James through his unfailing eye for the proper distribution of space and stress. The accent throughout the tale remains on Morris Gedge—on his reactions and on his strategy. Mrs. Gedge, necessary as she is to spotlight by contrast the intellectual and moral superiority of her husband and to make his conflict more poignant, is not given more attention than is sufficient for that purpose. She remains "the bareheaded goodwife talking in the street about the row in the house" (XVII, 208). Miss Putchin's function is to preside over the initiation of her successors—there were other initiators but they are barely mentioned—and it is remarkable how this funny person is kept under proper control and dispatched as soon as she has dismayed the hero by a glimpse of the ideal he is to approximate. A writer less concerned with proportions would have played ducks and drakes with such a character. The American couple have the function of a *ficelle* whose main purpose is to encourage the hero's urge to express himself. No time is wasted, however, in introducing them or in prolonging the preparatory phase of their conversation with the hero. The author concentrates on Gedge's reasons for opening up in their presence: "The reason—well, the reason would have been, if anywhere, in something naturally persuasive on the part of the couple; unless it had been rather again, in the way the young man, once he was in the place, met the caretaker's expression of face, held it a moment and seemed to wish to sound it" (XVII, 171). The first visit of Mr. Grant-Jackson—his name has in it at once the tinkle of sovereigns and the ring of cultural hollowness—is no doubt important. In order to stress this, James, with his usual disregard for such minor matters as the stigma that attaches to the use of coincidence, has it take place one afternoon while the young Americans are there, so that "the two occasions were, of a truth, related only by being so intensely opposed" (XVII, 182). But the visit is not important enough to usurp a whole scene, particularly when the same space can be employed to much greater effect for a scene, immediately after the visit, between Morris Gedge and his wife. The second visit of Mr. Grant-Jackson is given almost no space at all. It is enough that Gedge should be shown as extremely nervous when he goes to meet him and extremely amused as he rejoins his American friends and his wife. A less economy-conscious storyteller might have succumbed to the temptation to make one scene out of each visit.

The tonal consistency of the tale is even more remarkable, for very rarely do we come across a comparable example of such sustained irony. The opening paragraphs, with their intentionally exaggerated ponderousness of manner, set the key. In these paragraphs the source of the ironic undertones, of course, is the omniscient narrator himself: "Their friend, Mr. Grant-Jackson, a highly preponderant pushing person, great in discussion and arrangement, abrupt in overture, unexpected, if not perverse, in attitude, and almost equally acclaimed and objected to in the wide midland region to which he had taught, as the phrase was, the size of his foot—their friend had launched his bolt quite out of the blue and had thereby so shaken them as to make them fear almost more than hope" (XVII, 131). We notice the mock exaltation of Mr. Grant-Jackson to the position and power of a capricious, favor-dispensing god. There is a similar note in the passages where the author sums up the chief characteristics of his hero's personality through a few glimpses of his life before the new job:

Morris Gedge had for a few years, as a young man, carried on a small private school of the order known as preparatory, and had happened then to receive under his roof the small son of the great man, who was not at that time so great. . . . The school hadn't prospered but dwindled to a close. Gedge's health had failed and still more every sign in him of a capacity to publish himself as practical. He had tried several things, he had tried many, but the final appearance was of their having tried him not less. They mostly, at the time I speak of, were trying his successors, while he found himself, with an effect of dull felicity that had come in this case from the mere postponement of change, in charge of the grey town-library of Blackport-on-Dwindle, all granite, fog and female fiction. (XVII, 132-133)

The measured epigrammatic balance of these sentences, the opposition between the two uses of "trying," the connection between the "dwindled to a close" and the "town-library of Blackport-on-Dwindle," and the brilliant effect of surprise contained in the juxtaposition of "granite, fog and female fiction" should give some indication of the high quality of comic sensibility displayed in this portion of the tale.

From a preliminary delineation of the exhilarating effect of the offer on the two Gedges, the author moves to a subtle discrimination between their reactions: "Her knowledge of the needs of the case was as yet, thanks to scant information, of the vaguest, and she had never, more than her husband, stood on the sacred spot; but she saw herself waving a nicely-gloved hand over a collection of remarkable objects and saying to a compact crowd of gaping awestruck persons: 'And now, please, *this* way'" (XVII, 135). Mrs. Gedge, we are told, "was from the first surer of everything than he" (XVII, 136); she "dwelt on the gain, for that matter, to their income" (XVII, 137). But the greatest advantage to him of their new position would be the opportunity of knowing and loving the Poet. The difference in attitude is beautifully rendered in their last excited conversation before assuming the job:

By the time their appointment arrived in form their relation to Him had immensely developed. . . . "It's absurd," he didn't hesitate to say, "to talk of our not 'knowing.' So far as we don't it's because we are dunces. He's *in* the thing, over His ears, and the more we get into it the more we're with Him. I seem to myself at any rate," he declared, "to *see* Him in it as if He were painted on the wall."

"Oh doesn't one rather, the dear thing? And don't you feel where it is?" Mrs. Gedge finely asked. "We see Him because we love Him—that's what we do. How can we not, the old darling—with what He's doing for us? There's no light"—she had a sententious turn—"like true affection."

"Yes, I suppose that's it. And yet," her husband mused, "I see, confound me, the faults."

"That's because you're so critical. You see them, but you don't mind them. You see them, but you forgive them. You mustn't mention them *there*. We shan't, you know, be there for *that*."

"Dear no!" he laughed: "we'll chuck out any one who hints at them." (XVII, 140-141)

Mrs. Gedge's emphasis throughout is on love of Him motivated by frankly prudential considerations: "How can one not, the old darling—with what He's doing for us?" Morris Gedge's emphasis is on knowledge: "And yet . . . I see, confound me, the faults." Mrs. Gedge, moreover, is quite unconscious of the irony and the humor of her remarks—she is a comic character. Her husband, on the other hand, is aware of the ironic humor of his remarks and perceptions. The fun he provides is born of calculation and design, and even when it is at his own expense he fully knows it.

In a way, the tale can be taken as the depiction of the process by which Morris Gedge flowers into a superb ironic artist. We see the various stages of this process in his reactions to Miss Putchin, in his various conversations with his wife, in his first encounter with the American couple, in that delightful scene with his wife immediately after he has "seen Grant-Jackson's broad well-fitted back, the back of a banker and a patriot, move away" (XVII, 185-186), and, finally, in his mock sermon. Each stage brings him closer to this last, but I shall confine my attention to the final two stages. Soon after Grant-Jackson's admonition, we find Gedge with his wife, telling her how he has been taken to task by that grand visitor. He has told her how he must suppress his critical sense:

". . . So I must put it—I *have* put it—at the bottom."

"A very good place then for a critical sense!" And Isabel, more placidly now, folded her work. "*If*, that is, you can only keep it there. If it doesn't struggle up again."

"It can't struggle. . . . It's dead," he went on; "I killed it just now."

He really spoke so that she wondered. "Just now?"

"There in the other place—I strangled it, poor thing, in the dark. If you'll go out and see, there must be blood. Which indeed," he added, "on an altar of sacrifice is all right. But the place is for ever spattered."

"I don't want to go out and see." She locked her hands over the needlework folded on her knee, and he knew, with her eyes on him, that a look he had seen before was in her face. "You're off your head, you know, my dear, in a way." Then, however, more cheeringly: "It's a good job it hasn't been too late."

"Too late to get it under?"

"Too late for Them to give you the second chance that I thank God you accept."

"Yes, if it *had* been—!" And he looked away as through the ruddy curtain and into the chill street. . . . "The pinch," he pursued, "is that I can do nothing else."

"Nothing whatever!" she agreed with elation.

"Whereas here—if I cultivate it—I perhaps *can* still lie. But I must cultivate it."

"Oh you old dear!" And she got up to kiss him.

"I'll do my best," he said. (XVII, 189-190)

That throughout this scene Morris Gedge is being ironical is seen in the result of his promised "cultivation." The wife's elation at the promise is the measure of the safe margin by which she misses his irony. The American husband and wife repeat their visit after about a year and a half. Gedge has perfected his method. On the previous occasion he had given expression to his feelings about the place and its vulgarization by the fact-hungry votaries in a manner that now looks crudely direct in contrast with his new manner:

"We stand here, you see, in the old living-room, happily still to be reconstructed in the mind's eye, in spite of the havoc of time, which we have fortunately of late years been able to arrest. It was of course rude and humble, but it might have been snug and quaint, and we have at least the pleasure of knowing that the tradition in respect to the features that do remain is delightfully uninterrupted. Across that threshold He habitually passed; through those low windows, in childhood, He peered out into the world that He was to make so much happier by the gift to it of His genius; over the boards of this floor—that is over *some* of them, for we mustn't be carried away!—his little feet often pattered; and the beams of this ceiling (we must really in some places take care of *our* heads!) he endeavoured, in boyish strife, to jump up and touch. It's not often that in the early home of genius and renown the whole tenor of existence is laid so bare, not often that we are able to retrace, from point to point and from step to step, its connexion with objects, with influences—to build it round again with the little solid facts out of which it sprang. This, therefore, I need scarcely remind you, is what makes the small space between these walls—so modest to measurement, so insignificant of aspect—unique on all the earth. *There's nothing like it,*" Morris Gedge went on, insisting as solemnly and softly, for his bewildered hearers, as over a pulpit-edge; "there's nothing at all like it anywhere in the world. There's nothing, only reflect, for the combination of greatness and, as we venture to say, of intimacy. You may find elsewhere perhaps absolutely fewer changes, but where shall you find a *Presence* equally diffused, uncontested and undisturbed? Where in particular shall you find, on the part of the abiding spirit, an equally towering eminence? You may find elsewhere eminence of a considerable order, but where shall you find *with* it, don't you see, changes after all so few and the contemporary element caught so, as it were, in the very fact? . . . It is in this old chimney-corner, the quaint inglenook of our ancestors—just there in the far angle, where His little stool was placed, and where, I dare say, if we could look close enough, we should find the hearthstone scraped with His little feet—that we see the inconceivable child gazing into the blast of the old oaken logs and making out there pictures and stories, see Him conning, with curly bent head, His well-worn hornbook, or poring over some scrap of an ancient ballad, some page of some such rudely-bound volume of chronicles as lay, we may be sure, in His father's window seat." (XVII, 194-196)

This is a parody at once of both official and pseudocritical utterance, and like all great parody it is profoundly serious in its underlying intention. It is the sternest of James's numerous admonitions against sentimental curiosity about the private life of a great artist in preference to a genuine interest in his works; needless to add, it is also the most delightful. Inspired as it was by the case of a particular couple at a particular Birthplace,[16] the tale has been given a universal dimension. "The Birthplace" has many affinities with James's parables of writers and artists; in the preceding analysis I have taken these obvious affinities for granted. What is not so obvious is that here James concentrates far more on the characterization of his artist-hero: he shows, in fact, the process whereby an artist is born.

The Bench of Desolation

"The Bench of Desolation" (1909-1910) is James's last and perhaps best omniscient-narrator nouvelle. It is certainly better than the virtual absence of any detailed critical comment on it might suggest. Like the other four tales of *The Finer Grain* (1910)—in Ezra Pound's phrase "a book of tales with no mis-fire"[17]—it was probably completed too late for inclusion in the New York Edition. This may have something to do with the critical neglect it has suffered in comparison to some better known but less challenging tales, such as "Daisy Miller." Be that as it may, we are in what seems to me a fortunate position to discuss this tale, untrammeled by James's own opinion of it. For even the relevant entry in the *Notebooks* gives no inkling of the great nouvelle that was to result from the "good small 'short-story' *donnée* of the orthodox type" recorded there.[18]

The ordeal of Morris Gedge—the conflict between his own refinement and the vulgarity of the idolatrous herd

—originates in his troubled consciousness, but it is given release through his vengeful irony; he triumphs over the enemies of art with the aid of artifice. His is a battle of ideas and attitudes; his antagonists are the others; his mortification—and his victorious subterfuge—is largely intellectual. The tormented hero of "The Bench of Desolation" goes through an ordeal that is deeply spiritual; his passage is through the emptiness of his own inner spaces. It is quite appropriate, therefore, that for the better part of this story his darkened consciousness provides the scene of his mute but roaring agony. The atmosphere of this tale is consequently much more terrifying, much more ghostly.

We glimpse the deeply churned mind of the hero with the first sentence of the tale: "She had practically, he believed, conveyed the intimation, the horrid, brutal, vulgar menace, in the course of their last dreadful conversation, when, for whatever was left him of pluck or confidence—confidence in what he would fain have called a little more aggressively the strength of his position—he had judged best not to take it up" (M, XXVIII, 409). The intensity of his agitation, and of his revulsion, is suggested by the nervous pace of this sentence and by the string of charged adjectives chosen to reflect his state of mind. The author conceals his own hand by the carefully placed short clause "he believed" and by the parenthetical qualification of "confidence." The narrative, in the characteristic mature manner of James, is picked up after the scene between "him" and "her" is over. The scene itself is reflected piecemeal through the troubled consciousness of Herbert Dodd. James adopts this alternative to a straight dramatic depiction of the scene, in order to fix our attention from the very beginning on what the "dreadful conversation" does to the hero. He wants to evoke "the very atmosphere of [his] mind"[19] while the hero re-enacts the whole scene in his own consciousness. The reader is left in no doubt that it is a highly subjective re-enactment, and that as such it may be partially colored. Thus after we have been given "the ugly, the awful words, ruthlessly formed by her lips" (M, XXVIII, 409)—the words themselves designedly seem less ugly and awful—the author once again concentrates on Herbert Dodd's evaluation of Kate Cookham and the vulgarity of her stand. This evaluation does not proceed from the author, who only reports it. The reader at this stage does not accept the evaluation as final. In fact, much of James's skill consists in effectively preventing him from doing so, without at the same time injecting an overt authorial caution. This feat is accomplished by the tone imparted to the agitated murmur going on in Dodd's mind:

That she had pretended she loved him was comparatively nothing; other women had pretended it, and other women too had really done it; but that she had pretended he could possibly have been right and safe and blest in loving *her*, a creature of the kind who could sniff that squalor of the law-court, of claimed damages and brazen lies and published kisses, of love-letters read amid obscene guffaws, as a positive tonic to resentment, as a high incentive to her course—this was what put him so beautifully in the right. It was what might signify in a woman all through, he said to himself, the mere imagination of such machinery. Truly what a devilish conception and what an appalling nature! (M, XXVIII, 410)

There is just enough indication of smug self-righteousness in Dodd's thoughts to give the reader pause and a dim recognition of an ironic intention on the part of the author. The reader, to be sure, does not yet know what Kate Cookham's real motives are; but he does perceive that she is desperate enough to resort to anything. Furthermore, he is not quite sure that Dodd hates Kate as much as he believes he does. Take, for instance, the note on which their conversation in the scene ends:

"I take it, of course," he had swaggered on, "that your pretensions wouldn't be for a moment that I should—after the act of profanity—take up my life with you."

"It's just as much my dream as it ever was, Herbert Dodd, to take up mine with *you*! Remember for me that I can do with it, my dear, that my idea is for even as much as that of you!" she had cried; "remember that for me, Herbert Dodd; remember, remember!"

It was on this she had left him—left him frankly under a mortal chill. There might have been the last ring of an appeal or a show of persistent and perverse tenderness in it, however preposterous any such matter; but in point of fact her large, clean, plain brown face . . . presented itself with about as much expression as his own shop-window when the broad, blank, sallow blind was down. (M, XXVIII, 412-413)

Dodd, obsessed as he is with the shock to his sense of delicacy, hurriedly suppresses his insight into Kate's deeper motives and goes on to associate her with something—his shop-window with its drawn blind—that is distasteful to him.

At this point the omniscient narrator imperceptibly takes over for a few lines in order to provide the necessary information about Dodd's background and occupation. The transition from Dodd's consciousness to the narrator's omniscience is effected with James's usual regard for the invisibility of the author. We see a similar transition a few pages later, when the reader has to be given a minimal necessary account of Kate Cookham's background and the previous history of the relations between the two. The authorial interruptions are not blatant here because of the way in which they are fused with the hero's thoughts, as well as because of their brevity. The presence of the omniscient author needs to be pointed out now and then as a corrective to the oversimplifications of the "point of view" analysis of James's technique, according to which his most mature productions are held to be totally devoid of authorial presence and comment. That this is not so can be demonstrated by a close textual examination of any work of James, including *The Ambassadors*. What needs to be emphasized instead is that James exercises an unprecedented economy and restraint in performing his supervisory functions as an omniscient storyteller and almost succeeds in creating the illusion that his narratives are autonomous. More than that is neither possible nor perhaps desirable, and it serves no critical purpose to go on saying that the point of view in this, that, or the other tale is *entirely* the point of view of this, that, or the other character.

The author does not confine himself in this section to presenting the immediate reactions of Dodd after the encounter with his inexorable "adversary." He also succeeds in rendering as full a portrait of Dodd—the aspirant to gentlemanliness and the morbid analyst—as is commensurate with the essential indirection of his method. We see the collapse of Dodd's anger in helpless tears that evening, and then again the revival in him of "the glow of righteous resentment. Who should be assured against coarse usage if a man of his really elegant, perhaps in fact a trifle over-refined or 'effete' appearance, his absolutely gentlemanlike type, couldn't be?" (M, XXVIII, 416). This rhetorical question gives an idea of the subtlety with which James suggests the working of his hero's mind and, at the same time, his own ironic view of his blinding egotism. By the close of the section, we have not been ranged so completely on the side of the hero as to be incapable of suspending our own judgment of Kate Cookham until we have seen more of her. In the absence of some such mental reservation, we would not be able to appreciate her unexpected gesture in the second part of the story. Still, our interest in Herbert Dodd must be predominantly sympathetic, and its firm foundations must be laid in this section; otherwise we would fail to be moved by his suffering through long years of desolation. The success of this section lies in its achievement of both effects with astonishing economy and completeness.

One would normally expect the next stage in the narrative to be a straight account, scenic or otherwise, of the settlement arrived at by Dodd and Kate. Instead of any simple and space-wasting chronological progression, we have in the next section first of all a compressed account of Dodd's intimacy with Nan Drury following his final rupture with Kate. Nan has been already briefly mentioned in the first section: "She [Kate] never wore pretty, dotty, transparent veils, as Nan Drury did" (M, XXVIII, 414). At that time the reader was perhaps intrigued by this strange comparison and could not account for it. Now he realizes that "tender-souled" Nan is "the *kind* of woman, at least, that he liked; even if of everything else that might make life possible he was to be . . . for ever starved" (M, XXVIII, 419). We still do not know the part that she has played in taking Dodd away from Kate. In any case it is to Nan that he turns with, it is suggested, increased ardor. It is with her that he sits on his favorite bench where she begins "to take off and fold up and put away in her pocket her pretty, dotty, becoming veil" (M, XXVIII, 419). This unveiling dates from the day of Dodd's recital to Nan of the "quite appalling upshot of his second and conclusive 'scene of violence' with the mistress of his fortune" (M, XXVIII, 420). It is at this point that the "scene of violence" is captured briefly, after which the focus shifts back once again to Dodd's infatuation with Nan. Nan's first appearance on Dodd's horizon was after he had

struck for freedom by his great first backing-out letter. . . . The date of the letter, taken with its other connexions, and the date of her [Kate's] first give-away for himself, his seeing her get out of the Brighton train with Bill Frankle that day he had gone to make the row at the Station Parcels' office about the miscarriage of the box from Wales—those were the facts it sufficed him to point to, as he had pointed to them for Nan Drury's benefit, goodness knew, often and often enough. (M, XXVIII, 422)

We are beginning to get a glimpse of what has actually happened, but it is just a glimpse. Kate Cookham is implacable because she attributes his breach of promise to his interest in Nan, which—according to Dodd—is false; Dodd backed out presumably because he saw Kate getting out of the Brighton train with Bill Frankle. The tangle is only hinted at, not made quite clear, for in that case it would take away the tension of uncertainty. It will reappear later in the climactic scene between Kate and Dodd. For the present, the casual hint has served its purpose of suggesting the tragic misconception that caused the lovers' quarrel. In the last paragraph of this section we have another foreshadowing, this one concerning Dodd's disillusionment with Nan Drury: "It little mattered, meanwhile, if on their bench of desolation all that summer —and, it may be added, for summers and summers, to say nothing of winters, there and elsewhere, to come—she did give way to her artless habit of not contradicting him enough, which led to her often trailing up and down before him, too complacently, the untimely shreds and patches of his own glooms and desperations" (M, XXVIII,

422-423). This sentence is followed by a series of quoted remarks by Nan, all too smug, though well-meaning, to be anything but infelicitous. Thus in this tightly packed section—just five pages—we have a glimpse of Dodd's brief spell of dubious bliss with Nan, dubious because we notice the first signs of Dodd's recognition that, after all, the refined Nan too is becoming rather tiresome.

We may have looked forward now to an interesting violent scene between Dodd and Nan in the next section, but instead we are shown the process of Dodd's dignified occupation of the bench of desolation through years of general deprivation. This effect is achieved in a very short space without loss of any real value. Hence, James is not elaborately scenic; all details are strictly selective. The impression of Dodd's struggle to scrape together the two hundred and seventy pounds is conveyed through an expressive image instead of an accumulation of naturalistic detail: "These melancholy efforts formed a scramble up an arduous steep where steps were planted and missed, and bared knees were excoriated, and clutches at wayside tufts succeeded and failed, on a system to which poor Nan could have intelligently entered only if she had been somehow less ladylike" (M, XXVIII, 424). We note the reduction of Nan Drury to "poor Nan" in this bleak phase. The failure of Dodd's business is similarly conveyed through another brilliant image, which probably conveys more than any amount of detailed realistic description might have: "He could by this time at any rate measure his ruin—with three fantastic mortgages on his house, his shop, his stock, and a burden of interests to carry under which his business simply stretched itself inanimate, without strength for a protesting kick, without breath for an appealing groan" (M, XXVIII, 425). Nan's infelicities, and his attitude to them, are captured in yet another luminous image:

Everything came to seem equally part of this [his preparation for catastrophe]—in complete defiance of proportion; even his final command of detachment, on the bench of desolation (where each successive fact of his dire case regularly cut itself out black, yet of senseless silhouette, against the red west), in respect to poor Nan's flat infelicities, which for the most part kept no pace with the years or with change, but only shook like hard peas in a child's rattle, the same peas always, of course, so long as the rattle didn't split open with usage or from somebody's act of irritation. They represented, or they had long done so, her contribution to the more superficial of the two branches of intimacy—the intellectual alternative, the one that didn't merely consist in her preparing herself for his putting his arms round her waist. (M, XXVIII, 425-426)

The slow-motion depiction of the act of embrace, in the last clause above, shows how the thrill of companionship with Nan has completely disappeared. One feels, in the presence of the image of the child's rattle, the irritation created by Nan. However, her infelicities are also sampled through a concrete illustration: her persistent murmur that he should have taken legal advice in order to ascertain the validity of Kate's threat. He learns to ignore it while she is alive but after her death

it woke again as an echo of far-off things—far-off, very far-off, because he felt then not ten but twenty years older. . . . With all that had come and gone the bench of desolation was still there, just as the immortal flash of the westward sky kept hanging its indestructible curtain. . . . He might in these sessions, with his eyes on the grey-green sea, have been counting again and still recounting the beads, almost all worn smooth, of his rosary of pain—which had for the fingers of memory and the recurrence of wonder the same felt break of the smaller ones by the larger that would have aided a pious mumble in some dusky altar-chapel. (M, XXVIII, 427)

The bench of desolation thus becomes an open-air chapel of grief where he learns, as we are told in the next section, "the secret of the dignity of sitting still with one's fate" (M, XXVIII, 432). A succession of beautiful images unrelieved by fact would have had a cloying effect. So some actuality is reflected in the mirror of his brooding memory—his "recaptured sense . . . of the dismal unavailing awareness that had attended his act of marriage" (M, XXVIII, 428), his recollection of the "but two direct echoes of [Kate] in all the bitter years," his marriage with "poor Nan [who] had come to affect him as scarce other than red-nosed and dowdy by that time, but this only added, in his then, and indeed in his lasting view, to his general and his particular morbid bravery" (M, XXVIII, 428-429). Toward the close of the section, the persistent echo of poor Nan is repeated, to suggest the sharp point of all his wasted life: "Voices from far off would quaver to him therefore in the stillness; where he knew for the most recurrent, little by little, the faint wail of his wife. He had become deaf to it in life, but at present, after so great an interval, he listened again, listened and listened, and seemed to hear it sound as by the pressure of some weak broken spring. . . . Nothing remained to him in the world, on the bench of desolation, but the option of taking that echo—together with an abundance of free time for doing so" (M, XXVIII, 430-431).

I have mentioned only some of the images by which James achieves a poetical compression to express the duration and intensity of Herbert Dodd's suffering. These images are not ornaments of style but vehicles of emotion and feeling. They are, to echo a title of the late Ananda K. Coomaraswamy, figures of thought rather than figures of speech.[20] This section especially abounds in images because it is here that they are most needed to give a concentrated picture of the ten miserable years of Dodd's life, to lift the tale to the intensity of a poem of suffering and to give it the ring of universality. There are, of course, a few images in the first two sections as well. We have one, for instance, in the opening paragraph of the tale: "The ugly, the awful words, ruthlessly formed by her lips, were like the fingers of a hand that she might have thrust into her pocket for extraction of the monstrous object that would serve best for—what should he call it?—a gage of battle" (M, XXVIII, 409). But this image has just that hint of exaggeration necessary to give a slightly comic slant to Herbert Dodd's reactions. The same seems to be true of another much more elaborate image, in which the pulled blind of Herbert's shop-window is compared by him to Kate's "ominous visage" with "Herbert Dodd" on her lips (M, XXVIII, 412-414). The comic touch in these and other images is intentional, for there is an element of the ridiculous in the hero's recoil from vulgarity. But in the third section his suffering is too deep for either tears or laughter, and the function of the imagery appropriately becomes different: it serves to help us in identifying ourselves with him without reservation. The nature of the imagery undergoes a corresponding change.

Structurally, the first three sections form the first part of the tale, where the method of representation on the whole is not scenic. The expanse of time covered is great, particularly in the third section; equally great is the range of Dodd's spiritual development from a querulous young victim of self-pity to a serene old man of experience. Consequently the narrative is close-knit and heavily compressed in this part. The last three sections of the tale are more dramatic, each section embodying one scene and the temporal gap between one scene and the other being very brief. There is therefore quicker movement in the narrative. Another distinguishing feature of this part is that it seems to be dominated by Kate Cookham, just as the first part is dominated by Herbert Dodd. The focus, of course,

remains on Dodd in the sense that, apart from the dramatic dialogue that gives us a direct view of both of them,
the author allows us to see Kate only through Dodd's eyes;
but those eyes see differently now.

Kate's reappearance in section four is a momentous
event, and James renders it with measured emphasis.
Instead of bringing the two abruptly face to face, he lets
us see the process of Dodd's gradual recognition of his
old friend and foe. This heightens the drama of their
reunion. Before the recognition dawns, we are given a
view of Kate as she now strikes Dodd:

Yes, she stood there with the ample width of the Marina
between them, but turned to him, for all the world, as to
show frankly that she was concerned with him. And she
was—oh, yes—a real lady: a middle-aged person, of good
appearance and of the best condition, in quiet but "handsome"
black, save for very fresh white kid gloves, and with a pretty,
dotty, becoming veil, predominantly white, adjusted to her
countenance; which through it somehow, even to his imperfect
sight, showed strong fine black brows and what he would
have called on the spot character. . . . So this mature,
qualified, important person stood and looked at the limp,
undistinguished—oh, his values of aspect now!—shabby man
on the bench. (M, XXVIII, 434-435)

Reading the tale for the first time, we do not easily
imagine that this person with the significant "pretty,
dotty, becoming veil" will turn out to be Kate Cookham.
The suggestion is not only that a great change has taken
place in Kate but also that there is some change in the eye
of the beholder. The preliminary part of their reunion
takes place in appropriate silence: "She moved toward
him, she reached him, she stood there, she sat down near
him, he merely passive and wonderstruck, unresentfully
'impressed,' gaping and taking it in—and all as with an
open allowance on the part of each, so that they positively

and quite intimately met in it, of the impertinence for their case, this case that brought them again, after horrible years, face to face, of the vanity, the profanity, the impossibility, of anything between them but silence" (M, XXVIII, 435). It is a long, involuted sentence of the type that has earned James the reputation of a "difficult" writer. But once the drift is grasped, can one imagine how else James could have conveyed all that he tried to? As Pound has said, "He is seldom or never involved when a direct bald statement will accurately convey his own meaning, *all of it*."[21] Of the various explanations and justifications that have been given for James's "third" style, this seems to me the most satisfying and just.

The silence between them enables the author to elaborate Dodd's view of the greatly changed Kate and her effect upon him: "It wasn't thus execration that she revived in him; she made in fact, exhibitively, as he could only have put it, the matter of long ago irrelevant, and these extraordinary minutes of their reconstituted relation—how many? how few?—addressed themselves altogether to new possibilities" (M, XXVIII, 436). Dodd is considerably alarmed by the realization that she was still "in possession of him," that whereas "he had come there to flop, by long custom, upon the bench of desolation *as* the man in the whole place, precisely, to whom nothing worth more than tuppence could happen[22] . . . in the grey desert of his consciousness, the very earth had suddenly opened and flamed" (M, XXVIII, 437). This delay before speaking is of course natural in terms of verisimilitude; only in a third-rate film will two similarly situated persons make a dash into each other's arms or plunge into conversation, or perhaps do both. But it is also necessary to establish Dodd's strategy for meeting the new situation. Even when the conversation does break out, all of it is not reported directly: they are "yet keeping off and off, dealing with such surface facts as involved ancient acquaintance but kept abominations at bay" (M, XXVIII, 439). The author has correctly judged it more important to lay the basis for the next scene by concentrating here on the perturbation in Dodd's mind over an unexpected promise of new possibilities. Dodd is shown as trying his hardest to remain indifferent to his mystifying visitor and indeed to mystify her in return, even though the reader has already begun to guess that he will go on the next day to Kate's hotel for tea. The most remarkable thing about this scene, then, is its restraint; without this it could have burst into recriminations and sentimentality, thus disrupting the tone of the tale.

The next section opens with these revealing words: "Nothing in the world, on the Sunday afternoon, could have prevented him from going; he was not after all destitute of three or four such articles of clothing as, if they wouldn't particularly grace the occasion, wouldn't positively dishonour it. That deficiency might have kept him away, but no voice of the spirit, no consideration of pride" (M, XXVIII, 445). We are amused at the way Dodd rationalizes all objections away, and "whistled odd snatches to himself as he hung about on that cloud-dappled autumn Sunday, a mild private minstrelsy that his lips hadn't known since when?" (M, XXVIII, 445). We notice also a cheerful springiness in the narrative, corresponding to Dodd's mood. The scene, after Captain Roper has been summarily dismissed by Kate, much to Dodd's delighted enlightenment, proceeds rapidly to the essential point. Herbert Dodd stiffens at the thought that he has unwittingly betrayed a relaxation of rigor and utters his much-rehearsed speech about his desire to "know exactly where I am and to what you suppose I so commit myself"

(M, XXVIII, 448). Even as he utters it he is conscious that "perhaps he didn't give it, in her presence—this was impossible, her presence altered so many things—quite the full sound or weight he had planned" (M, XXVIII, 448). From this point on they are face to face over the abyss that has separated them; we see Dodd accepting the collapse of his indifference; we hear Kate explain her at first unacceptable "idea"; we watch Dodd's mystification and his recriminating allusions to the suffering she has caused him until "he caught from her dark eye a silver gleam of impatience. 'You've suffered and you've worked—which, God knows, is what I've done! *Of course* you've suffered,' she said—'you inevitably had to! We have to,' she went on, 'to do or to be or to get anything'" (M, XXVIII, 451).

This solemn declaration of the inevitability of suffering marks an important stage in their long-deferred hope for mutual understanding. After this he can refer to Bill Frankle and she to Nan Drury without letting the interest of the reader sag at the hint that they have both suffered only because of a tragic misconception. Moreover, the author is careful not to have Herbert Dodd promptly renounce all his stored-up rancor; as a matter of fact, the essential point of the story is to emphasize how long it takes Dodd to understand and accept not only Kate's love for him but his own love for her. He does finally understand "how she had loved him" (M, XXVIII, 456), but his next step is clouded by thoughts of "his little dead dissatisfied wife; across all whose final woe and whose lovely grave he was to reach out, it appeared, to take gifts. He saw them too, the gifts; saw them—she bristled with them—in his actual companion's brave and sincere and authoritative figure, her strangest of demonstrations. But the other appearance was intenser, as if their ghost had waved wild arms; so that half a minute hadn't passed before the one

poor thing that remained of Nan, and that yet thus became
a quite mighty and momentous poor thing, was sitting on
his lips as for its sole opportunity" (M, XXVIII, 457). The
tears that follow the "immense clearance between them"
(M, XXVIII, 458), after the ghost of poor Nan's lifelong
doubt has been laid, to no abatement of Dodd's misery, are
a sincere tribute to the unloved innocent Nan. The scene
can go no further without a false note, and so they part in
silence.

The next section opens with the promise of another
scene: "Off there on the bench of desolation a week later
she made a more particular statement, which it had taken
the remarkably tense interval to render possible" (M,
XXVIII, 459). Our curiosity is kept in abeyance while the
author reveals Dodd's thoughts during the "remarkably
tense interval," concentrating on his reflections immediately after leaving Kate's hotel. We are told he had gone to
the bench of desolation where "he began to look his extraordinary fortune a bit straighter in the face and see it
confess itself at once a fairy-tale and a nightmare" (M,
XXVIII, 459). He confirms his resolve not to return to
Kate, by nursing his memories of his dead wife and daughters until the week is over; on the following Sunday, instead of going to the church, he proceeds to his bench of
desolation, thinking of Kate, caught "between hope and
fear" of meeting her there. Here again, as in the scene of
their meeting in the fourth section, the author slows down
his narrative deliberately to let us see the confusion of
various impulses in Dodd's mind as he sees Kate from a
distance on his bench. It strikes him that "if he hadn't
been quite sure of her recurrence she had at least been
quite sure of his." He has "a sublime, an ideal flight, which
lasted about a minute," about turning his back on her (M,
XXVIII, 464); he watches her watch him and gathers that

she is "leaving him, not for dignity but . . . for kindness, free to choose"; he stands "rooted, neither retreating nor advancing, but presently correcting his own share of their bleak exchange by looking off at the sea. Deeply conscious of the awkwardness this posture gave him, he yet clung to it as the last shred of his honour" (M, XVIII, 465). Finally she comes to him and says: "There are twelve hundred and sixty pounds, to be definite, but I have it all down for you—and you've only to draw" (M, XXVIII, 466). This is the "more particular statement" referred to in the opening sentence of the section; but before coming to it the author has shown us the whole process of Dodd's step-by-step surrender. Without this the spectacle of his final response to Kate would not be moving enough.

The preliminary part of their conversation is again summarized in order to direct attention not to what is said but to what goes on in Dodd's mind. The climax of his thoughts is reached with his realization that "she had now created between them an equality of experience. He wasn't to have done all the suffering, *she* was to have 'been through' things he couldn't even guess at; and, since he was bargaining away his right ever again to allude to the unforgettable, so much there was of it, what her tacit proposition came to was that they were 'square' and might start afresh" (M, XXVIII, 467-468). There is still a vestige of resentment in him. His "pride," though compromised, prompts him to tell her that it was after all she who had come to him, to which her reply is a remarkable declaration of love: " 'Come to you, Herbert Dodd?' she imperturbably echoed. 'I've been coming to you for the last ten years!' " (M, XXVIII, 468). Just before this, we are now told, Dodd has been thinking of thrusting the sealed envelope back at her, thus refusing to accept her tacit offer of a fresh start; but a hush falls upon him that is broken only by her farewell. By now, however, Dodd is not sure that he wants her to go away like this, and the reader has his own uncertainty about what Dodd wants. It is what is called a "crucial" moment. The author knows the dramatic value of suspense at this juncture and knows also how to maintain it—he diverts our gaze away from Dodd's thoughts to what he says and to the conversation that follows. We notice, however, that all the questions now come from Dodd, until we come to the final stage of their strange and superbly managed conversation:

Thus confronted they stayed; and then, as he saw with a contentment that came up from deeper still, it was indeed she who, with her worn fine face, would conclude. "But I can take care of you."

"You *have!*" he said as with nothing left of him but a beautiful appreciative candour.

"Oh, but you'll want it now in a way—!" she responsibly answered.

He waited a moment, dropping again on the seat. So, while she still stood, he looked up at her; with the sense somehow that there were too many things and that they were all together, terribly, irresistibly, doubtless blessedly, in her eyes and her whole person; which thus affected him for the moment as more than he could bear. He leaned forward, dropping his elbows to his knees and pressing his head on his hands. So he stayed, saying nothing; only, with the sense of her own sustained, renewed and wonderful action, knowing that an arm had passed round him and that he was held. She was beside him on the bench of desolation. (M, XXVIII, 473-474)

"Suspense" is much too weak a term to convey the order of artistic calculation by which James involves us in this remarkably harmonious conjunction of nightmare and fairy tale. It is a story with a "happy ending"—another unprofitable cliché[23]—but the effect is not one of life lived "happily ever after." The hero and heroine are left not listening to wedding bells but together on the bench of desolation, possessed "of the secret of the dignity of sitting still with one's fate," where, in Blackmur's words, the "triumph consists . . . in the gradual inward mastery of the outward experience, a poetic mastery which makes of the experience conviction."[24]

CHAPTER VII

Anecdotes

(ALSO PARABLES)

TO READ almost any anecdote of James immediately after one of his great nouvelles, such as "The Bench of Desolation," is to become intensely aware of the fact that he was not a born short-story writer, in the same way that he was a born novelist or a born *nouvelliste*. Economy, as distinguished from brevity, was the soul of his technical concern as a fabulist; and the short story necessarily puts a premium on brevity. Thus, if we find him cramped for want of space in his first-person anecdotes, the problem is even greater in his omniscient-narrator anecdotes. Several of the latter are "novels intensely compressed" and they "but masquerade as little anecdotes."[1] Of the short tales that manage to be genuine anecdotes, there are only a few that are qualitatively comparable to the best of his nouvelles, even when we keep our minds clear about the individual peculiarities of these two categories of short fiction. I propose to analyze in this chapter three such anecdotes: "Fordham Castle" (1904), "The Great Good Place" (1900), and "The Middle Years" (1893). These tales share with one another an element of fantasy, and the last two have a markedly parabolic center of intention.

Fordham Castle

I started the previous chapter by observing that *"emphasised* internationalism" began to loosen its hold on James after about 1888.[2] In two very short tales, however, he reverts to the international subject. In "Miss Gunton of Poughkeepsie" (1900), James's shortest tale except for "A Problem" (1868), we see once again the triumphant innocence of the American girl abroad. Miss Lily Gunton, a less famous sister of Daisy Miller, baffles her smug Roman suitor, the Prince, who is evidently in love only with her "extraordinary number of dollars" (XVI, 391); and she is no less an enigma to her elderly English confidante, Lady Champer, whose remark "With Americans one's lost!" (XVI, 392) closes this amusing story. Miss Gunton's own interest in the Prince is more that of a typical Jamesian "Europophile" than that of a lover. Her case is presented with charm and dexterity, the omniscient author making his own mildly ironical view of the situation quite clear in the process. This is one of the few tales in which James successfully approximates Maupassant's technique, allowing the objective action of the tale to reveal all its characters and values, without trying to probe much into the inner consciousness of any of the three characters. Consequently, the style of "Miss Gunton of Poughkeepsie" is as simple and uninvolved as any disapprover of the characteristic later manner of James would like it to be.

"Fordham Castle" is more complex in both subject and treatment. In it James was conscious of having been "reduced to finger once more, not a little ruefully, a chord perhaps now at last too warped and rusty for complicated music at short order."[3] The chord was the international theme, and James's ruefulness stemmed from the fact that he had "waited with something of a subtle patience . . . [for] just enough of a wandering air from the down-town penetralia as might embolden, as might inform, as might . . . even conceivably inspire . . . ; all to the advantage of my extension of view and my variation of theme."[4] Thus in "Fordham Castle" he found it difficult, despite all his ingenuity of effort, "to create for my scrap of an up-town subject . . . a certain larger connexion."[5] However, "as to my pressing the clear liquor of amusement and refreshment from the golden apple of composition, *that* blest freedom, with its infinite power of renewal, was still my resource, and I felt myself invoke it not in vain."[6] But did James really fail to achieve any larger connection? I think it may be said that he did, after all, succeed in a direction other than the one leading to "down-town penetralia."

The most obvious thing about "Fordham Castle" is the symmetry of its plot. Abel Taker has been exiled under a false name, C. P. Addard, by his wife Sue, who considers him a drag on her social ambitions. Mrs. Magaw has been similarly disposed of under a false name, Mrs. Vanderplank, by her daughter Mattie, who considers her an obstacle in the way of her campaign for a "high" marriage. Both the pairs are American. The husband and the mother are drawn together in a Swiss pension by an intuitive recognition of each other's plight; later they confide their real identities and develop even a greater mutual affection. The wife and the daughter come together at Fordham Castle—it is significant that their hunting ground is the same—and recognize each other as kindred spirits. The wife is ashamed of her past: she "only wanted a fair start" and could not get it "so long as he was always there, so terribly cruelly there, to speak of what she *had* been," although in her husband's view "she had been nothing worse . . . than a very pretty girl of eighteen out in Peoria, who had seen at that time no one else she wanted more to marry, nor even any one who had been so supremely struck by her" (XVI, 403). The daughter too is ashamed of her past, her parentage: she "found her two names, so dreadful even singly, a combination not to be borne, and carried on a quarrel with them no less desperate than Sue's quarrel with—well, with everything" (XVI, 411). There are other minor parallels. Both Abel Taker and Mrs. Magaw receive a letter by the same post from their respective relatives. Even their lies, before they have revealed their true identities, are similar: he has just been to Constantinople to visit Mrs. Addard's grave; she has made a similar pilgrimage to her daughter's grave in Rome. If these amusing symmetrical touches seem to strain our sense of verisimilitude, one can only suggest that we should not look for such literalness in James, particularly not in his fantasies.

An even greater source of amusement, however, is the dissimilarity between the situations and sensibilities of the two principal characters. Abel Taker may have failed in the "conduct of the coal, the commission, the insurance and, as a last resort, desperate and disgraceful, the book-agency business" (XVI, 409), but, as C. P. Addard at least, he feels and talks like a supreme ironist; with regard to Sue, in particular, his irony has the sting of an adder. Mrs. Magaw, on the other hand, is not "formed for duplicity, the large simple scared foolish fond woman, the vague anxiety in whose otherwise so uninhabited and unreclaimed countenance, as void of all history as an expanse of Western prairie seen from a car-window, testified to her scant aptitude for her part" (XVI, 408). This vast continental image, characteristic of James as it is, gives us the measure of contrast between the simple-minded Mrs. Magaw and the ironical Abel Taker. Their conversations derive many of their comic tones from her inability to cope with his devastating sarcasm. Thus while talking of the fictitious graves of Sue and Mattie, she innocently refers to Constantinople and Rome as "places that mightn't have so *very* much" but for the "fact" that their relatives are buried there. Abel Taker, naturally surprised at her ridiculous observation, notices "the cautious anxious sound of her 'very'" (XVI, 405). The tale is full of similar juxtapositions of conscious irony on the part of Abel Taker and unconscious humor provided by Mrs. Magaw's failure to understand him:

"By Gosh then, she [Mattie] has struck Sue!"

"'Struck' Mrs. Taker—?"

"She isn't Mrs. Taker now—she's Mrs. Sherrington Reeve." It had come to him with all its force—as if the glare of her genius were, at a bound, high over the summits. "Mrs. Taker's dead: I thought, you know, all the while, she must be, and this makes me sure. She died at Fordham Castle. So we're both dead."

His friend, however, with her large blank face lagged behind. "At Fordham Castle too—died there?"

. . . . .

Mrs. Magaw's understanding was still in the shade. . . . "But how has she become Mrs. Sherrington Reeve?"

"By my death. And also after that of her own. . . . She simply became, the day I became C. P. Addard, something as different as possible from the thing she had always hated to be. . . . Her baser part, her vulgar part, has ceased to be, and she lives only as an angel."

It affected his friend, this elucidation, almost with awe; she took it at least, as she took everything, stolidly. "Do you call Mrs. Taker an angel?" (XVI, 422-423)

The dissimilarity between their situations is equally important and adds to the amusement provided by the tale. Mrs. Magaw is naturally interested in her daughter's future: "It was clear that Mattie's mother couldn't be expected not to want to see her married" (XVI, 420). She accepts her exile; she strikes Abel Taker as "sacrificed— without blood, as it were; as obligingly and persuadedly passive" (XVI, 399). She is therefore quite happy at the thought of rejoining Mattie, whose engagement to Lord Dunderton opens up the exciting possibility of going to Fordham Castle (XVI, 425). Like Greville Fane she is perhaps inwardly proud of her daughter's prospective enlistment in the aristocracy. Abel Taker, on the other hand, can take no such satisfaction in the social triumphs of his wife at Fordham Castle. He cannot get excited over the thought of going there—"he'd be hanged if he wasn't willing, on his side, to take Sue's elevation quite on trust" (XVI, 417-418). Unlike Mrs. Magaw, he is permanently "dead."

In the context of these differences, his incipient love for Mrs. Magaw—"his senior by several years" (XVI, 409) —takes on a pathetic overtone, even as it indicates the intensity of his loneliness. He is ready to "give Mrs. Taker up, definitely, just to remain C. P. Addard" with her (XVI, 419). Mrs. Magaw, of course, sanctimoniously evades his overtures, but he desperately clings to his one connection with the "living":

"Then you'll come back to me? If you only will, you know, Sue will be delighted to fix it."

"To fix it—how?"

"Well, she'll tell you how. You've seen how she can fix things, and that will be the way, as I say, you'll help her."

She stared at him from her corner, and he could see she was sorry for him; but it was as if she had taken refuge behind her large high-shouldered reticule, which she held in her lap, presenting it almost as a bulwark. "Mr. Taker," she launched at him over it, "I'm afraid of you."

"Because I'm dead?"

"Oh sir!" she pleaded, hugging her morocco defence. (XVI, 425)

It must be pointed out, however, that this element of love is not introduced to give a "romantic" tinge to the story, which is romantic enough without it. It is congruous with the comic-fantastic mode of the story and serves to heighten the impression of Taker's curious reduction to life-in-death. With the departure of Mrs. Magaw he feels "left, in his solitude, to the sense of his extinction. He faced it completely now, and to himself at least could express it without fear of protest. 'Why certainly I'm dead'" (XVI, 426).

Needless to say, Abel Taker's insistence on his being dead is not meant to be a sign of his morbidity. This is his sardonic defense against the anonymity imposed on him by the hard, ominously named Sue; it is his desperate protest against a loss of identity. It is perhaps a weak man's defense, but then on the face of it Abel Taker is a weak man. His wife, by the same token, is "strong" but completely hollow. It is interesting to note that her character is established *in absentia*, just as Mrs. Newsome's is in *The Ambassadors*. We see Mrs. Taker quite as distinctly as we do Mrs. Newsome, though the one is perched on the heights of Fordham Castle, Wilts, and the other enveloped in the vagueness of Woollett, Mass. Sue takes her place along with James's "eternity of mere international young ladies" in spite of the fact that she is not in "the foreground of the general scene."[7] And yet "Fordham Castle" is an international tale with a difference. In James's own words, its few pages are packed with an "exceedingly close complexus of intentions."[8] Some of these intentions bothered him again and again, and in the *Notebooks* we can trace the interesting record of his continual preoccupation with them.[9] The story did not succeed, for him, in embodying these ideas clearly enough. But on close scrutiny we find that, in the first place, it renders the effect on a sensitive character of a loss of identity. It is also a parable of the

American Eve in search of a European Eden and of the American Adam consequently relegated to oblivion. Finally, it touches very significantly on the "phenomenon of the social suppression" of American parents by their children.[10] In these respects, this parable has as much relevance today as it had at the turn of the century, considering the current complaints about the domination of the American male by the female and of the American parent by the child.

In describing the narrative principle of "Fordham Castle" it would be an oversimplification to say that the "point of view" is entirely Abel Taker's. For one thing, in no tale, whether of James or of Joyce, can the point of view ever entirely belong to any character. The author as narrator is always present, the manner of his presence or the mode of his intervention differing from writer to writer and from tale to tale. A story never gets told of itself; it has to be told by someone. For another thing, this formula often is a convenient but misleading substitute for the more rewarding task of close analysis. We can appreciate the narrative complexity of "Fordham Castle" better when we recognize the subtlety with which the omniscient narrator effects his numerous transitions

It [his identity] was denied there in his wife's large straight hand; his eyes, attached to the envelope, took in the failure of any symptom of weakness in her stroke; she at least had the courage of his passing for somebody he wasn't; of his passing rather for nobody at all, and he felt the force of her character more irresistibly than ever as he thus submitted to what she was doing with him. He wasn't used to lying; whatever his faults—and he was used, perfectly, to the idea of his faults— he hadn't made them worse by any perverse theory, any tortuous plea, of innocence; so that probably, with every inch of him giving him away, Madame Massin didn't believe him a bit when he appropriated the letter. He was quite aware he could have made no fight if she had challenged his right to it. That would have come of his making no fight, nowadays, on any ground with any woman; he had so lost the proper spirit, the necessary confidence. It was true that he had had to do for a long time with no woman in the world but Sue, and of the practice of opposition so far as Sue was concerned the end had been determined early in his career. (XVI, 396-397)

In this passage it is clear that the omniscient narrator is recording the thoughts of Abel Taker as he looks at his wife's letter. But is must also be conceded that there is a well-designed principle of selection at work, that it is not an interior monologue—not that an interior monologue is altogether free of any selective principle. Up to "He wasn't used to," the omniscient narrator's voice is not there. After that we can hear his voice until we come to "He was quite aware." Then the omniscient narrator adds his voice again at "It was true." A similar examination of the rest of the tale would indicate that simply to say that the point of view is entirely that of Abel Taker is to say little beyond the fact that Abel Taker is the most important character in the tale. It is true that the focus generally is on his thoughts more than on Mrs. Magaw's, but occasionally we see it moved to a point at which we have a simultaneous view of both of them: "Their instinct was unmistakably to cling to each other, but it was as if they wouldn't know where to take hold till the air had really been cleared" (XVI, 410). Again, while the authorial comment or generalization is kept to a minimum, it is never completely suppressed: "Deep emotion sometimes confounds the mind—and Mrs. Magaw quite flamed with excitement. But on the other hand it sometimes illumines, and she could see, it appeared, what Sue meant" (XVI, 424). This observation does not proceed from Abel Taker, or from within his consciousness, but from the author himself.

It is surprising that "Fordham Castle" should have been neglected so thoroughly by critics, one exception being Ezra Pound, who calls it a "comedietta, excellently, perhaps flawlessly done. Here, as so often, the circumstances are mostly a description of the character, of the personal tone of the 'sitters'; for his people are so much more, or so much more often, 'sitters' than actors. . . . Compare Maupassant's *Toine* for treatment of case similar to *Fordham Castle*."[11] We may also compare it to Hawthorne's "Wakefield," where the husband voluntarily, but whimsically, absents himself from his wife for twenty years, during which time he lives on the next street, unknown and unrecognized. The emphasis of Hawthorne's tale is of course on a different issue: acting upon an eccentric impulse Wakefield becomes "the Outcast of the Universe."

The Great Good Place

"The Great Good Place" is a late Jamesian version of "Benvolio," its hero an elderly, more integrated Benvolio. In "Benvolio" the omniscient narrator, true to the early Jamesian manner, is perceptibly and audibly present throughout the narrative. The conflict of the hero is illustrated through a series of descriptive scenes, and the intensity of the conflict is not rendered independently of the narrator's supporting comments and elucidations, which add up to a running gloss on the vacillations of the hero. The conflict, essentially internal, is externalized through an allegorical structure of easily interpretable events. The supernormal does not enter into the picture, except through allusive names of characters and places. In "The Great Good Place" the omniscient narrator, true to the later Jamesian manner, is imperceptibly and almost inaudibly present. The conflict of the hero is dramatized more fully, so that the narrator's commentary is all but gone. The drama takes place in the inner consciousness of the protagonist, and it is appropriately embodied in a dream vision that, spatially as well as otherwise, takes up most of the tale. The allegorical element is refined into fantasy, and a dreamlike atmosphere pervades the whole tale. Dimensionally, "The Great Good Place" conforms to the anecdotic type in spite of its division into sections, which give it the illusory shape of a nouvelle. It has the compactness and the pointedness of a short story.

The quality that distinguishes this tale among all the Jamesian tales of artists is its larger meaning. It may be called a spiritual fantasy, with a meaning that transcends the problems peculiar to the artist. Like other fantasies, such as "The Altar of the Dead," "The Beast in the Jungle," *The Sacred Fount*, and "The Jolly Corner," it invites all sorts of conjectures about the inner life of James. Beguiling as these matters doubtless are, I shall restrict the discussion to its more purely literary aspects.

George Dane, an elderly writer weary not so much with his work as with the distracting consequences of success, wakes up after a late night of work. He finds himself surrounded by "the bristling hedge of letters," by "newspapers too many . . . each with its hand on the neck of the other," by the "huddled mound" of unopened journals and periodicals, by "books from publishers, books from authors, books from friends, books from enemies, books from his own book-seller," and by the reminders of "his systematic servant," Brown, who presently comes in with the "absurd solemnity of two telegrams on a tray" (XVI, 225-227). All this strikes the hero as "the old rising tide [which] had been up to his shoulders last night [and] was up to his chin now" (XVI, 226). The tale opens with this mock-heroic exaggeration of Dane's helplessness, his baffled consciousness of the contrast between his own reluctance to "touch" anything and "the great staring egotism of [the world's] health and strength [which] wasn't to be trusted for tact or delicacy" (XVI, 227). It is followed by an amusing scene, in which the external pressures are further concretized through Dane's exaggerated revulsions at Brown's various reminders. Dane talks of "a happy land—far far away" from the world that has grown too much with him (XVI, 230). This foreshadows the "scene of his new consciousness" (XVI, 234), into which he soon drifts at the "touch" of his young admirer's hand. It also indicates his awareness of the existence of that great good place and of the possibility of escape from all that is oppressive. The reader is made sharply aware of the parabolic nature of Dane's dream.

In the next section the dream is not explicitly announced as having had begun. Instead, the reader approaching the tale for the first time is agreeably mystified, since he does not understand the whereabouts of this scene of Dane's new consciousness. Even on subsequent readings, with the clue at the end, the reader is not completely unmystified, which suggests the powerful magic of this midsummer day's dream. The "place" is rendered progressively through the various stages of Dane's acclimatization to it. His perception of it is at first "pleased but . . . slightly confused"; the "general charm" of his surroundings strikes him as "such an abyss of negatives, such an absence of positives and of everything." He finds himself in "the broad deep bath of stillness," with water up to his chin, thinking vaguely of that other flood "of rushing waters in which bumping and gasping were all" (XVI, 234, 235). The flood image, which had appeared in his waking consciousness in the first section, is repeated here and later in the story and given the compulsiveness and comprehensiveness of a poetic symbol. The "great glare of recommencement" which he had then found in nature (XVI, 225) is contrasted now with the "long afternoon creeping to its end" and with the absence of any change "in the element itself" (XVI, 235). The "labyrinth" of his room is contrasted with the "great cloister, enclosed externally on three sides and probably the largest fairest effect, to his charmed sense, the human hands could ever have expressed in dimensions of length and breadth" (XVI, 235). And in this restful atmosphere he sits on the bench of consolation with the Brother who "turned to him a look different from the looks of friends in London clubs" (XVI, 237).

In this first stage of his habitation in the great good place, Dane is "still immensely aware" (XVI, 235), comparing and contrasting the "place" with the places of the workaday world. In the course of the conversation that ensues, Dane first wants to know where it is and then what it is. The answers of the Brother point to the "reality" symbolized by the wonderful place:

"I shouldn't be surprised if it were much nearer than one ever supposed."
"Nearer 'town,' do you mean?"
"Nearer everything—nearer every one." (XVI, 238)

To Dane's question "*What* is it?" the Brother replies: "'Oh it's positively a part of our ease and our rest and our change, I think, that we don't at all know and that we may really call it, for that matter, anything in the world we like—the thing for instance we love it most for being" (XVI, 238). The reader can, of course, infer whatever he likes, from the description and effect of the place, about its location and nature. To Dane it appears in various images that punctuate his conversation with the

Brother, but one underlying hint seems to be that the place represents no less than the still center of one's own being, access to which is generally obstructed by innumerable irrelevancies: The Great Good Place is within you. The whole dream in this case becomes a verbalized representation of that trancelike state, the *samadhi* of Indian tradition, in which man is face to face with his Self and which opens his eyes to the heart of things. James presents this in secular terms, in an effort perhaps to prevent this dreamland from seeming too utopian, but the mystical meaning also seems inherent in the total picture.

This meaning is missed by readers who, like Matthiessen, make the mistake of regarding it as "a fantasy of escape."[12] If it is an escape at all, it is one into the inner reality, a "place" which rejuvenates Dane, puts him in possession of his lost peace, and restores "the vision and the faculty divine" (XVI, 248). The whole of the fourth section is devoted to a depiction of Dane's sense of the awakening of his inner life, of his having recovered something: "He had not had detachment, but there was detachment here—the sense of a great silver bowl from which he could ladle up the melted hours" (XVI, 253). According to Matthiessen again, "such a fantasy sprang from his uprooted religious sense which had been deprived in childhood of any normal development."[13] It may or may not be so, but on the evidence of this tale it is possible to say that James here succeeds in rehabilitating that religious sense, unless of course we confuse it with any particular theological dogma.

The last section opens with Dane looking at rain, "one of the summer sprinkles that bring out sweet smells" (XVI, 256). The rain, which had inspired him before with a fantastic hope that it "might clear the ground by floating out to a boundless sea the innumerable objects among which his feet stumbled and strayed" (XVI, 227), now gives him pause, for it reminds him "of all that friction of which the question of weather mostly forms a part" (XVI, 256). The pause is brief, and soon we find Dane once again absorbed in puzzling out, with the Brother, what the place is. Here the Brother makes another of his pronouncements: "The thing is so perfect that it's open to as many interpretations as any other great work—a poem of Goethe, a dialogue of Plato, a symphony of Beethoven" (XVI, 257). Their conjectures multiply—it is "liberty-hall," "a convalescent home," "a sort of kindergarten," and so on. This constant effort to arrive at the identity of the place is clearly meant to suggest the validity of "many interpretations" and not to impose on the reader any single referent of the symbol.

Another thing that preoccupies Dane both here and in the previous section is the fact that the occupants of the place have to pay even as those of the other, the worldly, places. This detail is not really meant to provide any realistic bridge linking the two worlds, once we realize that "payment" like all other elements in the tale is symbolic: it represents the effort necessary to attain the blissful consciousness symbolized by the place. The rain I spoke of above does indirectly remind Dane of "the increasing rage of life," which produces in him and the Brother a passing "faint small fear" that they may not find their way back to the sanctuary after their "return to the front" (XVI, 259). The fear passes, however, and their confidence returns, for Dane has already "got it," and to the Brother "it is coming" (XVI, 260). Consequently, Dane's relapse into his ordinary consciousness is not accompanied by that pang with which Keats returns from his sojourn with the nightingale. As Dane "rose and looked about his room, [it] seemed disencumbered, different, twice as large. It *was* all right" (XVI, 263). His visit to the great good place has given him sufficient calm and detachment, sufficient, one may hope, until another trip becomes necessary.

The Middle Years

James opens his preface to Volume XVI of the New York Edition with a few remarks about "The Middle Years," expressing his sense of satisfaction and pride at the success of his "struggle to keep compression rich, if not, better still, to keep accretions compressed." It leads him unwittingly to miscalculate the length of the tale, which is a couple of thousand words more than the 5550 he counts for the benefit of "the curious."[14] He goes on to mention the "fond formula" by which he was able to achieve this concise anecdote, in spite of the developmental proclivities of the subject—by following "it as much as possible from the outer edge in, rather than from its centre outward."[15] The formula seems rather vaguely phrased, or at least is not quite clear to me, but the compression itself is evident in the tale. Formula or not, on the other hand, the tale does not achieve the desired effect, which obviously is to render the change that comes over Dencombe, the total acceptance with which he meets his end.

"Poor Dencombe" is shown first standing in the garden of his hotel at Bournemouth, feeling "thankful . . . for the commonest conveniences," then, with an unopened parcel in hand, "creeping to a bench he had already haunted, a safe recess in the cliff" (XVI, 77). This, we soon see, is his bench of desolation as well as reflection. There he sits lost in unhappy reverie, postponing the opening of the parcel containing his latest book, staring "at the sea, which appeared all surface and twinkle, far shallower than the spirit of man," thinking of "the abyss of human illusion that was the real, the tideless deep," looking vaguely at the trio—two ladies and a gentleman—weaving by sheer force of his novelistic habit inconsequent fancies about their relationships, and finally returning to the book in hand (XVI, 77-79). His state of extreme physical and mental weariness could not be rendered better in such a short space. On opening the parcel, he becomes "conscious of a strange alienation" and is tormented by "the pang that had been sharpest during the last few years—the sense of ebbing time, shrinking opportunity; and now he felt not so much that his last chance was going as that it was gone indeed." With his "mild eyes" already filled with tears, he now feels the "laceration . . . as violent as a grip on his throat" and rises "from his seat nervously—a creature hunted by a dread" (XVI, 80). The image begun by "creeping" on an earlier page is finally completed by "a creature hunted by a dread": Dencombe has been reduced by anguish and regret to the helplessness of a hunted animal. Similarly the image of the sea used earlier to describe the "abyss of human illusion" is further augmented by "ebbing time."

As we go further and watch Dencombe reading his book—his "rare compression" (XVI, 80)—we find him temporarily "pacified and reassured," for he is "drawn down, as by a siren's hand, to where, in the dim underworld of fiction, the great glazed tank of art, strange silent subjects float" (XVI, 81). The sea image is repeated now with a variation: the "siren's hand" foreshadows not only his physical end but also his beguilement into a longing for a "second age, an extension": his murmur, "Ah for another go, ah for a better chance!" (XVI, 82). Thus his recognition of the power of his latest book accentuates the fear that it may be his last and the desire that it shouldn't be so. These first five pages are the most effective, and the most compressed, in the tale.

From this painful preoccupation with the double-edged question of his art and life, Dencombe takes refuge in the ebullient praises of his young admirer, Dr. Hugh. Given the form of the tale, essentially that of a parable, this happy coincidence is quite acceptable to the reader who has already suspended disbelief. However, the space devoted to the other members of the trio—"the large lady, a massive heterogenous person with bold black eyes and kind red cheeks" and "the angular lady" (XVI, 82, 83)—seems an unnecessary concession to realism, which the reader rightly resents. These two personages, particularly Miss Vernham, could have been easily eliminated from the tale; interesting as they are, they do not have to be physically present to enable Dencombe to appreciate Dr. Hugh's sacrifice. As a matter of fact, their presence tends to belittle this sacrifice considerably; it also causes a structural disproportion in the narrative by tempting the author into an account, however foreshortened, of their peculiarities as well as of the way Dr. Hugh came to meet them. The fact of the fortune Dr. Hugh sacrifices in order to be near the master could have been established otherwise, and it might then have been more in tune with the fabulistic tone of the tale.

Dr. Hugh's sacrifice, it has been correctly pointed out by Clifton Fadiman, "is but a symbolical device. Call it the lever with which James uprears in Dencombe's mind his final vision of himself, the meaning of his life, of the lives of all creators."[16] Nevertheless, this device does not seem to be a powerful enough lever. The reader has been led to see the despair of Dencombe as a profound state of mind; he cannot accept its sudden alteration by so mundane and external a factor as Dr. Hugh's surrender of a problematic fortune. There is a gap between this act of homage and the vision it is supposed to give rise to. Dencombe's anguished longing for a second chance has reasons too psychologically deep to permit their abrupt disappearance under the pressure of a gesture that has little integral relation to those reasons. Consequently, we remain unconvinced when the author tells us: "A response so absolute, such a glimpse of a definite result and such a sense of credit, worked together in his mind and, producing a strange commotion, slowly altered and transfigured his despair. The sense of cold submersion left him—he seemed to float without an effort" (XVI, 105). We would have liked to hear more about the "strange commotion" and the process of slow transfiguration of Dencombe's despair. This might have been possible, even within the limited space James allowed himself in this tale, had he not given away so much of that space to Miss Vernham, the Countess, and Dr. Hugh's expectations. The point of my objection, then, is the incongruity between the parabolic character of the tale and its partial lapse into a realistic account. It seems to come very close to falling between the proverbial two stools.

It may be pointed out that in his *Notebooks* James had thought of rendering the change in Dencombe's attitude through a different device, which would have been more effective and congruous: "A deep sleep in which he dreams he *has* had his respite. Then his waking to find that what he has dreamed of is only what he has *done*."[17] He employed this device, as we have seen, in "The Great Good Place" with good effect. Incidentally, there are several other resemblances between "The Middle Years" and "The Great Good Place": the weariness of the two writer-protagonists, the change that comes over them, the master-disciple motif, the "bench" they occupy, the sea imagery, and so on. The dream would also have been a more appropriate symbolical and psychological agent of the change in Dencombe, and his famous utterance—"We work in dark—we do what we can—we give what we have. Our doubt is our passion and our passion is our task. The rest is the madness of art" (XVI, 105)—would then be coming more naturally from a spiritually rehabilitated hero.

Dissatisfaction with the story in its present form has led one commentator, Perry D. Westbrook, to work up an altogether untenable interpretation. Westbrook believes that there is a satirical intention in the tale, that "the strength of the story lies in the contrast between the dying man's distortion of events and the actual happenings as indicated by the somewhat subtle but unmistakable clues that James provides."[18] "What has actually happened," according to this view, "is that Dr. Hugh—a staunch admirer of Dencombe, to be sure—has written a laudatory review himself and has got it published in a newspaper with whose editors he has influence, and that he has pretended to have forgone the fortune, since this idealistic author rather ironically can appreciate no token of esteem except a monetary one."[19] The actual tale does not seem to bear out this interesting interpretation; nor does one find any trace of those "unmistakeable clues" either in the tale or in Westbrook's discussion of it. The reason for this "supersubtlety," however, is unwittingly made clear by Westbrook, who cannot imagine that James wanted to give such "a maudlin presentation of 'the plight of the artist in an unundestanding world.' "[20] A purely textual approach, which Westbrook claims to be making in his essay, must lead one to a recognition of the existing elements of self-pity, not to a denial of those elements. In this connection it is interesting that Clifton Fadiman should maintain "The Middle Years" to be the one

Jamesian tale of writers that is not "diluted by a certain infusion of self-pity."[21] The fact, clearly adducible from the tale itself, is that self-pity is an important element, perhaps both causal and consequential, in the depressed mental state of Dencombe; the failure of the tale lies in James's failure to render artistically the transfiguration of self-pity into self-acceptance.

I have analyzed two fairly representative parables of the artist in order to see how James varies his method for adorning his tale and pointing his moral. In both tales—together with "The Lesson of the Master" (1888), which is a successful cross between the parable and the realistic tale—the problems and peculiarities of the artist are central; "The Great Good Place," I have mentioned, also has a larger application. As distinguished from James's first-person tales about artists, these are more somber in tone and less comic, as well as less melodramatic, in treatment. This difference is attributable partly to the fact that they are told impersonally and partly to the comparatively abstract nature of the issues involved.

Before going on to a few parables of another variety and of larger dimension, in the next chapter, I may refer briefly to "The Real Right Thing" (1899) and "The Story in It" (1900) in view of their general kinship with the tales discussed above. "The Real Right Thing" conveys its point, about the sacredness of a writer's private life and its irrelevance to a consideration of his writings, through the agency of the supernatural. The supernatural in this tale, however, does not make for an intense ghostly atmosphere. George Withermore is entrusted by the widow of his friend, Ashton Doyne, with the flattering task of constructing her husband's biography from "diaries, letters, memoranda, notes, documents of many sorts" (XVII, 411). Gradually he divines the mute admonition in the intensely felt "presence" and then the "absence" of the deceased master.

The only appearance of the ghost takes place off page and is referred to in passing in order to clinch the truth of Withermore's growing conviction that the master would like his "private life" left unexcavated. The tale is a neat enough dramatization of this idea; it is concise and the motive stands out sharply. But it could hardly be ranked among James's great tales, for it convinces us without moving us.

"The Story in It" is unique among James's parables of artists in that none of its three characters is an artist. It is a dialectical parable, very much akin to his essays, "Daniel Deronda: A Conversation" (1876) or "After the Play" (1889).[22] The subject is illuminated through a lively dialogue between two interesting disputants, and the excitement is that of an intellectual argument. As the dialogue proceeds, we veer closer to the author's own point of view, represented in the tale by a charming widow, which is a cunning refutation of the "general truth" that inspired him to fabricate the story: *L'honnête femme n'a pas de roman.*[23] It is the most important, if not the most successful, single dramatization of some of James's deepest artistic convictions. With these same convictions he achieves, in his best work, a frequent union of honesty and adventure, of innocence and experience, showing the growth and decline of "relations" without letting his heroes and heroines forgo their innocence or their adventures become dull. It also conveys the implicit admonition not to fix upon such terms as "passion," "life," "novel," "adventure," "romance," "relation," in inelastic *a priori* definitions. As the demure Mrs. Maud Blessingbourne repeatedly points out, all these terms express only what you mean by them and you can mean different things depending on who and where you are. "The Story in It," in short, may not in itself be a great story, but it is an ingenious fictional explanation of why James wrote the way he did.

CHAPTER VIII

A Jamesian Triptych

D. W. JEFFERSON remarks that "one of James's characteristic devices in [his] late period was to choose fantastic subjects involving either a complete departure from literal possibility or a bold distortion or simplification."[1] This tendency is seen in an unmistakable form in the numerous late tales where the adventures of his heroes and heroines are either completely internalized or else take place in the rarer regions of fantastic allegory.

I have examined two parables that are also fantasies; I come now to three fantasies that are also parables. "The Great Good Place" and "The Middle Years," along with several other tales with the artist theme, form a virtual *Künstlerroman*. Taken together, "The Altar of the Dead" (1895), "The Beast in the Jungle" (1903), and "The Jolly Corner" (1908) form a triptych depicting man in quest of his Self; they constitute James's most successful attempt at a spiritual odyssey.

The Altar of the Dead

Both in the *Notebooks* and the preface James refers to "The Altar of the Dead" as a "conceit." In the *Notebooks*, however, this term is used in the context of his doubt whether "it is worth going on with"—he had already written a part of it—and is intended to be pejorative: "One's claim for it is, on the very face of the matter, slight. Let me remember that I have always put things through."[2] But, as the editors of the *Notebooks* comment, this apologetic feeling must have been momentary, for he included it as a title story in the canon and prefaced it with remarks that betray no dissatisfaction with the finished product. Still, it is as an extended conceit, which here is synonymous with parable or apologue, that the tale holds together so well.

It is laid out in nine sections that fall into three more or less distinct and equal parts. The first part is given to the raising of the altar by "poor Stransom" first in his "spiritual spaces," later in a suburban Catholic church. The early phase of the worship of the dead—its genesis and growth—is presented in the form of a concentrated summary covering a few pages. Stransom's tenacious devotion to the memory of Mary Antrim is telescoped into two sentences: "He had needed no priest and no altar to make him for ever widowed. He had done many things in the world—he had done almost all but one: he had never, never forgotten" (XVII, 4). Then the extension of this devotion into a pious observance of the memory of all his dead is briefly mentioned until we come to this significant sentence: "Quite how it had risen he probably never could have told you, but what had come to pass was that an altar, such as was after all within everybody's compass, lighted with perpetual candles and dedicated to these secret rites, reared itself in his spiritual spaces" (XVII, 5). We are now informed that Stransom has no other religion but "the religion of the Dead. It suited his inclination, it satisfied his spirit, it gave employment to his piety" (XVII, 6). The narrative passes from summary to scene, from a general account of Stransom's devout preoccupation with his dead to a specific instance of the way it is deepened by an accidental encounter with Paul Creston and his second wife.

The encounter occurs before a shop front "that lighted the dull brown air with its mercenary grin" (XVII, 7). The scene, however, is not rendered in dramatic detail, since it would take unnecessary space and contribute nothing of value to the picture of Stransom's revulsion at Creston's infidelity. The meeting has an obvious symbolic function—it takes place before a jeweler's shop where "Stransom lingered long enough to suspend, in a vision, a string of pearls about the white neck of Mary Antrim" (XVII, 7), and into which Creston is accompanying his new wife perhaps to buy her a real string of pearls. It fits into the parabolic structure of the tale. Stransom represents the few who never forget their dead, Creston the many who never remember them. The contrast is felt by Stransom, and it makes his own devotion even more profound. He spends the evening visualizing Kate Creston through his mind's eye: "He thought for a long time of how the closed eyes of dead women could still live—how they could open again, in a quiet lamplit room, long after they had looked their last. They had looks that survived—had them as great poets had quoted lines" (XVII, 11). The image conveys the sensitivity of Stransom and the restfulness that the contemplation of the dead induces in him. It should be noticed that James does not specify any details of Stransom's reminiscences regarding Kate Creston, for the image suffices vividly to convey his silent session with the dead.

The only flaw, if it may be so called, in this scene is James's deviation, probably by force of habit, into what seems an inopportune dig at the American woman: "The happy pair had just arrived from America, and Stransom hadn't needed to be told this to guess the nationality of the lady" (XVII, 9). The new Mrs. Creston could have had a "face that shone as publicly as the jeweller's win-

dow" (XVII, 8) and "shrieked into the fog 'Mind now
you come to see me right away!'" (XVII, 9) without
having to be identified as an American. The detail, even
as a glimpse into Stransom's mind, is quite out of place in
this uninternational tale.

That same evening Stransom has another shock, of a
different kind, when he reads of Sir Acton Hague's death.
It reminds him of his rupture of years ago with this old
friend. He thinks of him as "Hague," but the death leaves
him absolutely cold, which contrasts in the reader's mind
with Stransom's warmth for his other dead and gives him
the measure of his relentlessness in regard to Hague. Here
again it should be noticed that no specific details of the
estrangement are allowed to enter the picture of Stransom's reaction; it is enough for the purpose of the tale to
mention the fact and effect of that rupture. Both incidents—Stransom's encounter with Creston and his reading
of Hague's death—happen on the eve of Mary Antrim's
death anniversary; the coincidence might not have occurred
in a realistic tale in which the author wishes to maintain
verisimilitude. Since, however, it is not a realistic tale,
we have a few more coincidences. The most important
one is Stransom's happening to enter on the following day
the very church frequented by the unnamed lady in whom
he later discovers a fellow apostle. Even at first glance he
is struck by her: "He wished he could sink, like her, to the
very bottom, be as motionless, as rapt in prostration"
(XVII, 14). Soon he himself is lost in thought, "floating
away on the sea of light," comparing the shrine before
him to the shrine within him, taking "the silent roll-call
of his Dead," and he is suddenly possessed by the idea of
translating "the mere chapel of his thoughts" into "some
material act, some outward worship" (XVII, 14-15). Finding an unused chapel, he decides to "make it a masterpiece

of splendour and a mountain of fire" (XVII, 15). This decision represents the union, in his mind, of his aesthetic and religious cravings. It also illustrates James's recurrent tendency in his later work to invest his several central characters, even when they are not artists, with a highly refined imagination and sensibility; all the "poor sensitive gentlemen" of James's late fiction are men of vision and of visions. The practical difficulties encountered by Stransom in raising the altar are dealt with summarily. By the end of this third section Stransom has had his "mountain of fire" for a year or two; and his "plunge . . . into depths quieter than the deep sea-caves" (XVII, 17) has become his most cherished form of saturation in his inner life. Meanwhile, the star-tipped tapers at his altar "were gathering thick at present, for Stransom had entered that dark defile of our earthly descent in which some one dies every day." The only exclusion from this "huddled flock" is the taper for Acton Hague: "For Acton Hague no flame could ever rise on any altar of his" (XVII, 18, 19). The passage of time is thus reflected in the "gathering" thickness of Stransom's altar, and his apostolic function is seen through the "huddled flock."

The account of the time in which Stransom and the unnamed lady grow "old together in their piety" is also presented in the form of a concentrated summary, enlivened by occasional scenic glimpses, such as their first meeting outside the church at a concert, their first walk together, or their infrequently reported conversations during the long years of communion with the dead. This is as it has to be in a tale that spans a long stretch of time and is meant to exemplify an idea without the "solidity of specification"[3] expected of a realistic narrative. Thus, for instance, the passage of time is suggested through a deliberately vague but meaningful indirection:

"For long ages he never knew her name, any more than she had ever pronounced his own." And again, "it had taken him months and months to learn her name, years and years to learn her address" (XVII, 26, 31). Neither the name nor the address is disclosed to the reader, although the general location of her house is captured in a vivid image: "He knew the small vista of her street, closed at the end and as dreary as an empty pocket, where the pairs of shabby little houses, semi-detached but indissolubly united, were like married couples on bad terms" (XVII, 31). Similarly the growing desolation of Stransom's contact with the living is rendered through the corresponding proliferation of his dead: "Friend by friend dropped away till at last there were more emblems on his altar than houses left him to enter" (XVII, 28-29). The spectacle of their growing old together, along with the difference in their ages, is beautifully compressed into one sentence: "She had reached the period of life he had long since reached, when, after separations, the marked clockface of the friend we meet announces the hour we have tried to forget" (XVII, 31). Summary, rather than scene (by which I mean the dramatic scene), is the main narrative ingredient in the composition of "The Altar of the Dead."

There is, however, one fully realized scene in the tale. It begins at the end of the sixth section with the shock of recognition Stransom registers on seeing the portrait of Acton Hague in the unnamed lady's apartment. His going to her house has already struck him as "an event, somehow; and in all their long acquaintance there had never been an event" (XVII, 32). We are led to anticipate the reverberations of this event as we read the story—their impersonal friendship is now heading toward a personal complication. Stransom is overwhelmed by the sudden illumination that the object of his fellow apostle's devotions is Hague, the one person of whose memory he had "inveterately tried to rid himself," "the greatest blank in the shining page" (XVII, 19). The scene is carried over into the next section. This new element, which threatens to put an end to their joint piety as well as to their mutual kinship, is represented fully to add tension to the narrative in its concluding phase and to dramatize the central theme of the story. Stransom's religion of the dead is incomplete as long as he does not make what from his point of view is the supreme sacrifice: he must give up his egotistical resolve to exclude Acton Hague from his dead; he must fully forgive him. It takes him some time to persuade himself to take this opportunity, and the rest of the tale gives us the measure of the change that finally does take place, leading up to his last epiphanous experience before the altar. For a while, however, the altar, particularly the one in his spiritual spaces, ceases to exist: "His altar moreover had ceased to exist; his chapel, in his dreams, was a great dark cavern. All the lights had gone out—all his Dead had died again. He couldn't exactly see at first how it had been in the power of his late companion to extinguish them since it was neither for her nor by her that they had been called into being. Then he understood that it was essentially in his own soul the revival had taken place, and that in the air of this soul they were now unable to breathe" (XVII, 50).

This marks the first turning point in his thoughts. Thereafter he resumes his visits to the church, where he sits thinking constantly of the unnamed lady, feeling "a sharper and sharper pang in the imagination of her darkness" as he himself once again "wandered in the fields of light; he passed, among the tall tapers, from tier to tier, from fire to fire, from name to name, from the white intensity of one clear emblem, of one saved soul, to another"

(XVII, 52). As he loses himself once again "in the large lustre . . . as dazzling as the vision of heaven in the mind of a child" (XVII, 52), her "plea for just one more" (XVII, 53) humming in his mind, he persists for a while in the thought that his altar is after all "compact and complete" and that there is no room in the arrangement of rows for one more, even "if there were no other objection" (XVII, 52). He takes refuge, in other words, in an aesthetic objection to any addition to the tapers before arriving, under pressure of a final sincerity, at a new "conception of the total, the ideal, which left a clear opportunity for just another figure" (XVII, 53). The demand of the spirit and of aesthetics is thus demonstrated to be one—but his first impulse is to propel *himself* into the gap. This impulse is countered by the thought that once he is with the "Others" the altar will cease to matter, for who will tend it "since his particular dream of keeping it up had melted away?" (XVII, 54). After a long process of inner conflict he goes, following a brief illness, for the last time to his shrine: "It seemed to him he had come for the great surrender. . . . He had come, as he always came, to lose himself; the fields of light were still there to stray in; only this time, in straying, he would never come back. He had given himself to his Dead, and it was good: this time his Dead would keep him" (XVII, 55).

In his conscious mind the "surrender" may appear only as his prospective death; but somewhere deeper it must also be connected with the surrender he has resisted so far. Kneeling before his altar, he has the vision of Mary Antrim smiling "at him from the glory of heaven—she brought the glory down with her to take him" (XVII, 55). Simultaneous with the joy of this vision is the pain of another recognition: "It suddenly made him contrast that very rapture with the bliss he had refused to another. . . .

The descent of Mary Antrim opened his spirit with a great compunctious throb for the descent of Acton Hague. It was as if Stransom had read what her [Mary Antrim's] eyes said to him" (XVII, 55-56). Stransom finds himself face to face with "the partner of his long worship" who also has undergone an important change. During these last moments the two transformed friends vie with each other in renouncement, and Stransom dies, leaning on her.[4] A virtual identification takes place between Stransom and Acton Hague; the candle he would have her add to their "mountain of light" is not for himself but for Hague.

Thus the ritual is completed and the priest, having made the supreme sacrifice, passes on the apostleship of his altar to the priestess. It should be noticed that the last sacrificial rite he observes at the altar is an act of immolation both for the dead—it is Mary Antrim's vision that liberates him from his ego—and for the living—it is for the unnamed lady that he gives up his resistance to "one more, just one." If his own end coincides with his surrender, it is as it should be in a parable: it is the "reward" for his last act of simultaneous piety for the dead and the living, for the candle that will burn for Acton Hague will also burn for him.[5]

R. P. Blackmur says this tale "can be thought of with *Lycidas* and *In Memoriam* and *Adonais,* and without their particularity of reference."[6] This is a sound grouping and a sound distinction, for "The Altar" is indeed a requiem. Nevertheless, there is a meaning behind this meaning: the "altar" is a symbolic bridge between the living and the dead, and the fable exemplifies the point that this bridge is never complete, aesthetically or spiritually, so long as there is even the last vestige of egotism in the devotee. Stransom must give up his self to gain his Self. This metaphysical pun, I believe, is also embedded in the tale.

From the numerous quoted phrases and passages, it should be clear that the mortar that goes into the making of "The Altar" is supplied by its rich and refulgent images. Concrete statistics would not be to the point. Suffice it to say that the recurrent images—of the feast, of the mountain of fire and light, of fields of light, of the seas of contemplation and thought, of the concert and the choir—and the general rhythms of the prose combine to give this tale the shape almost of an emblem and the tone almost of an incantation. It is a little surprising that Allen Tate, while recognizing its "great tone," should characterize it as "James's great failure."[7] In its tone, more than in anything else, lies its success, and it seems to me wrong to set as little store by tone as Tate seems to do.

Finally, it is an interesting paradox that a tale so exclusively concerned with the dead should also be the least "ghostly" of all of James's ghostly tales. It is in fact, in Clifton Fadiman's words, "far removed from the ghostly or the morbid. . . . The story is crowded, not with terror, but with love. Indeed it *is* a love story, the death of Stransom being a true *Liebestod*."[8] This view seems to do greater justice to the tale than the view of Q. D. Leavis, who finds it "unprofitably unpleasant,"[9] or of F. R. Leavis, to whom it exemplifies a "very unpleasantly sentimental morbidity."[10]

The Beast in the Jungle

If "The Altar of the Dead" is a fable based on its hero's sense of the sacred past and its beneficent influence on him, "The Beast in the Jungle" can be taken as a fable depicting its hero's dread of the future and its maleficent influence on him. George Stransom haunts the past; John Marcher is haunted by the future. The difference, however, is that Stransom's obsession has a liberating and enriching influence; Marcher's obsession only drains his

spirit and emotions. Another difference between the two
protagonists is that Stransom renounces his ego in time
for final redemption; to Marcher the impulse for this
renunciation comes too late, and even in that terrible
moment he is more appalled by the spring of the "Beast"
than by the tremor of regret at not having responded to
May Bartram's love. Stransom joins his dead soon after
the blissful vision of Mary Antrim and, we can imagine,
his soul will rest in peace. Marcher mourns his dead after
his baleful vision of the Beast and, we can imagine, he will
never be at peace. After such knowledge there can be no
rest.

The wider thematic context of "The Beast" is perhaps
too obvious to merit more than a bare mention: it is a
"fantastic" embodiment of the central Jamesian theme of
the unlived life, dealt with most amply in *The Ambassadors*. What gives "The Beast" its distinctive place among
James's shorter masterpieces, however, is its spell-binding
power. Without this special quality, even with all its
thematic meaningfulness, it might have been as ordinary
a tale as, for instance, "The Friends of the Friends" or
"Maud-Evelyn," the two tales written during the same
phase and around a similar idea. We need not dwell any
longer on the theme, then, for James has clearly disengaged in his preface the "treated theme for the reader's
benefit."[11] As he goes on to say, "any felt merit in the thing
must all depend on the clearness and charm with which
the subject just noted expresses itself."[12] In what follows
I shall be almost exclusively concerned with evaluating
this "clearness and charm."

Each of the six sections contains at least one dramatized
scene that is embedded in an analytical summary. The
summary is a heavily foreshortened account of the long
intervals separating one scene from another and an anal-

ysis of the progressive stages of Marcher's obsession. The scenes dramatize these stages through increasingly tense conversations between Marcher and May, except in the last scene where Marcher faces the Beast alone. Thus in the first section, the summary is used to provide the background for the scene in which Marcher and May reminisce about their meeting of ten years ago. The less essential part of this conversation is also given through indirect narration, editorially compressed, with the accent on Marcher's response to this unexpected renewal of an old acquaintance. The scenic half of the section begins with May's speech, mentioned in the opening sentence of the tale. By the close of the scene, the nature of Marcher's obsession has been dramatically defined and the partnership he offers May clearly established.

In the second section, the summary is employed to give us the idea of their growing "older together" (XVII, 82)—the phrase, like several others, echoes similar phrases in "The Altar of the Dead." Marcher does not have the ghost of a perception that May is in love with him; he himself does not love her. He satisfies his conscience by trying not to appropriate her entirely for his own selfish purpose—but this is a veneer beneath which his egotism still lives. Marcher himself is not quite conscious of the veneer, but the reader is left in very little doubt. As L. C. Knights has pointed out, everything is "'seen' largely through the eyes of Marcher, but the seeing is flecked with unobtrusive irony so that we are aware of two views—Marcher's and that of James himself—existing simultaneously."[13] The simultaneity of views can be seen, for instance, in the tone of the passages that show Marcher grappling with the question of his selfishness: "This was why [the fact that he "had thought himself, so long as nobody knew, the most disinterested person in the world" and "hadn't disturbed people with the queerness of their having to know a haunted man" (XVII, 77-78)] he had such good—though possibly such rather colourless—manners; this was why, above all, he could regard himself, in a greedy world, as decently—as in fact perhaps even a little sublimely—unselfish" (XVII, 78). Or later, when he knows of "a deep disorder in her blood," his reactions are given in these words: "This indeed gave him one of those partial recoveries of equanimity that were agreeable to him—it showed him that what was still first in his mind was the loss she herself might suffer. 'What if she should have to die before knowing, before seeing—?'" (XVII, 94). Even when he thinks he is being least selfish, the reader is made subtly aware of the telltale error in his thought. Many more illustrations can be adduced to refute the notion that "the point of view is consistently that of Marcher."[14] In addition to the ironic interplay of the author's and Marcher's point of view, we also have a brief glimpse of May's—for instance in the passage that begins, "So while they grew older together she did watch with him, and so she let this association give shape and colour to her own existence. Beneath *her* forms as well detachment had learned to sit, and behaviour had become for her, in a social sense, a false account of herself" (XVII, 82).

The summary gives way to the scene in the second half of the section: "What we are especially concerned with is the turn it happened to take from her one afternoon when he had come to see her in honour of her birthday" (XVII, 83). A good deal has happened, and time has elapsed, since the scene in the first section. The vigil May had agreed to keep with Marcher has not yet been rewarded by any sign of the long-awaited Beast. But what this scene establishes most trenchantly is Marcher's disconcerting suspicion that May has perhaps already seen the Beast. This suspicion is shared by the reader, who is free to read something more into May's speeches and silences and guarded hints—for instance, he knows without being explicitly told that she is in love with Marcher and can almost predict what the dreadful Beast will turn out to be, although he has no idea of how and when it will spring.

The third section opens with the summary, giving the effect on Marcher of their last important conversation, passes on to a brief scene, dramatizing his slight uneasiness about what she has "got" out of her long association with him—a question she answers with all the characteristic evasiveness of a Jamesian lover—and turns again to a summary conveying Marcher's fear that he might lose her. The agony of his fear comes from his dependence on her as well as from his knowledge that "she 'knew' something and that what she knew was bad—too bad to tell him" (XVII, 92). But he is shown as having rationalized this fear into the flattering appearance of an unselfish concern for the loss *she* would suffer by her death. The irony of this subtle self-deception has been mentioned above. And of course there is the further irony that will flash out only at the end: he will realize that she died in full knowledge of his fate, a knowledge she scrupulously spared him out of tenderness. The idea that his "great accident" might after all be "nothing more than his being condemned to see this charming woman, this admirable friend, pass away from him" crosses his mind, only to be dismissed as "an abject anti-climax" (XVII, 95-96). Another thought that has begun to torment him is the dread that "it was overwhelmingly too late" for anything to happen to him (XVII, 96): "It wouldn't have been failure to be bankrupt, dishonoured, pilloried, hanged; it was failure not to be anything" (XVII, 97). The scene in this section has an insignificant function in comparison to the summary, through which James conveys the very atmosphere of his hero's mind.

In the next section the scene is given predominance to dramatize Marcher's supreme failure in deciphering May's answer to his riddle and in grasping the sole opportunity to escape the Beast. Apart from the scene in the opening section, this is the only other scene provided with some kind of setting, although the setting in this case is more atmospheric than physical: it conveys his impression of May as he visits her "one afternoon, while the spring of the year was young and new."[15] He sees her as "the picture of a serene and exquisite but impenetrable sphinx," as "an artificial lily, wonderfully imitated and constantly kept," as someone sitting "with folded hands and nothing more to do" (XVII, 98-99). It is against the background of his alarm and bafflement that the scene is played out, with Marcher remaining blank in the presence of what she tries to communicate to him. It is a scene whose importance and terror Marcher grasps later, while the reader grasps it at the moment. It is perfectly placed in the total design of the tale and is attended by the full involvement of the author and the reader. Its reverberations remain with us throughout the rest of the tale.

This is followed by a companion scene in the next section, which in its opening paragraphs depicts Marcher's anguished efforts to read the riddle of the sphinx; he fails to do so even though she spoke "with the perfect straightness of a sibyl" (XVII, 110). The approaching death of May Bartram lends poignancy to her assurance to Marcher that his danger has passed. The scene is followed by a picture of Marcher's desolation after May's death. But as the shock of that death fades, his unlaid obsession begins to haunt him once again: "What it presently came to in truth was that poor Marcher waded through his beaten grass, where no life stirred, where no breath sounded, where no evil eye seemed to gleam from a possible lair, very much as if vaguely looking for the Beast, and still more as if acutely missing it" (XVII, 116). As this quotation indicates, the jungle which Marcher now threshes has already receded into his past: "What was to happen *had* so absolutely and finally happened that he was as little able to know a fear for his future as to know a hope, so absent in short was any question of anything still to come. He was to live entirely with the other question, that of his unidentified past, that of his having to see his fortune impenetrably muffled and masked" (XVII, 117).

This calls for a slight modification of my initial statement that Marcher is haunted by his future, for at this stage the habitation of the Beast shifts and so does the direction of Marcher's obsession. Had he followed May's advice, he would not have tried to "win back by an effort of thought the lost stuff of consciousness" (XVII, 117), and he would have perhaps enjoyed the bliss that lies in ignorance. But constituted as he is, this new turn of the obsession takes an even greater hold on his mind. So far he has waited intensely but almost passively for his fate. Now his search becomes more active as well as more desperate: "The lost stuff of consciousness became thus for him as a strayed or stolen child to an unappeasable father; he hunted it up and down very much as if he were knocking at doors and enquiring of the police" (XVII, 118). This vivid image expresses the fever with which he now hunts the Beast. The encounter, however, does not take place as a direct result of his own effort of thought. Before setting out on his travels, he makes a pilgrimage to May Bartram's grave, which is pictured as a part of "the wilderness of tombs" (XVII, 118). Later, just before his final revelation, the graveyard will bloom appropriately into an image of the "garden of death" (XVII, 121). Meanwhile, however, as he kneels on the stones beside the grave, "beguiled into long intensities," his question remains unanswered and not even the "palest light" breaks (XVII, 118).

The last section rapidly summarizes his cheerless travels abroad. On returning home he makes straight for "the barely discriminated slab in the London suburb" that "had become for him, and more intensely with time and distance, his one witness of a past glory" (XVII, 119). He is mentioned as having "wandered from the circumference to the centre of his desert," back to "the part of himself that alone he now valued" (XVII, 120). The reader is conscious of no abruptness in this reported transition from a harassed hunter of the Beast to a devoted worshiper of his dead friend, the change from a tormented questioner to a stoical accepter: "Whatever had happened —well, had happened" (XVII, 120). In this new state of mind Marcher begins to visit regularly May Bartram's grave, which "had lost for him its mere blankness of expression. It met him in mildness—not, as before, in mockery; it wore for him the air of conscious greeting that we find, after absence, in things that have closely belonged to us and which seem to confess of themselves to the connexion" (XVII, 120). The wilderness of tombs has now become the garden of death, where "he settled to live— feeding all on the sense that he once *had* lived, and dependent on it not alone for a support but an identity" (XVII, 121).

The garden, however, is a place associated with knowledge, and, after a year of comparative peace, knowledge comes to him on an autumn day, not "on the wings of experience" but through "the disrespect of chance, the insolence

of accident" (XVII, 125). Had it come by his own effort
of thought—a course perhaps equally open to the author
—the point of John Marcher's "great negative adventure"
would have been somewhat blunted, though his lot would
have been somewhat redeemed. But the point is not only
his inability to "do" anything, but also his tragic inability
to "see" anything except as he finally does see. The spectacle of his waking to the horror of this knowledge is great;
layer after layer of ignorance is removed, the whole back-
ward reach of the emptiness of his life reflected, till he
stands stripped before himself. The anti-hero, instead of
remaining a mere pathetic figure, becomes a tragic hero,
arousing pity and terror because of the single-mindedness
with which he has looked forward to his destiny and the
intensity with which he experiences his doom.

Allen Tate cautiously expresses several objections to the
tale, among them: "The foreground is too elaborate, and
the structure suffers from the disproportion of the Mis-
placed Middle"; the grief-stricken stranger is introduced
too suddenly and "could better be described as *deus ex
machina*"; and the symbolism tends to allegory in the Haw-
thornian way.[16] What Tate dismisses as foreground—the
first two sections—is structurally proportionate, well integrated in the tale, and very necessary to an appreciation of
Marcher's obsession and his relationship with May. The
middle of the tale is in the third section, where Marcher's
suspicion, that May knows something he does not, first
turns into a virtual conviction; this is almost exactly the
dimensional middle of the tale. The grief-stricken stranger
may be termed a *deus ex machina,* but his descent at the
opportune moment is not at all ruled out by the tenor
of the tale. Here perhaps we have the basic reason for
Tate's objections to the tale: it should not be evaluated
as a realistic tale or be read as a mere allegory. It is a

disservice both to Hawthorne and to James to dismiss "The Beast," and "The Altar" as failures *because* they are allegories. Instead, we should perhaps revise our opinion of allegory, as well as our definition of it, in the light of "The Great Good Place," "The Altar," "The Beast," and "The Jolly Corner."[17]

As contrasted with "The Altar of the Dead," there are more scenic effects in "The Beast in the Jungle," but even here the task of creating the haunting effect of the tale falls to what I have expressed by the somewhat unimpressive, but quite Jamesian, term "summary." As used here, the term expresses those narrative resources of the storyteller by which he both bridges the gaps between his crucial scenes and lets us hear the musings of his hero without surrendering his privilege to stand beside him and, in Knights's phrase, to fleck unobtrusively these musings occasionally with his own.

The Jolly Corner

Blackmur has caught the connection between "The Jolly Corner" and "The Altar of the Dead" in a well-phrased epigram: "If in *The Altar of the Dead* James made a fable of the dead who must be kept alive for the sake of the living, in *The Jolly Corner* he made a fable of the living who must be slain for the sake of the living, which if at first it sounds like nonsense can easily enough be cleared up."[18] "The Jolly Corner" can also be seen as "The Beast in the Jungle" in reverse. Marcher is obsessed by what he will be, Spencer Brydon by what he would have been. In the end, of course, Marcher is appalled by what he has been, Brydon by what he might have been.[19] As Edwin Honig puts it in his admirable essay, "Marcher wakes to the 'horror' and not, like Spencer Brydon, to the 'joy' of knowledge."[20]

Spencer Brydon's pilgrimage to his ancestral home is in several respects a reversal of Clement Searle's pilgrimage to his ancestral home in "A Passionate Pilgrim." But the two tales, in spite of this situational kinship, are so different in details of treatment and technique that a mere passing mention of the connection will suffice. We also have James's own account of the fact that he "was filching in a small way" from *The Sense of the Past* for "The Jolly Corner."[21] Going still further back, we have the connection of this tale, and of *The Sense of the Past,* with his "immense hallucination" about "the Galerie d'Apollon of my childhood," recaptured so vividly in *A Small Boy and Others.*[22] Furthermore, James's visit to America in 1904-1905 must have contributed to the soil of memory and desire from which "The Jolly Corner," biographically considered, emanates.[23] Finally, and this particular point seems to me farfetched and least relevant to any critical purpose, we have Saul Rosensweig's theory about the link between "The Story of a Year" and "The Jolly Corner" and the autopsychoanalytical implications of this link.[24]

To all these connections I may add that the theme of "The Jolly Corner," and to a certain extent that of "The Beast in the Jungle" and "The Altar of the Dead," overflows into "Crapy Cornelia" (1909) and "A Round of Visits" (1910). In both these tales the protagonist returns to America after several years abroad. In "Crapy Cornelia" White-Mason, an old man "shifting . . . his posture on his chair of contemplation" and debating indecisively whether he should propose to Mrs. Worthingham, is an ancestor of J. Alfred Prufrock. Like Spencer Brydon, he is struck by the contrast between the old and the new as symbolized by Cornelia and Mrs. Worthingham. Like Stransom and Marcher, he cannot forget the girl whom he might have married but for a misunderstanding and who is now dead.

In the end he accepts his old age, which has been a source of uneasiness to him up to then, and his past. In the light of this self-realization the question of his marrying Mrs. Worthingham fades away:

Cornelia marvelled—or looked as if she did. "Not for all she has?"

"Yes—I know all she has. But I also know all she hasn't. And, as I told you, she herself doesn't—hasn't a glimmer of a suspicion of it; and never will have."

Cornelia magnanimously thought. "No—but she knows other things."

He shook his head as at the portentous heap of them. "Too many—too many. And other indeed—*so* other. Do you know," he went on, "that it's as if *you*—by turning up for me—had brought that home to me?"

"For you," she candidly considered. "But what—since you can't marry me!—can you do with me?"

Well, he seemed to have it all. "Everything. I can live with you—just this way." To illustrate which he dropped into the other chair by her fire; where, leaning back, he gazed at the flame. "I can't give you up. It's very curious. It has come over me as it did over you when you renounced Bognor. That's it—I know it at last, and I see one can like it. I'm 'high.' You needn't deny it. That's my taste. I'm old." And in spite of the considerable glow there of her little household altar he said it without the scowl. (M, XXVIII, 360-361)

Although this passage suggests the restful note on which the tale ends, it does not give a full picture of the dense imagery of "Crapy Cornelia," which is in many ways akin to the stylistic bias of "The Jolly Corner."

In "A Round of Visits" Mark Montieth returns to New York in order to look into business matters. He finds he has been swindled by his friend and factotum, Phil Bloodgood.[25] He is appalled at the hugeness, newness, and blaring vulgarity of the city—"bright and bleak, fresh and harsh, rich and evident somehow, a perspective like a page of florid modern platitudes. He didn't quite know what he had expected for his return—not certainly serenades and deputations; . . . Phil Bloodgood had gone off not only with so large a slice of his small *peculium*, but with all the broken bits of the past, the loose ends of old relationships, that he had supposed he might pick up again" (M, XXVIII, 377). The burden of grief that Montieth carries with him is suggestive of Chekhov's "Lament." But more relevant, to my purpose, is the similarity of the myth created in "A Round of Visits" to the central idea of "The Jolly Corner." The two tales differ, of course, in emphasis and conclusion.[26] But I may suggest, without forcing the point, that Phil Bloodgood and Newton Winch also represent the alter ego of Mark Montieth—represent him as he might have been if he had stayed on in the business world of New York. Let us not, however, get entangled in this maze of "connections"; the strictly biographical-psychoanalytical ones especially should not be allowed to distract us from the task of examining "The Jolly Corner" itself.

The tale opens dramatically, with Spencer Brydon's remark to Alice Staverton, indicating his impatience with people who are constantly after him for his impressions "of everything" (XVII, 435). The scene from which this remark is extracted is resumed several pages later: "It was a few days after this that, during an hour passed with her again, he had expressed his impatience of the too flattering curiosity—among the people he met—about his appreciation of New York" (XVII, 447). The intervening pages give a compact account of the total setting of this scene. A summary of this summary cannot be accomplished without attenuating the rich picture of Brydon's preliminary confrontation with his past. At best I can only point to the range of information that is abbreviated pictorially through a fusion of the omniscient narrator's voice and the consciousness of the hero. Thus we learn about the hero's "so strangely belated return to America" (XVII, 435), about "the newness, the queerness, above all the bigness . . . that at present assaulted his vision wherever he looked" (XVII, 436), about his "house on the jolly corner" and the general purpose of his homecoming (XVII, 437), about his amused perception of his "dormant" business capacities as he supervises the conversion of his other house into flats (XVII, 438), about the "communities of knowledge" he shares with his old friend Alice Staverton (XVII, 440), about the effect on him of Miss Staverton's ironical remarks about his "real gifts" (XVII, 440), about their talk of the "ghosts" during their visit together to the jolly-corner house (XVII, 441-447), and so on. The order of this information is not exactly chronological, and the process by which it is conveyed not entirely without scenic effects. Brydon's "morbid obsession" with his alter ego clings to him in the form of the "most disguised and most muffled vibrations" (XVII, 441). The form that this obsession is to take, and the ghost it will give rise to, is foreshadowed by his image of "some strange figure, some unexpected occupant, at a turn of one of the dim passages of an empty house," an image that he further improves upon: "that of his opening a door behind which he would have made sure of finding nothing, a door into a room shuttered and void, and yet so coming, with a great suppressed start, on some quite erect confronting presence, something planted in the middle of the place and facing him through the dusk" (XVII, 441). His actual nightmare is thus anticipated by this glimpse of his acutely developed visual imagination. The "actual" ghost and his adventure with it are here preceded by a mention of the "real" ghost and his preoccupation with it, for the ghost is but a symbolical embodiment of the phantom self he must exorcise.

The scene itself is not all dialogue, much of which is reported indirectly. It gives a hint, among other things, of Spencer Brydon's ambivalence toward what he might have been. The images in which he thinks of his alter ego are informed with the tenderness of desire—an "important letter unopened" and "the full-blown flower . . . in the small tight bud" (XVII, 448, 449); the words in which he describes it, taking his cue from his interlocutress, show the extent of his dread—"Monstrous above all . . . and I imagine, by the same stroke, quite hideous and offensive" (XVII, 450). Alice Staverton's even more ambiguous attitude to his alter ego, whom she tells him she has seen twice in a dream, is contained in the various enigmatic remarks she makes to quench his curiosity: "I feel it would have been quite splendid, quite huge, and monstrous" (XVII, 450). We gather that she loves him for whatever he is and would have loved him for whatever he might have been: "How should I not have liked you?" is her twice-repeated answer to his question of whether she would have liked him "that way" (XVII, 450). With the close of this section we have all that we need to know about the nature of Brydon's obsession and his determination to see the "wretch," an appellation that beautifully indicates the interlocked knot of his desire and his dread. No further scenes between the hero and his friend are necessary to demonstrate the intensity of his obsession, and Alice Staverton is appropriately absent from the second, and central, section of the tale.

This section can be subdivided into two parts. In the first part, we have a summarized account of Spencer Brydon's "particular form of surrender to his obsession"; in the second, covering about sixteen pages, we have a scenic depiction of the climactic episode in this surrender. The first part spans the initial stages of his nocturnal adventures in the house on the jolly corner; temporally it extends over several weeks. Brydon's life in this period is mentioned as having been split into two halves:

He circulated, talked, renewed, loosely and pleasantly, old relations—met indeed, so far as he could, new expectations and seemed to make out on the whole that in spite of the career, of such different contacts, which he had spoken of to Miss Staverton as ministering so little, for those who might have watched it, to edification, he was positively rather liked than not. He was a dim secondary social success—and all with people who had truly not an idea of him. It was all mere surface sound, this murmur of their welcome, this popping of their corks—just as his gestures of response were extravagant shadows, emphatic in proportion as they meant little, of some game of *ombres chinoises*. He projected himself all day, in thought, straight over the bristling line of hard unconscious heads and into the other, the real, the waiting life; the life that, as soon as he had heard behind him the click of his great house-door, began for him, on the jolly corner, as beguilingly as the slow opening bars of some rich music follows the tap of the conductor's wand. (XVII, 454-455)

I have quoted this passage to point out how, in a typical summary, the author imperceptibly merges his own voice with the consciousness of his central character so that the two are nearly inextricable. The very choice of descriptive words is determined by their dual origin—they seem to proceed simultaneously from the author's and the character's mind. It may be postulated that this is so where the author does not want to maintain an ironic distance between his own point of view and that of his hero. For instance, in similar passages in "The Beast in the Jungle" and "The Bench of Desolation," we are conscious of the intended ironic margin maintained by the author in regard to what goes on in the mind of John Marcher and

Herbert Dodd. Another point illustrated by the passage just quoted is the remarkable pictorial economy of a Jamesian summary. Thus the spectacle of Spencer Brydon's social "circulation" and its irrelevance to his own preoccupation is inimitably caught in the "mere surface sound, this murmur of their welcome, this popping of their corks." Notice also the contrast of the "surface sound" with "the click of his great house-door" and "the slow opening bars of some rich music [that] follows the tap of the conductor's wand." The wide distance between his waking and his nocturnal life—his "unreal" and his "real" life—could hardly be better expressed.

Brydon's obsessive probe into the "mystical other world . . . of all the old baffled forsworn possibilities" (XVII, 455) is shown as it progresses from stage to stage. At first by his "hushed presence" he wakes "them [the "possibilities"] into such measure of ghostly life as they might still enjoy" (XVII, 455-456). Then these possibilities take "the Form" he imagines himself to be hunting; the Form then is pictured by him as a Beast,[27] "the conviction of [whose] probable, in fact [whose] already quite sensible, quite audible evasion of pursuit grew for him from night to night, laying on him finally a rigour to which nothing in his life had been comparable" (XVII, 456). The image of the chase is presented as elaborating itself in his mind until, after many nights of daring pursuit, he begins to strike himself as "some monstrous stealthy cat" (XVII, 458). This transference of the beast image to himself is another fine stroke; it perhaps would take a "monstrous stealthy cat" to waylay that other beast. The crucial stage in this preparatory phase of his adventure is reached when he becomes conscious of a partial reversal of the roles played by himself and the still invisible Form of his alter ego. He becomes aware "of his being definitely followed, tracked at a distance carefully taken and to the express end that he should the less confidently, less arrogantly, appear to himself merely to pursue. It worried, it finally broke him up, for it proved, of all the conceivable impressions, the one least suited to his book" (XVII, 460). When Brydon has reached this stage of his probe, which allegorically speaking represents his developed awareness of the survivals of his other self within him—he is both the haunter and the haunted—the author switches the narrative from a summary to a fully sustained scene.

Since, however, there is no other visible character in the greater part of this scene—even when toward the end of it the "presence" appears in a visible form, it is not vocal—it resembles what we may call, taking our cue from Brydon's own image of Pantaloon and Harlequin, a pantomime.[28] We watch his movements and overhear his thoughts as he accomplishes his fateful ritual in the dark. What passes in his mind is dramatized through the use of inverted commas: "I've hunted him till he has 'turned': that, up there, is what has happened—he's the fanged or the antlered animal brought at last to bay" (XVII, 461). A later writer would perhaps have rendered such thoughts in the hero's mind by an attempted emulation or adaptation of Joyce's stream-of-consciousness technique. James employs an earlier convention and does not flinch from commenting on the limitations of his method: "There came to him, as I say—but determined by an influence beyond my notation!—the acuteness of this certainty; under which however the next moment he had broken into a sweat that he would as little have consented to attribute to fear as he would have dared immediately to act upon it for enterprise" (XVII, 461). It may be mentioned here that the presence of the author throughout this scene is clearly noticeable even when it is not so obvious as in the authorial "I" of the above quotation.

The first striking moment in the scene is when Spencer Brydon experiences a "duplication of consciousness" (XVII, 461) and rejoices in the fear that his hitherto frightened other self has begun to cause in him: "It was as if it would have shamed him that a character so associated with his own should triumphantly succeed in just skulking, should to the end not risk the open; so that the drop of this danger was, on the spot, a great lift of the whole situation" (XVII, 462). This lift, however, is compatible with the brief spell of panic that he masters and after which "the room, the other contiguous rooms, extraordinarily, seemed lighter—so light, almost, that at first he took the change for day" (XVII, 463). Thus the picture of struggle with his fears is achieved with an exceptional psychological realism and vividness and its successful outcome reflected in the increase he sees in the surrounding light. The tempo of his agitation is accelerated when he soon becomes aware of the door "closed *since* his former visitation, the matter probably of a quarter of an hour before" (XVII, 465). Explaining this anomaly to himself at first by the thought that "another agent" had closed the door, he finds himself up against a new surge of terror: "Ah this time at last they *were,* the two, the opposed projections of him, in presence; and this time, as much as one would, the question of danger loomed. With it rose, as not before, the question of courage—for what he knew the blank face of the door to say to him was 'Show us how much you have!'" (XVII, 466-467). Soon, however, Brydon reads an altogether opposite meaning in "the blank face of the door"—it seems to suggest the value of the proverbially better part of valor. To prove to himself that he can act upon this hint, he walks up to the closed door and addresses a silent communication to the imagined presence behind it: "If you won't then—good: I spare you and I give up. You affect me as by the appeal positively for pity: you convince me that for reasons rigid and sublime—what do I know?—we both of us should have suffered. I respect them then, and, though moved and privileged as, I believe, it has never been given to man, I retire, I renounce—never, on my honour, to try again. So rest for ever—and let *me!*" (XVII, 468).

With this ritualistic farewell Brydon retreats to the front of the house, thinking that the spell is now broken, and opens half a casement; but the outer world fails to respond to him. His ordeal is not yet over: he has not yet faced his alter ego, and the discretion he has read into the phenomenon of the mysteriously closed door is probably just a rationalization of his fear of facing it. This seems to be implicit in his going back toward the closed door to see if it is open now and in his stopping short before he reaches it, for "*should* he see the door open, it would all too abjectly be the end of him" (XVII, 471). This turn in his thoughts dramatizes the inconsistency of his reasoning and his intense fear of the lurking presence. Under the pressure of this fear we see him descending the stairs in a markedly harassed state, rendered through the audible harshness of his feet on the floors and the elaborated image of "some watery underworld" (XVII, 472, 473).

But he cannot escape an encounter with the Form that his own ruthless "interrogation of the past"[29] has caused to wake. So Brydon, in spite of the fear that has driven him down the stairs, finally "let himself go with the sense that here *was* at last something to meet, to touch, to take, to know—something all unnatural and dreadful, but to advance upon which was the condition for him either of liberation or of supreme defeat" (XVII, 474-475). He ultimately faces his alter ego not so much in fear as in desperation. The encounter is rendered in a manner that resembles the slow solemn unveiling of a terrible masterpiece. The veil itself is made of a rare fabric: "the vague darkness to which the thin admitted dawn, glimmering archwise over the whole outer door, made a semicircular margin, a cold silvery nimbus that seemed to play a little as he looked—to shift and expand and contract" (XVII, 474). Only by quoting it can one do full justice to the way in which the portrait behind the veil is projected:

Rigid and conscious, spectral yet human, a man of his own substance and stature waited there to measure himself with his power to dismay. This only could it be—this only till he recognised, with his advance, that what made the face dim was the pair of raised hands that covered it and in which, so far from being offered in defiance, it was buried as for dark deprecation. So Brydon, before him, took him in; with every fact of him now, in the higher light, hard and acute—his planted stillness, his vivid truth, his grizzled bent head and white masking hands, his queer actuality of evening-dress, of dangling double eye-glass, of gleaming silk lappet and white linen, of pearl button and gold watch-guard and polished shoe. No portrait by a great modern master could have presented him with more intensity, thrust him out of his frame with more art, as if there had been 'treatment,' of the consummate sort, in his every shade and salience. The revulsion, for our friend, had become, before he knew it, immense—this drop, in the act of apprehension, to the sense of his adversary's inscrutable manoeuvre. That meaning at least, while he gaped, it offered him; for he could but gape at his other self in this other anguish, gape as a proof that *he*, standing there for the achieved, the enjoyed, the triumphant life, couldn't be faced in his triumph. Wasn't the proof in the splendid covering hands, strong and completely spread?—so spread and so intentional that, in spite of a special verity that surpassed every other, the fact that one of these hands had lost two fingers, which were reduced to stumps, as if accidentally shot away, the face was effectually guarded and saved. (XVII, 475-476)

The high quality of visual imagination displayed in this passage needs no comment. The last jerk to the veil is given when the hands are dropped and the face is uncovered. The effect of this final exposure on Brydon is overwhelming. It is rendered through the quickened pace of the concluding paragraph, which throbs with the horror produced in him just before he faints, and through the aggressively advancing figure of the "evil, odious, blatant, vulgar" stranger (XVII, 477).

Had the tale ended here, its effect might have been like that of "The Beast in the Jungle." Also in that case our interpretation of it would have been constricted by several puzzling ambiguities about the author's attitude to Spencer Brydon. But the tale goes on for another brief section, which dispels the notion that Brydon has been vanquished by the terrible vision of his might-have-been past. On the contrary, we gather from this section that he has been reassured about what he has been to the extent of virtual rejuvenation. The most remarkable feature of this section is its profoundly peaceful tone as contrasted with the profoundly peaceless tone of the preceding section. Brydon has been dispossessed of the lingering remnants of his undesirable self: "He had come back, yes—come back from further away than any man but himself had ever travelled; but it was strange how with this sense what he had come back *to* seemed really the great thing, and as if his prodigious journey had been all for the sake of it" (XVII, 478-479). A few lines further we are told that he has been brought back "to knowledge, to knowledge—yes, this was the beauty of his state; which came to resemble more and more that of a man who has gone to sleep on some news of a great inheritance, and then, after dreaming it away, after profaning it with matters strange to it, has waked up again to serenity of certitude and has only to lie and watch it grow. This was the drift of his patience—that he had only to let it shine on him" (XVII, 479). "Serenity of certitude" is indeed the essence of the change that has taken place in him.

At one crucial stage of his nocturnal adventure, Brydon had seen himself as a hero of the age of romance, "since what age of romance, after all, could have matched either the state of his mind or 'objectively,' as they said, the wonder of his situation?" (XVII, 464). This image is now completed when Alice Staverton rewards him with a kiss. "It was the seal of their situation—of which he tasted the impress for a long blissful moment of silence" (XVII, 480-481). The scene of their tender conversation in which they compare notes and exchange endearments is one of the most moving, and one of the rarest, love scenes in the wide expanse of James's works. Alice's solicitous "acceptance" of Brydon's alter ego does not confuse the meaning of the tale, provided we do not tear it out of context:

"And when this morning I again saw I knew it would be because you had—and also then, from the first moment, because you somehow wanted me. *He* seemed to tell me of that. So why," she strangely smiled, "shouldn't I like him?"

It brought Spencer Brydon to his feet. "You 'like' that horror—?"

"I *could* have liked him. And to me," she said, "he was no horror. I had accepted him."

"'Accepted'—?" Brydon oddly sounded.

"Before, for the interest of his difference—yes. And as *I* didn't disown him, as *I* knew him—which you at last, confronted with him in his difference, so cruelly didn't, my dear —well, he must have been, you see, less dreadful to me. And it may have pleased him that I pitied him." (XVII, 484)

This suffices to suggest that Alice is less hard on Brydon's alter ego chiefly because she would have loved Brydon in any shape, even as May Bartram of "The Beast" loved

Marcher, and we should recall her assertion earlier in the tale: "How should I not have liked you?" (XVII, 450). Also, her pity is for someone who has indirectly brought them together. Finally, it is pity for someone who is now at last dead. Her last sentence, the last sentence of the tale, is significant: "'And he isn't—no, he isn't—*you!*' she murmured as he drew her to his breast" (XVII, 484). It suggests unmistakably that she is not ignoring the enormous difference between Brydon as he might have been and Brydon as he has been, is, and will probably be.

The last section, then, depicts the calm after the storm. It marks the end of Brydon's obsession and shows the salubrious effect of that end; Brydon is reborn, and the sweetest fruit of this rebirth is the consummation of his love for Alice Staverton. The "moral" of the tale is clear: given the type of alternative self that Brydon, or any man like him, might have had, his wholeness and health follow an exorcization of that other self. In other words, it does not celebrate the repudiation of all the unfulfilled possibilities of one's past, but only of certain kinds of unfulfilled possibilities. The supreme power of the tale, however, lies in its avoidance of a simple didactic approach to this idea, in its adoption of an exceptionally complex artistic approach.

In the foregoing analyses of these three interconnected tales, I have denied myself the psychoanalytical insights offered by Saul Rosensweig and Robert Rogers. Rogers, for instance, suggests that "The Jolly Corner" is "like 'The Beast in the Jungle' . . . a tragic lament for a life unlived, for deeds undone."[30] To me "The Jolly Corner," unlike "The Beast," is a joyous embodiment of a life lived, of deeds done. Again Rogers considers it "noteworthy that throughout the story Alice Staverton likes—in fact, prefers—the *alter ego* to Brydon himself."[31] This also seems to me a distortion of what Alice Staverton actually likes and prefers in the tale. The real trouble with Rogers' reading of "The Jolly Corner" is that it is subservient to the biographical-psychoanalytical ax that he wants to grind. An examination of this grinding would involve me in too detailed a refutation of all the phallic and womb symbols that he so blandly points out in the tale. Instead, perhaps, I should invoke Harry Levin's admonition of much that passes for psychoanalytic criticism: "It reduces our vocabulary of symbols to a few which are so crudely fundamental and so monotonously recurrent that they cannot help the critic to perform his primary function, which is still—I take it—to discriminate. Nature abounds in protuberances and apertures. Convexities and concavities, like Sir Thomas Browne's quincunxes, are everywhere. The forms they compose are not always enhanced or illuminated by reading our sexual obsessions into them."[32]

These three tales, together with "The Bench of Desolation," represent, in my opinion, the apex of James's method in his shorter omniscient narratives. In them we see the end of the story as a simple story. The focus shifts almost entirely from external to internal reality. The importance of what happens lies exclusively in how it happens. By a proper control of his omniscience, the narrator succeeds in dramatizing the consciousness of the protagonist to a degree that is unrivaled in the other tales of James. By a careful organization of summary and scene, the author achieves economy and concentration to an extent that is not seen elsewhere. The effect of terror produced, the spectacle of the protagonists' alienation, the torment of their quest and the ecstasy of their self-realiza-

tion, the relentlessness with which they pursue their ends
—all these factors combine to give these tales an atmosphere of contemporaneity. We see the modern man—his
terrifying loneliness and his strivings to confront that loneliness—reflected in a mirror that is also modern. After
reading these tales, one can see the truth of the assertion
that James is indeed our contemporary.

Conclusion

IT HAS been implied in the first part of this study that, in his first-person tales, James employs the age-old convention of first-person oral narration, adapting it to suit his unusually sophisticated compositional concerns and rigors. Except in two early tales—"A Light Man" and "The Diary of a Man of Fifty"—he almost never uses the first-person narrator primarily as an autobiographer. More often than not, the Jamesian narrator is a biographer, a raconteur, or a perceptive reporter of things that have happened to others. In a way, James denied himself the gripping immediacy of an autobiographical narrative, where the autobiography concerns not so much the external events as the internal reflections of the narrator-hero, his lonely conversations with himself about himself. Of course, this is not to deny or underestimate the peculiar pitfalls and challenges of this narrative mode; but James never fully faced them. In the preface to *The Ambassadors* he tries to explain why he did not make Strether "at once hero and historian" so that he could have enjoyed "the double privilege of subject and object": he thought, on the basis of the lesson provided by *Gil Blas* and *David Copperfield,* that "the first person, in the long piece, is a form foredoomed to looseness"; he was afraid of "the terrible *fluidity* of self-revelation."[1]

We hear an echo of the same view in James's letter to

H. G. Wells of March 3, 1911, where he chides his discomforting younger friend for "riding so hard again [in *The New Machiavelli*] that accurst autobiographic form which puts a premium on the loose, the improvised, the cheap and the easy."[2] There is an ostensible divergence from these views in James's comments on Conrad's *Chance,* where successive first-person narrators seem to pass muster with him, albeit with a few reservations, because their "circumferential tones . . . keep so clear of the others, the central, the numerous and various voices of the agents proper, those expressive of the action itself and in whom the objectivity resides"—because, in simpler words, they are not really autobiographers.[3] This is not the place to dispute at length James's rather summary dismissal of the autobiographical form of the novel, but it may be pointed out that *Gil Blas* and *David Copperfield* are but nominally autobiographical and that James did not perhaps fully take into account the possible distinction between a first-person novel and an autobiographical novel in which the hero, like Strether and unlike David Copperfield, is not a mere technical hero but the main center of the novelist's intention. In other words, I think it is possible to write a subtle and complex psychological novel, without any fluidity, in the autobiographical form.

Be that as it may, the point I wish to emphasize is that even in his tales—and in his only first-person novel *The Sacred Fount*[4]—James never really conceded the "double privilege" to his narrators. Thus even the governess of "The Turn of the Screw" is not primarily an autobiographical narrator, and this in spite of her involvement in the action, which is deeper than that of any other Jamesian narrator. The overwhelming terror and the rich psychological tone of that tale are vitally connected with her relatively greater absorption in the action. Yet this does not controvert my point, demonstrated through the several analyses, that the first-person narrator, as James used him, is more of a method and less of a character in his own right. This can be reinforced by evidence provided in the *Notebooks* where, again and again, he chooses a first-person narrator not for his interest as a character but because of his suitability as a compositional device.[5]

By way of illustration, we may look at how James decided upon the narrator of "The Next Time." He begins by ruminating over "the idea of the poor man, the artist, the man of letters, who all his life is trying . . . to do something *vulgar,* to take the measure of the huge, flat foot of the public."[6] Then, after he has reminisced about his own experience with Whitelaw Reid of the *New York Tribune,*[7] he goes on to develop the idea further: "A little drama, climax, a denouement, a small tragedy of the *vie litteraire* —mightn't one oppose to him some contrasted figure of another type—the creature who, dimly conscious of deep-seated vulgarity, is always trying to be refined, which doesn't in the least prevent him—or her—from suc-ceeding. Say, it's a woman."[8] By now the subject is clear to James. And then he comes to the problem of its presentation: "Mightn't *she* be the narrator, with a fine grotesque *inconscience?* So that the whole thing becomes a masterpiece of close and finished irony? There *may* be a difficulty in that—I seem to see it: so that the necessity may be for the narrator to be conscient, or SEMI-CONSCIENT, perhaps, to get the full force of certain effects."[9] In his next encounter with the subject, he returns to the problem of the narrator, this time to reject his original choice altogether: "The difficulty is that the narrator must be fully and richly, must be ironically, *conscient:* that is, *musn't* he? Can I take such a person and make him—or her —narrate my little drama *naïvement?* I don't think so—

especially with so *short* a chance: I risk wasting my material and missing my effect. I must, I think, have my real ironic painter; but if I take that line I must presumably include the vulgarian somehow in my little tale. *I* become the narrator, either impersonally or in my unnamed, unspecified personality. Say I chose the latter line, as in the *Death of the Lion,* the *Coxon Fund,* etc."[10]

Apart from indicating the intimate relation of the Jamesian narrator to his subject, these remarks also suggest the point that James's first-person narrator is generally a "conscient," sometimes a "semi-conscient," but almost never a fully "inconscient" person. It seems that James was so apprehensive of "wasting [his] material and missing [his] effect" that he seldom employed an inconscient narrator. The few exceptions, as I have noted above, are made quite unambiguous through the tone of the tales concerned. Not to take James's narrators, in the absence of clear internal evidence, as reliable personae would therefore force us into perverse readings of almost all his first-person tales. One feels surprised, for instance, why H— of "The Madonna" has not been taken to task by someone as *the* person responsible for the death of Theobald; or why should not the narrator of "Four Meetings" be castigated as a tempter of poor Caroline; or why is the narrator of "The Author of Beltraffio" not blamed for the death of Dolcino? Why should the governess alone be suspect?

The truth seems to be that all of James's narrators are made to conceal their detachment as outsiders behind a convincing pretense of personal involvement in the action. Wherever they precipitate the catastrophe, an irony is produced because their intentions are almost always unquestionable—the only exception to this formulation would be, not the governess, but the narrator of

"The Aspern Papers." To say this is not to suggest that the personae should be identified completely with James himself, but that their individual traits, insofar as they have any, should not be confounded with the generic traits they owe to their employment as James's deputies. This confusion is bound to play havoc with the meaning of a given tale, as best exemplified by the controversy over "The Turn of the Screw."

If the choice of the persona is partly determined by the subject—although it would be very hard to generalize or to lay down a rigid formula about what kind of subject is suitable only to the first-person narrative—the persona, once chosen, has an even more decisive influence on the tone, structure, and style of James's first-person narratives. On the basis of the tales studied, it can be said that the tone is generally light—even when the subject is serious or painful—that the structure often corresponds to a chronological succession of events, interspersed by the narrator's persuasive comments and conjectures, and that the style is much less involuted as contrasted with the omniscient-narrator tales. The precise manner in which the Jamesian narrator functions varies from tale to tale, depending upon the particular theme, the intended emphasis, the desired scope, and so on.

Thus in the stories of artists, the narrator, himself an artist of sorts, is employed mainly in the interest of what James called an "operative irony," which "implies and projects the possible other case, the case rich and edifying where the actuality is pretentious and vain."[11] In all these tales, with the exception of "The Figure in the Carpet" (whose ironic peculiarities have already been pointed out), the narrator is a mouthpiece for those points of view which the impersonal author would like to impress upon the reader. If the comments and observations of this narrator strike the reader as either boring or unpersuasive, the tale is an obvious failure. Similarly, in the tales of the supernatural, the narrator must, above everything else, succeed in exploiting that "blest faculty of wonder," that "strange passion planted in the heart of man for his [the novelist's] benefit, a mysterious provision made for him in the scheme of nature."[12] This task is most successfully performed by the governess of "The Turn of the Screw," which is one important reason for that tale's superiority over all the other first-person ghost tales of James or of any other American or English writer. We can, moreover, trace the application of this narrative principle in tales belonging to any other thematic category, in the international tales, for instance. Finally, the Jamesian narrator is more or less expansive in accordance with the scope of the given situation. Thus in tales of nouvelle length, we find him more relaxed, less hardpressed for space, than in tales of the genuinely anecdotic variety where he is called upon to deal with either a single incident or a single character.

Underlying all these variations, however, we can recognize a family likeness among all the Jamesian personae. Their outstanding features are intelligence, wit, curiosity, skepticism, and, above all, an infallible intuitive faculty. These are what have been previously described as the generic traits of the Jamesian narrator, traits that should be understood in their relation to the technical procedures of James and not subjected to psychoanalysis. Of all these traits, the intuitive faculty has evidently given rise to the greatest number of misconceptions. One does not have to invoke Bergson or Proust in order to justify the validity of the narrator's intuitive approach. To begin with, this approach is not confined to James's first-person narrators. Several, if not all, of his important characters are addicted to the habit of intuiting, of anticipating one another's thoughts, of divining those events still in the offing. The most important single exemplification of this habit is the charming telegraphist of "In the Cage" (1898)—which is not a first-person narrative—about whom James remarked: "My central spirit, in the anecdote, is, for verisimilitude, I grant, too ardent a focus of divination; but without this excess the phenomena detailed would have lacked their principle of cohesion."[13] The point is that the phenomena detailed in "In the Cage" are not false just because, in the interest of "their principle of cohesion," James has chosen to detail them through the telegraphist's inordinately developed power of divination. By the same token, the phenomena detailed in "The Turn of the Screw" are not unreal just because, in the interest of suspense, James has chosen to reflect them through the governess' gradually developing power of divination. To adapt an observation of Albert J. Guerard, all Jamesian narrators anticipate "the Faulknerian device of narration through speculative commentary, of reporting disguised as conjecture," for "the conjectural method is particularly useful where the narrator does not want to report a scene, or cannot, and where it is desirable for the reader to do a good deal of active imagining."[14] Further, in James, the narrators' intuitions occasionally serve the purpose of depicting what goes on in the minds of the principal characters. Through this device James seeks to transcend some of the limitations of the first-person narrator, the observer from outside; he bestows upon him a certain degree of disguised omniscience and directs our attention to what goes on behind the screen of external incidents.

Here I have thought it fit to concentrate upon James's use of the first-person-singular in order to call the reader's attention to the technical problems of the tales. The first part of the study emphasizes the method of James in his first-person tales, although other matters have naturally been mentioned along the way. The essence of this method cannot be grasped without a clear idea of the narrator's central role in it.

In the second part of my study I have tried to demonstrate how in his third-person tales James masks his presence and controls his omniscience. "Point of view," as I understand the term—although I have deliberately avoided its frequent use—means the relation in which a writer happens or, in the case of an exceptionally deliberate craftsman like James, chooses to stand with regard to his narrative. In his first-person narratives James solves this problem through a carefully chosen deputy; in his impersonally narrated tales he tackles it through the agency of the omniscient narrator, who doubtless often identifies himself with the point of view (used now in its normal, nontechnical sense) of the principal character. However, in cases where this identification is not intended to be complete, as in "The Beast in the Jungle" and to a limited extent in "The Bench of Desolation," we can notice some gleams of irony, which proceed precisely from the duplicity of the point of view. Again, occasionally—and this is of course a minor matter—we see the authorial "I" in almost all his fictions, including *The Ambassadors*. Lastly, it needs to be pointed out that a story never can tell itself.[15] The teller is always there, and it is the task of the critic to evaluate the effectiveness of the variety of ways in which the author seeks to become invisible.

In the narrative structure of these tales there is a far more deliberately controlled alternation of summary and scene than is common with most writers. James attached

great importance to what he called the "'scenic' law."[16]
He saw many of his tales "as little constituted dramas,
little exhibitions founded on the logic of the 'scene,' the
unit of the scene, the general scenic consistency"; he saw
the passages between one scene and the other as "prepara-
tive," and compared the alternations between summary
and scene to the various instruments in an orchestra.[17]
In some tales, depending on such factors as the lapse of
time involved and the degree of compression desired,
summary takes predominance over the scene. The "scene"
again is not always to be equated with a dramatized scene,
for it can be, as in "The Jolly Corner," a picture of the protagonist's consciousness in turmoil. In the anecdotes—and
this would cover first-person anecdotes as well—James
often resorts to summary more than to scene, particularly
where the anecdote happens to be more in the nature of a
compressed nouvelle. The same consideration would also
apply to a case where the nouvelle is a compressed novel,
as in "Julia Bride."

This raises once again the problem of an apposite
description for James as a writer of short fiction. If we
view him as a short-story writer, applying the standards
derived from Poe or Maupassant, he is bound to cause
dissatisfaction. We must take him primarily as a *nouvelliste*
in his shorter fiction, since most of his great tales fall into
the category of "the beautiful and blest *nouvelle*."[18] The
short story no doubt represented a persistent challenge to
him, so that in the *Notebooks* we hear him invoking
Maupassant—"Oh, spirit of Maupassant, come to my
aid!"[19]—more often than any other single writer. He
undertook to meet this challenge more than once and
wrote an impressive number of anecdotes, several of which,
however, remain far below the excellence of his nouvelles.
He achieved relatively greater success in those anecdotes

which lean either to the character sketch or to the parable.

In connection with his many parables, it is instructive to note what James had to say about his great American predecessor, Hawthorne:

Hawthorne, in his metaphysical moods, is nothing if not allegorical, and allegory, to my sense, is quite one of the lighter exercises of the imagination. Many excellent judges, I know, have a great stomach for it; they delight in symbols and correspondences, in seeing a story told as if it were another and a very different story. I frankly confess that I have, as a general thing, but little enjoyment of it, and that it has never seemed to me to be, as it were, a first-rate literary form. . . . it is apt to spoil two good things—a story and a moral, a meaning and a form; and the taste for it is responsible for a large part of the forcible-feeble writing that has been inflicted upon the world. The only case in which it is endurable is when it is extremely spontaneous, when the analogy presents itself with eager promptitude. When it shows signs of having been groped and fumbled for, the needful illusion is of course absent, and the failure complete. Then the machinery alone is visible, and the end to which it operates becomes a matter of indifference.[20]

James goes on to quote Poe, with approval, on this matter.[21] Poe bore down even more heavily on allegory— "In defence of allegory (however or for whatever object employed) there is scarcely one respectable word to be said"—but he also suggested an important, though somewhat grudging, exception: "Where the suggested meaning runs through the obvious one in a *very* profound undercurrent, so as never to interfere with the upper one without our own volition, so as never to show itself unless *called* to the surface, there only, for the proper uses of fictitious narrative, is it available at all."[22]

Thus both James and Poe, while expressing their dissatisfaction with allegory as employed by Hawthorne, also attempted an extension of the term; and it is interesting that neither of them altogether banished allegory from his works, even in the sense in which they most strongly disapproved of it.[23] When James published his book on Hawthorne in 1879, he was, indirectly at least, trying to assess his own indebtedness to that "beautiful, natural, original genius."[24] By then he had properly assimilated the influence of Hawthorne. As Matthiessen has correctly pointed out, in his earliest stories James "had depended on allegory in the manner of Hawthorne. . . . As he went on to master all the skills of realism, he grew dissatisfied with allegory's obvious devices; and yet, particularly towards the end of his career, realistic details had become merely the covering for a content that was far from realistic."[25] This journey from simple allegory in the early tales—"The Romance of Certain Old Clothes" and "Ben-volio"—to complex parable in the late tales—"The Great Good Place" and "The Beast in the Jungle"—is reflected in the spontaneous fusion of images and ideas. In my discussion of his last tales I have tried to focus attention on this fusion.

On comparing the omniscient-narrator tales with those discussed in the first part, one is bound to notice great differences in tone, style, and structure. Some of these differences, as I have hinted, cut across the chronological groupings of the early, middle, and late periods. The tone of the omniscient-narrator tales is more haunting; their style gets more involuted and nuanced as James probes with greater self-assurance into the inner sanctuaries of his characters; their structures are more dense because they are not structures so much of incidents as of perceptions inwardly attained. Barring a few exceptions, such as "The Turn of the Screw" and "The Birthplace," James's first-person tales are essentially comic in mode and impact, while his major omniscient-narrator tales are essentially tragic. An accompanying generalization would be that the first-person tales deal with the surface, which is not the same as superficial, aspects of human affairs, while the omniscient tales illuminate the hidden mysteries of the human condition. From this, however, it does not follow that the first-person singular as such is inimical to a tragic approach. But considering that James employed his first-person narrators more or less as objective outsiders, he could not have achieved the inwardness and depth of his omniscient-narrator tales. Perhaps I should add that the best of James's first-person tales, according to their own nature and aims, succeed as well as the omniscient-narrator tales; the two combine to give us a measure of the great breadth and depth of James's observations of human life.

Finally, I would like to end on the note with which I began this book. The tales of James are as important in their own right as his novels. I have concentrated on the technical aspects of the tales in view of my belief that technique should occupy a central position and that it is generally ignored in favor of other, seemingly more impressive, matters. Besides, as Mark Schorer has said, "When we speak of technique, then, we speak of nearly everything."[26] Of course, I do not claim that I have spoken of nearly everything. According to Ezra Pound, "Honest criticism . . . cannot get much further than saying to one's reader exactly what one would say to the friend who approaches one's bookshelf asking: 'What the deuce shall I read?' "[27] I have told this hypothetical friend something of what, in my opinion, he should read from James's tales and given him some of my reasons for his doing so.

CHRONOLOGY
OF THE TALES
NOTES · INDEX

Chronology of the Tales

ALL THE tales of Henry James are listed below in chronological order according to their dates of first publication. The
number of words given in each case is approximate. The
first-person tales, including those in the diary or the epistolary
form, are starred. In cases where the titles were later revised
by James, the original titles are indicated parenthetically.
For fuller information, consult *A Bibliography of Henry James*
by Leon Edel and Dan H. Laurence (London: Rupert Hart-
Davis, 1957; rev. ed., 1961).

1.	A Tragedy of Error	1864	7,500
2.	The Story of a Year	1865	15,000
3.	A Landscape Painter*	1866	12,000
4.	A Day of Days	1866	8,000
5.	My Friend Bingham*	1867	7,500
6.	Poor Richard	1867	22,000
7.	The Story of a Masterpiece	1868	11,000
8.	The Romance of Certain Old Clothes	1868	7,000
9.	A Most Extraordinary Case	1868	16,000
10.	A Problem	1868	5,000
11.	De Grey: A Romance	1868	13,500
12.	Osborne's Revenge	1868	14,000
13.	A Light Man*	1869	10,500
14.	Gabrielle de Bergerac*	1869	21,500
15.	Travelling Companions*	1870	19,000
16.	A Passionate Pilgrim*	1871	28,000
17.	At Isella*	1871	11,000
18.	Master Eustace*	1871	11,500
19.	Guest's Confession*	1872	24,500

20.	The Madonna of the Future*	1873	14,500
21.	The Sweetheart of M. Briseux*	1873	12,000
22.	The Last of the Valerii*	1874	12,000
23.	Madame de Mauves	1874	33,000
24.	Adina*	1874	16,000
25.	Professor Fargo*	1874	13,500
26.	Eugene Pickering*	1874	17,000
27.	Benvolio	1875	17,000
28.	Crawford's Consistency*	1876	10,500
29.	The Ghostly Rental*	1876	11,000
30.	Four Meetings*	1877	11,500
31.	Rose-Agatha* (Theodolinde)	1878	6,500
32.	Daisy Miller (Daisy Miller: A Study)	1878	25,000
33.	Longstaff's Marriage	1878	10,500
34.	An International Episode	1878–79	32,000
35.	The Pension Beaurepas*	1879	23,000
36.	The Diary of a Man of Fifty*	1879	11,000
37.	A Bundle of Letters*	1879	14,000
38.	The Point of View*	1882	19,000
39.	The Siege of London	1883	35,000
40.	The Impressions of a Cousin*	1883	27,000
41.	Lady Barbarina (Lady Barberina)	1884	38,000
42.	Pandora	1884	19,000
43.	The Author of Beltraffio*	1884	19,000
44.	Georgina's Reasons	1884	25,000
45.	A New England Winter	1884	22,000
46.	The Path of Duty*	1884	14,000
47.	Mrs. Temperly (Cousin Maria)	1887	11,500
48.	Louisa Pallant*	1888	14,500
49.	The Aspern Papers*	1888	38,000
50.	The Liar	1888	20,500
51.	The Modern Warning (Two Countries)	1888	23,000
52.	A London Life	1888	44,000
53.	The Lesson of the Master	1888	26,000
54.	The Patagonia*	1888	23,000
55.	The Solution*	1889–90	18,000
56.	The Pupil	1891	18,000
57.	Brooksmith*	1891	6,500
58.	The Marriages	1891	12,000

59.	Sir Edmund Orme*	1891	10,500
60.	The Chaperon	1891	18,000
61.	Nona Vincent	1892	11,000
62.	The Private Life*	1892	13,000
63.	The Real Thing*	1892	10,000
64.	Lord Beaupre (Lord Beauprey)	1892	19,000
65.	The Visits* (The Visit)	1892	6,000
66.	Sir Dominick Ferrand (Jersey Villas)	1892	20,500
67.	Collaboration*	1892	7,500
68.	Owen Wingrave	1892	13,000
69.	Greville Fane*	1892	7,000
70.	The Wheel of Time	1892–93	16,000
71.	The Middle Years	1893	7,500
72.	The Death of the Lion*	1894	14,500
73.	The Coxon Fund*	1894	24,000
74.	The Next Time*	1895	16,000
75.	The Altar of the Dead	1895	15,000
76.	The Figure in the Carpet*	1896	15,500
77.	Glasses*	1896	19,000
78.	The Friends of the Friends* (The Way It Came)	1896	11,000
79.	The Turn of the Screw*	1898	44,500
80.	John Delavoy*	1898	13,500
81.	In the Cage	1898	38,000
82.	Covering End	1898	40,000
83.	The Given Case	1898–99	10,000
84.	Europe* ("Europe")	1899	7,500
85.	The Great Condition	1899	16,000
86.	Paste	1899	6,000
87.	The Real Right Thing	1899	5,500
88.	The Great Good Place	1900	10,000
89.	Maud Evelyn*	1900	11,000
90.	Miss Gunton of Poughkeepsie	1900	5,400
91.	The Special Type*	1900	7,500
92.	The Tone of Time*	1900	7,500
93.	The Two Faces (The Faces)	1900	6,000
94.	Broken Wings	1900	7,500
95.	The Tree of Knowledge	1900	6,500
96.	The Abasement of the Northmores	1900	8,500

97.	The Third Person	1900	12,500
98.	Mrs. Medwin	1901	9,000
99.	The Beldonald Holbein*	1901	9,500
100.	The Story in It	1902	7,000
101.	Flickerbridge	1902	8,000
102.	The Beast in the Jungle	1903	18,000
103.	The Birthplace	1903	22,500
104.	The Papers	1903	33,000
105.	Fordham Castle	1904	8,500
106.	Julia Bride	1908	14,500
107.	The Jolly Corner	1908	13,500
108.	The Velvet Glove	1909	10,000
109.	Mora Montravers	1909	21,500
110.	Crapy Cornelia	1909	10,500
111.	The Bench of Desolation	1909–10	18,000
112.	A Round of Visits	1910	11,000

Notes

1. Charles G. Hoffmann, *The Short Novels of Henry James* (New York: Bookman Associates, 1957). My point about the inappropriateness of the title becomes clear subsequently.

2. Joseph Warren Beach, *The Method of Henry James* (Philadelphia: Albert Saifer, rev. ed., 1954), p. 3. This book was first published in 1918; in the new edition the original text was left untouched, but a long introduction and a few notes were added. It must be mentioned in fairness to Beach that he qualifies his remark about the tales in the new notes (see p. 285).

3. Introduction to *The Odd Number: Thirteen Tales by Guy de Maupassant*, trans. Jonathan Sturges (New York: Harper, 1889), p. xiv.

4. *The Letters of Henry James*, 2 vols., ed. Percy Lubbock (New York: Charles Scribner's Sons, 1920), I, 31; cited hereafter as *Letters*.

5. *Letters*, I, 135.

6. *The Notebooks of Henry James*, ed. F. O. Matthiessen and Kenneth B. Murdock (New York: Oxford University Press, 1947), p. 269; cited hereafter as *Notebooks*.

7. *Letters*, I, 163.

8. *Notebooks*, p. 106.

9. *Selected Letters of Henry James*, ed. Leon Edel (London: Rupert Hart-Davis, 1956), p. 176. For two similar statements in two letters to Stevenson, see *Letters*, I, 157, 189.

10. *Letters*, I, 232.

11. *Notebooks*, p. 135.

12. *Notebooks*, p. 269.

13. James's expression in a letter, March 5, 1907, to Grace Norton; see *Letters*, II, 70.

14. The volumes referred to are XII, XIV, XV, XVI, XVII, and X, XI, XIII.

15. See *The Short Stories of Henry James*, ed. Clifton Fadiman

(New York: Random House, 1945); *Henry James: Selected Short Stories,* ed. Quentin Anderson (New York: Rinehart, 1950); and *The Great Short Novels of Henry James,* ed. Philip Rahv (New York: Dial Press, 1944).

16. See Hoffman, *The Short Novels of Henry James,* pp. 85-86, about "The Turn of the Screw."

17. Bowen, "Introduction: The Short Story," in *The Faber Book of Modern Stories* (London: Faber and Faber, 1937), p. 8. Similar views are expressed, a little more harshly, by Somerset Maugham in his introduction to *Tellers of Tales* (New York: Doubleday, Doran, 1939), pp. xxxvi-xxxvii: "When for this book I read, yet once again, the short stories of Henry James, I was troubled by the contrast offered by the triviality of so many of his themes and the elaboration of his treatment. He seems to have had no inkling that his subjects might be too slight to justify so intricate a method."

18. *The Art of the Novel: Critical Prefaces by Henry James,* introduction by Richard P. Blackmur (New York: Charles Scribner's Sons, 1934), p. 180; cited hereafter as *The Art of the Novel.*

19. *The Art of the Novel,* p. 4.

20. *Notebooks,* pp. 146, 346.

21. *The Art of the Novel,* pp. 139, 220, 231, 262.

22. *Ibid.,* p. 220.

23. *Ibid.,* p. 220.

24. *Ibid.,* p. 232.

25. *Ibid.,* p. 181. James is here speaking with reference to *The Reverberator,* which appeared to him "in the light of an exemplary anecdote, and at the same time quite in that of a little rounded drama" (*ibid.,* p. 180).

26. *Notebooks,* p. 212.

27. *The Art of the Novel,* p. 179.

28. *Ibid.,* p. 285.

29. *Ibid.,* p. 232-233.

30. Introduction to *Notebooks,* p. xvi.

31. *The Art of the Novel,* p. 240.

32. A recent exception to this is Richard Poirier, *The Comic Sense of Henry James: A Study of the Early Novels* (New York: Oxford University Press, 1960).

Chapter I. Three Early Tales

1. *The Art of the Novel,* p. 180.

2. The earliest of these tales, "A Landscape Painter," appeared in 1866 and the latest, "Maud-Evelyn," in 1900.

3. This is the form (volume and page) in which citations from

The Novels and Tales of Henry James (New York: Charles Scribner's Sons, 1907-1909), 24 vols., will be made throughout the text. Reference to works not included in the New York Edition, unless otherwise specified, are to *The Novels and Stories of Henry James* (London: Macmillan, 1921-1923), 35 vols. Citations from this edition will follow the same form as those from the New York Edition, with the addition of "M" for the publisher's name.

4. *The Art of the Novel,* p. 327.

5. See Cornelia Pulsifer Kelley, *The Early Development of Henry James* (Urbana: University of Illinois, 1930), pp. 149-150, for a more detailed account of the resemblance between Balzac's tale and "The Madonna"; also for the latter's partial indebtedness to Musset's *Lorenzaccio.*

6. *The Comedie Humaine of Honore de Balzac,* ed. George Saintsbury (New York: Croscup and Sterling, 1901), II, 240.

7. *Ibid.,* p. 227.

8. *The Early Development of Henry James,* p. 152.

9. *The Art of the Novel,* p. 192.

10. See Albert F. Gegenheimer, "Early and Late Revisions in Henry James's 'A Passionate Pilgrim,'" *American Literature,* XXIII (May 1951), 233-242.

11. *The Art of the Novel,* p. 290.

12. See *The Art of the Novel,* pp. 12-15.

13. Ford Madox Ford, whose lavish praise of James but rarely attains the balance of true criticism, has an interesting remark about one aspect of this tale: "For *A Passionate Pilgrim* is the apotheosis of the turf, the deer, the oak trees, the terraces of manor houses. It had never been so 'done' before and never again will it be so done." *Henry James: A Critical Study* (London: M. Secker, 1913), p. 110.

14. The situation of "A Passionate Pilgrim" was taken up again by James in his incomplete *The Sense of the Past* and somewhat reversed in "The Jolly Corner" (1908). In both works, however, the idea of the *Doppelgänger* is made central, and the ghostly element is emphasized to a much greater degree.

15. See, for example, Henry James, *Hawthorne* (London: Macmillan, 1879), pp. 3, 42-43.

16. *The Art of the Novel,* p. 177.

17. Ford, *Henry James,* p. 25.

Chapter II. Anecdotes

1. Henry James's amusing characterization of his dramatic years is from a letter, dated February 6, 1891, to William James. *Letters,* I, 181.

2. *The Art of the Novel,* p. 179; James is referring to "The Two Faces," one of his shortest tales.

3. "Europe" is one of the few tales in which James successfully achieved the brevity originally intended (7,500 words); no wonder therefore that he felt jubilant over this success in the preface. See *The Art of the Novel,* pp. 239-240.

4. Clifton Fadiman, ed., *The Short Stories of Henry James* (New York: Random House, 1945), p. 291.

5. Q. D. Leavis, "Henry James: The Stories," *Scrutiny,* XIV (Spring 1947), 223.

6. *The Art of the Novel,* p. 234.

Chapter III. Nouvelles (Also Parables)

1. See *The Art of the Novel,* p. 224; also R. P. Blackmur's views on the subject in "In the Country of the Blue," in *The Question of Henry James: A Collection of Critical Essays,* ed. F. W. Dupee (London: A. Wingate, 1947).

2. *The Art of the Novel,* p. 221.

3. *Ibid.*

4. *Ibid.,* p. 252.

5. *Ibid.,* p. 227.

6. *Ibid.,* p. 252. See also *Notebooks,* pp. 109-110.

7. This schizoid condition is common enough among writers— for instance, Balzac, Flaubert, Thomas Mann, and James himself to an extent. But James is concerned not with the pathological aspect of this condition, only with its salubrious effect on Clare Vawdrey's work.

8. *The Art of the Novel,* p. 224.

9. James probably had Dickens' Mrs. Leo Hunter in mind while creating Mrs. Wimbush with her fondness for the lions. See *The Pickwick Papers,* chap. 15.

10. James wrote two highly amusing tales wholly in the epistolary mode—"A Bundle of Letters" (1879) and "The Point of View" (1882).

11. *The Art of the Novel,* p. 229.

12. *Ibid.*

13. Matthiessen, Introduction to *Henry James: Stories of Writers and Artists* (Norfolk: New Directions, n.d.), p. 6.

14. *The Art of the Novel,* p. 228.

15. Blackmur, "In the Country of the Blue," p. 214.

16. *Ibid.,* pp. 214-215.

17. *The Art of Fiction and Other Essays by Henry James,* ed. Morris Roberts (New York: Oxford University Press, 1948), p. 216.

18. Westbrook, "The Supersubtle Fry," *Nineteenth-Century Fiction,* VIII (September 1953), 137-138.

19. *Ibid.,* p. 139.

20. Roditi, *Oscar Wilde* (Norfolk: New Directions, 1947), p. 111.

CHAPTER IV. THE TURNS OF THE SCREW

1. The history of this battle can be traced in *A Casebook on Henry James's "The Turn of the Screw,"* ed. Gerald Willen (New York: Crowell, 1960), a convenient anthology of most of the important controversial articles on the tale; hereafter cited as *Casebook.*

2. "The Ambiguity of Henry James," in *Casebook,* p. 121.

3. *Ibid.,* pp. 145, 147.

4. *Ibid.,* p. 153.

5. See *Notebooks,* pp. 220-223, and Chapter III above.

6. *Casebook,* p. 124.

7. *Ibid.,* p. 153.

8. *The Art of the Novel,* p. 245. Italics mine.

9. The original title of "The Friends of the Friends" was "The Way It Came," which James changed in the New York Edition. Wilson, misled by Marius Bewley (see *The Complex Fate* [London: Chatto and Windus, 1952], pp. 84-87), refers also to "The Liar" as if it were a first-person narrative, which it is not: "As has been noted by Mr. Marius Bewley . . . the liar is not the harmless romancer who is adored and protected by his wife, but the painter who is telling the story. This narrator has been in love with the wife" (*Casebook,* p. 153). The text of the tale provides no basis whatever for denying that the liar is Colonel Capadose, however harmless he may be.

10. *Casebook,* p. 146.

11. Leon Edel, ed., *The Ghostly Tales of Henry James* (New Brunswick: Rutgers University Press, 1948), p. 396. I do not, however, agree with Edel in his view that "the personality of the jealous woman—as indeed all the elements of this tale—foreshadows the governess of *The Turn of the Screw.*"

12. I have not referred to *The Sacred Fount* because, like "The Turn of the Screw," the whole case for this novel's ambiguity rests on some critics' willingness to take it as an ironic portrait of its narrator.

13. Wellek and Warren, *Theory of Literature* (New York: Harcourt, Brace, 1949), p. 34. For James's own views on the importance

of a writer's intention, consider "The Figure in the Carpet," and see *The Art of the Novel*, pp. 3, 56, 79, 134. James, it seems, was old-fashioned enough to attach great value to artistic intentions.

14. The best single refutation of the Freudian interpretation is R. B. Heilman, "The Freudian Reading of 'The Turn of the Screw,'" *Modern Language Notes*, LXII (November 1947), 433-445. Some others are: Nathan Bryllion Fagin, "Another Reading of *The Turn of the Screw*," 1941, *Casebook*, pp. 154-159; A. J. A. Waldock, "Mr. Edmund Wilson and *The Turn of the Screw*," 1947, *Casebook*, pp. 171-173; Glenn A. Reed, "Another Turn on James's 'The Turn of the Screw,'" 1949, *Casebook*, pp. 189-199; Charles G. Hoffmann, "Innocence and Evil in James's *The Turn of the Screw*," 1953, *Casebook*, pp. 212-222; Alexander E. Jones, "Point of View in *The Turn of the Screw*," 1959, *Casebook*, pp. 298-318. See also Robert Wolff, "The Genesis of 'The Turn of the Screw,'" *American Literature*, XIII (March 1941), 1-8.

15. *Casebook*, pp. 115-116. See also "Freudian Reading," pp. 442-443; Heilman, of course, believes in the testimony of Douglas.

16. It may, however, be suggested that the elaborateness of the prologue to "The Turn of the Screw" is in part due to the way James got his *donnée*; the prologue is essentially a dramatization of the *Notebooks* entry concerning the tale. See *Notebooks*, pp. 178-179.

17. See *The Art of the Novel*, p. 174: "She has 'authority,' which is a good deal to have given her, and I couldn't have arrived at so much had I clumsily tried for more." See also Edmund Wilson's distortion of this statement in *Casebook*, pp. 120, 121, and Heilman's explanation of it in "Freudian Reading," p. 434: "In the context he is talking merely about technical problems of composition, and what he is saying is, to use the trite terms of the rhetoric book, that he is telling the story entirely from the governess's point of view."

18. We may also keep in mind the fictional convention of the English governess, as in Charlotte Bronte, who was in James's mind while writing "The Turn of the Screw": "Was there a 'secret' at Bly—a mystery of Udolpho or an insane, an unmentionable relative in unsuspected confinement?" (XII, 179).

19. Marius Bewley uses the expression "appearance and reality" almost like a talisman in *The Complex Fate*; his discussion of "The Turn of the Screw" (pp. 96-111, 132-143) seems to me both confused and confusing, thanks to his reliance on Wilson's theory and to his desperate effort to prove his own.

20. Wilson, *Casebook*, p. 116.

21. See "Freudian Reading," pp. 436-437.

22. For other instances of her candid expression of love for the master, see XII, 162, 198-199, 240. Katherine Anne Porter seems to

miss the technical purpose of this insistence when she says: "In her attempt to vindicate herself she's doing the whole thing really at the expense of the children—I have always believed for the sake of destroying them, of putting them out of the way in some manner or other in order to clear a road to the master." "James: 'The Turn of the Screw': A Radio Symposium," in *Casebook*, p. 161.

23. See *Casebook*, pp. 117, 145.

24. *Ibid.*, p. 153, Wilson's brief note from which this is excerpted was specially written for the *Casebook* and is dated 1959.

25. *Ibid.*, pp. 242-243.

26. *Casebook*, p. 243.

27. "Symbolism in Coleridge," *Publications of the Modern Language Association*, LXIII (March 1948), 230. Stoll makes this observation in the context of his disagreement with Edmund Wilson's interpretation of "The Turn of the Screw."

28. See *Casebook*, p. 243.

29. *The Art of the Novel*, p. 176.

30. *Ibid.*, p. 173.

31. *Ibid.*, p. 172. Edna Kenton misinterpreted this observation years ago, in 1924, by tearing it out of context (*Casebook*, pp. 105, 108). So far as I know, Heilman was the first to restore it to its context: "His tone is simply not that of one who has proudly hoaxed the credulous; it is that of one meditating upon an aesthetic problem." "Freudian Reading," p. 433.

32. The string of adjectives is from John Lydenberg, "The Governess Turns the Screws," *Casebook*, p. 276.

33. *Casebook*, p. 118.

34. *Ibid.*, p. 118.

35. Cargill, "Henry James as Freudian Pioneer," in *Casebook*, p. 228.

36. *Ibid.*, p. 234.

37. Heilman, "The Turn of the Screw as Poem," *Casebook*, p. 183.

38. See in this connection Donald P. Costello's "The Structure of *The Turn of the Screw*," *Modern Language Notes*, LXXV (April 1960), 312-321. Costello's analysis of the structure is brilliant, but his conclusion is, I think, erroneous: "It helps us to discover how James keeps up a feeling of horror, by forcing us to accept the ghosts; and how he keeps up a feeling of mystification, by forcing us to doubt the ghosts" (p. 321). Costello should not have forced a separation between mystification and horror, since the mystification only adds to the horror and hence to the reality and the acceptability of the ghosts.

39. "Freudian Reading," p. 441.

CHAPTER V. THREE EARLY TALES

1. See Edel, *Henry James: The Untried Years (1843-1870),* (Philadelphia and New York: Lippincott, 1953), pp. 215-219. The text of the tale was reprinted for the first time in 1956: "'A Tragedy of Error': James's First Story, with a Prefatory Note by Leon Edel," *New England Quarterly,* XXIX (September 1956), 291-317. Page references to the tale are to this source and are incorporated in the text.

2. We can notice this in almost all the tales chosen for analysis in this study.

3. *Henry James: The Untried Years,* p. 217.

4. "A Note on Henry James's First Short Story," *Modern Language Notes,* LXXII (January 1957), 104.

5. *Ibid.,* p. 105.

6. *Eight Uncollected Tales of Henry James,* ed. Edna Kenton (New Brunswick: Rutgers University Press, 1950), p. 24.

7. *Ibid.,* pp. 25, 35, 37, 39, 41, 45.

8. Cornelia Pulsifer Kelley, *The Early Development of Henry James* (Urbana: University of Illinois, 1930), p. 35. See also Joseph Warren Beach, *The Method of Henry James* (Philadelphia: Albert Saifer, rev. ed., 1954), pp. 174-175.

9. See *The Untried Years,* p. 220, where Edel draws attention to its "considerable originality when considered in the context of its time and weighed as the performance of a young man."

10. Kelley, *The Early Development of Henry James,* p. 84.

11. See *Eight Uncollected Tales,* pp. 103-109.

12. *The Art of the Novel,* p. 197.

13. Christof Wegelin, *The Image of Europe in Henry James* (Dallas: Southern Methodist University Press, 1958), p. 39.

14. Allusions to Shakespeare are quite frequent in James; in this particular case they contribute to the romantic atmosphere of the tale.

15. Kelley, *The Early Development of Henry James,* p. 233.

16. Quentin Anderson has drawn attention to the point that this sentence "presages the theme of *The Princess Casamassima.*" *The American Henry James* (New Brunswick: Rutgers University Press, 1957), p. 39n.

17. We can recognize here an anticipation of Mrs. Wimbush of "The Death of the Lion."

18. Scholastica's remark is very close in substance to James's own advice to the would-be novelist: "Try to be one of the people on whom nothing is lost!" "The Art of Fiction," in *Partial Portraits* (London and New York: Macmillan, 1888), p. 390.

CHAPTER VI. NOUVELLES

1. *The Art of the Novel*, p. 199.

2. *Ibid.*, p. 200. This would be equally true of "Daisy Miller" (1878), "Pandora" (1884) insofar as it is a companion piece to "Daisy Miller," and "The Modern Warning" (1888) —this last tale is not included in the New York Edition.

3. *Ibid.*, p. 133.

4. *Ibid.*, p. 134.

5. *Ibid.*, p. 153.

6. *Ibid.*, p. 136.

7. "What Maisie Knew: A Disagreement by F. R. Leavis," in Marius Bewley, *The Complex Fate* (London: Chatto and Windus, 1952), p. 120.

8. *Ibid.*, p. 123.

9. *Ibid.*, p. 122.

10. *The Complex Fate*, p. 121.

11. It is perhaps on the basis of such details that Clifton Fadiman has suggested: "The relation between them goes beyond mutual respect and affection. Its roots reach deep into the dark soil of their emotional under-lives. The conventions of his day (which James, through his subtle logic, both obeyed and evaded) prevented him from making any more explicit the perfectly unconscious homosexual love—of a type that could never ripen into overt action—binding Morgan and Pemberton. . . . It adds still another dimension to this rich narrative, endowing it with a troubling beauty whose parallel is perhaps to be found nowhere else save in Thomas Mann's 'Death in Venice.'" *The Short Stories of Henry James* (New York: Random House, 1945), p. 272. However, I hesitate in accepting the idea that James was consciously positing a latent homosexual bond between Morgan and Pemberton. Textual evidence for such a reading is as ambiguous in "The Pupil" as it is in "The Turn of the Screw." Moreover, it is doubtful if "another dimension" is really added to "The Pupil," even if Fadiman's suggestion is accepted.

12. The children of James—Randolph Miller, Dolcino, Morgan, Maisie, Miles, Flora—are all quite as precocious as those of Shakespeare, Dickens, and Ivy Compton-Burnett; and it is quite probable that James was influenced by Dickens in this respect.

13. *The Art of the Novel*, p. 248.

14. *Notebooks*, p. 306.

15. *The Art of the Novel*, p. 248.

16. See *Notebooks*, p. 306, and *The Art of the Novel*, pp. 248-249. It should be noted that, in the tale as written, James nowhere names Shakespeare, although the allusion is obvious. The ironic impact of

the tale is considerably enhanced if we remember the devouring curiosity—still unabated—about the life of the poet.

17. "Henry James," in *Make It New* (New Haven: Yale University Press, 1934), p. 284; first appeared in *The Little Review* (August 1918).

18. *Notebooks*, p. 330; for full details, see pp. 330-331. It is surprising that the editors' comment on the tale is also rather cold; see *Notebooks*, p. 332.

19. James's phrase, "The Art of Fiction" (1884) in *Partial Portraits*, p. 388.

20. Coomaraswamy, *Figures of Speech or Figures of Thought* (London: Luzac, 1946).

21. Pound, *Make It New*, p. 271.

22. This is an easily audible echo of "The Beast in the Jungle"; the thematic and imagistic affinities between these two tales are numerous and obvious.

23. "The 'ending' of a novel is, for many persons, like that of a good dinner, a course of dessert and ices, and the artist in fiction is regarded as a sort of meddlesome doctor who forbids agreeable aftertastes." James, "The Art of Fiction," in *Partial Portraits*, p. 382.

24. "In the Country of the Blue," in *The Question of Henry James*, ed. F. W. Dupee (London: A. Wingate, 1947), p. 205.

CHAPTER VII. ANECDOTES (ALSO PARABLES)

1. *The Art of the Novel*, p. 235. James is referring specifically to "The Abasement of the Northmores" and "The Tree of Knowledge."

2. Critics of James's "major phase" would do well to remember that, according to James, "the subject [of *The Wings of the Dove* and *The Golden Bowl*] could in each case have been perfectly expressed had *all* the persons concerned been only American or only English or only Roman or whatever" (*The Art of the Novel*, p. 199). It is difficult, however, to agree with him on this point.

3. *The Art of the Novel*, p. 276.

4. *Ibid.*, p. 275.

5. *Ibid.*, p. 276.

6. *Ibid.*, p. 277.

7. *Ibid.*, p. 277.

8. *Ibid.*, p. 276.

9. See *Notebooks*, pp. 116, 267-268, 274-275, 292, 293-294.

10. *Notebooks*, p. 267.

11. Pound, "Henry James," *Make It New* (New Haven: Yale University Press, 1934), pp. 291-292.

12. Matthiessen, *Henry James: The Major Phase* (New York: Oxford University Press, 1944), p. 143. See also Elizabeth Stevenson, *The Crooked Corridor: A Study of Henry James* [New York: Macmillan, 1949), p. 72.

13. *The Major Phase*, p. 144.

14. *The Art of the Novel*, p. 232.

15. *Ibid.*, p. 233.

16. Fadiman, *The Short Stories of Henry James* (New York: Random House, 1945), p. 317.

17. *Notebooks*, p. 122.

18. Westbrook, "The Supersubtle Fry," p. 136.

19. *Ibid.*, p. 135.

20. *Ibid.*, p. 134.

21. Fadiman, *The Short Stories of Henry James*, p. 316.

22. Included respectively in *Partial Portraits* (1888) and *Picture and Text* (New York: Harper, 1893).

23. *Notebooks*, p. 267. See also James's prefatory remarks in *The Art of the Novel*, pp. 285-286.

CHAPTER VIII. A JAMESIAN TRIPTYCH

1. Jefferson, *Henry James* (New York: Grove Press, 1961), p. 75.

2. *Notebooks*, p. 166; see also *The Art of the Novel*, pp. 241-242, and p. 245, where he calls it his "more or less vivid fable."

3. The quoted expression is from James, "The Art of Fiction," in *Partial Portraits*, p. 390. James says in his first entry in the *Notebooks* (p. 165) about this tale, "The thing takes place in London, vaguely, fancifully, obscurely, without 'realism' or dots upon the *i*'s."

4. "But there is a virtue more distinctively Christian than honor that figures largely in the stories [which in the context implies both novels and tales] of James. That is unselfishness, or self-devotion to the happiness of others." Beach, *The Method of Henry James* (Philadelphia: Saifer, 1954), p. 140.

5. I disagree with Edwin Honig when he says: "It is the only one of these romances in which the gaining of the small prize is permitted its ambiguous victory directly in the shadow of the larger," and "The last candle, she knows, must be for Stransom, and not for Acton Hague." "The Merciful Fraud in Three Stories of Henry James," *The Tiger's Eye*, IX (October 1949), 91, 92.

6. Blackmur, "The Sacred Fount," *Kenyon Review*, IV (Autumn 1942), 338.

7. Tate, "Three Commentaries: Poe, James, and Joyce," *The Sewanee Review*, LVIII (Winter 1950), 101. See also William Troy,

"The Altar of Henry James," in *The Question of Henry James* (London: A. Wingate, 1947), p. 277. Troy finds it "fluttering on the edge of morbid emotionalism and sustained only by a marvelous tonality of style."

8. Fadiman, *The Short Stories of Henry James,* p. 359. See also Rebecca West, *Henry James* (New York: Holt, 1916), p. 10, where in her characteristically purple phraseology she says about "The Altar of the Dead": "Once at least Henry James poured into his crystal goblet the red wine that nourishes the soul."

9. Q. D. Leavis, "Henry James: The Stories," *Scrutiny,* XIV (Spring 1947), 223.

10. F. R. Leavis, "Henry James and the Function of Criticism," *Scrutiny,* XV (Spring 1948), 103. In *The Great Tradition* (London: Chatto and Windus, 1948), p. 163, Leavis parenthetically refers to "the significant badness of *The Altar of the Dead,* that morbidly sentimental and extremely unpleasant tale which—it is, of course, late—also illustrates poor James's weary, civilized loneliness of spirit."

11. *The Art of the Novel,* p. 247.

12. *Ibid.,* p. 248. See pp. 245-247 for James's comments on the theme of the tale.

13. Knights, "Henry James and the Trapped Spectator," *Southern Review,* IV (Winter 1938), 612.

14. Tate, "Three Commentaries," p. 7.

15. For the symbolical importance in this tale of the characters' names in relation to the seasons, see John L. Sweeney, "The Demuth Pictures," *Kenyon Review,* V (Autumn 1943), 527, and Edward Stone, "James's 'Jungle': The Seasons," *University of Kansas City Review,* XXI (Winter 1955), 142-144.

16. Tate, "Three Commentaries," pp. 9-10.

17. For an excellent exploration of the question of allegory, see Edwin Honig, *Dark Conceit: The Making of Allegory* (Evanston: Northwestern University Press, 1959). See also F. E. Smith, " 'The Beast in the Jungle': The Limits of Method," *Perspective,* I (Autumn 1947), 33-40. Smith's reading of the tale is very perceptive in several places, but his concluding judgment suffers from the same fixation on "realism": "And the final irony is that [James] has preached his lesson too well, that his method is here too specialized, too barren of action, too empty of emotion, that his characters lose what life they have in the mazes of logical inference until they have more of the nature of propositions than of human beings" (p. 40).

18. Blackmur, "The Sacred Fount," p. 340.

19. I have obviously, but with no regrets, "fallen into James's trap in reading the story as that of a man who discovers what he

would have been. What Spencer Brydon really discovers is what he has been." Quentin Anderson, *The American Henry James* (New Brunswick: Rutgers University Press, 1957), pp. 177-178. However, I do not subscribe to the theory of "traps."

20. Honig, "The Merciful Fraud in Three Stories of Henry James," p. 90.

21. *Notebooks,* p. 364.

22. James, *A Small Boy and Others* (New York: Charles Scribner's Sons, 1913), pp. 347-349.

23. For more detailed biographical connections, see Leon Edel, *Henry James: The Untried Years* (Philadelphia: Lippincott, 1953), pp. 75-79, and *The Ghostly Tales of Henry James,* ed. Edel, pp. viii-x, 720-725.

24. Rosensweig, "The Ghost of Henry James," *Partisan Review,* XI (Fall 1944), 436-455; appeared originally as "The Ghost of Henry James: A Study in Thematic Apperception" in *Character and Personality,* XII (December 1943).

25. It is interesting to note that James's first published tale ("A Tragedy of Error") and his last ("A Round of Visits") both deal with the theme of betrayal and contain violence. These, along with several other tales and novels on similar subjects, provide considerable basis for Graham Greene's remark that James's "ruling passion was the idea of treachery, the 'Judas Complex.'" *The Lost Childhood and Other Essays* (London: Eyre and Spottiswoode, 1951), p. 44.

26. Matthiessen remarks about the conclusion of "A Round of Visits": "Such an ending breaks the situation to pieces rather than resolves it, but what James achieved here was at the opposite pole from the ethical tenuosities and withdrawals of *The Special Type.* He had penetrated into a world so corrupted by money that the only escape seemed to be by violence." *The Major Phase,* p. 117.

27. The allusive echo of "The Beast in the Jungle" may be noted.

28. See Honig, "The Merciful Fraud in Three Stories of Henry James," pp. 84-85: "Despite the presence of other characters, Spencer Brydon seems to exist alone in an action which resembles a pantomime, in a commentary verging on interior monologue."

29. James's phrase in *A Small Boy and Others,* p. 1.

30. Rogers, "The Beast in Henry James," *The American Imago,* XIII (Winter 1956), 429.

31. *Ibid.,* p. 438.

32. *Symbolism and Fiction* (Charlottesville: University of Virginia Press, 1956), p. 12. Reprinted in Harry Levin, *Contexts of Criticism* (Cambridge: Harvard University Press, 1957).

Conclusion

1. *The Art of the Novel,* pp. 320, 321.

2. *Henry James and H. G. Wells: A Record of Their Friendship,* ed. Leon Edel and Gordon N. Ray (Urbana: University of Illinois Press, 1958), pp. 128-129.

3. "The New Novel" in *Notes on Novelists* (New York: Charles Scribner's Sons, 1914), pp. 347-348. For a fuller account of James's comment on *Chance,* see *ibid.,* pp. 345-353.

4. The narrator of *The Sacred Fount,* I believe, is even more definitely a "mere" narrator. It is significant that only two critics of this novel have given importance to its narrator *as* narrator, and consequently are not baffled by it or misled into unnecessary conjectures either about James or his persona. See Claire J. Raeth, "Henry James's Rejection of *The Sacred Fount,*" *Journal of English Literary History,* XVI (December 1949), 308-324, and Edward Sackville-West, *Inclinations* (London: Secker and Warburg, 1949), pp. 63-71.

5. See *Notebooks,* pp. 58, 73, 88, 94, 95, 109, 148, 149, 160, 179, 180, 200, 220, 275, 300.

6. *Ibid.,* p. 180.

7. For a full account of this experience, see the introduction to *Henry James: Parisian Sketches, Letters to the New York Tribune 1875-1876,* ed. Leon Edel and Ilse Dusoir Lind (New York: New York University Press, 1957).

8. *Notebooks,* p. 180.

9. *Ibid.,* p. 180.

10. *Ibid.,* p. 201.

11. *The Art of the Novel,* preface to *The Lesson of the Master,* p. 222.

12. *The Art of the Novel,* p. 253.

13. *Ibid.,* p. 157.

14. *Conrad the Novelist* (Cambridge: Harvard University Press, 1958), pp. 270, 271. Guerard is, in the context, commenting upon *Chance.*

15. See in this connection Percy Lubbock's rather extreme view in *The Craft of Fiction* (London: J. Cape, 1921), p. 147: "It is given as nobody's view—not his own, as it would be if he told the story himself, and not the author's, as it would be if Henry James told the story. The author does not tell the story of Strether's mind; he makes it tell itself, he dramatizes it." The statement, however, becomes acceptable only if we lay a good deal of emphasis on "he makes it tell itself," in which case the author as omniscient narrator returns to the fictional domain from which Lubbock would have him

banished. See, in this connection, Sister Kristin Morrison, "James's and Lubbock's Differing Points of View," *Nineteenth-Century Fiction*, XVI (December 1961), 245-255.

16. *The Art of the Novel*, p. 157.

17. *Ibid.*, pp. 157, 158.

18. *Ibid.*, p. 220.

19. *Notebooks*, p. 89; see pp. 92, 102, 104, 135, 293; see also James's introduction to *The Odd Number: Thirteen Tales by Guy de Maupassant* (New York: Harper, 1889) and his "Guy de Maupassant" in *Partial Portraits* (London and New York: Macmillan, 1888).

20. Henry James, *Hawthorne* (Ithaca: Cornell, Great Seal Books, 1956), pp. 49-50. The book was originally published in Macmillan's English Men of Letters series in 1879.

21. See *ibid.*, p. 51. It is amusing to note what James has to say about Poe and Baudelaire in another place: "An enthusiasm for Poe is the mark of a decidedly primitive stage of reflection. Baudelaire thought him a profound philosopher, the neglect of whose golden utterances stamped his native land with infamy. Nevertheless, Poe was vastly the greater charlatan of the two, as well as the greater genius." *French Poets and Novelists* (London: Macmillan, 1878), p. 76.

22. *The Works of Edgar Allan Poe,* ed. Edmund Clarence Stedman and George Edward Woodberry (New York: Colonial Co., 1903), VII, 25.

23. The question of affinity between Poe and James has never been given much attention. One immediately thinks of their preoccupation with the supernatural, with the dead—James seems to share Poe's concern with the "posthumous heroine" (Harry Levin's expression in *The Power of Blackness* [New York: A. A. Knopf, 1958], p. 156) —and with the alter ego—one is reminded of Poe's "William Wilson" in connection with "The Jolly Corner."

24. *Hawthorne*, p. 144.

25. Matthiessen, *Henry James: The Major Phase* (New York: Oxford University Press, 1944), p. 71; we must, however, remember his "Yet James was no *symboliste*" (*ibid.*). See also *American Renaissance* (New York: Oxford University Press, 1941), pp. 301-304, where Matthiessen discusses James's use of symbolism in non-Freudian terms.

26. Schorer, "Technique as Discovery" in *Critiques and Essays on Modern Fiction: 1920-1951,* selected by John W. Aldridge (New York: Ronald Press, 1952), p. 67.

27. Pound, *Make It New* (New Haven: Yale University Press, 1934), p. 266.

Index